CHAKRAS

A Beginner's Guide to Healing

To Sudha Carolyn Lundeen
whose encouragement made this book possible.

FALL RIVER PRESS

New York

An Imprint of Sterling Publishing Co., Inc.
1166 Avenue of the Americas
New York, NY 10036

FALL RIVER PRESS and the distinctive Fall River Press logo are
registered trademarks of Barnes & Noble Booksellers, Inc.

© 2014 F+W Media, Inc.
Originally published as *The Everything® Guide to Chakra Healing*

ISBN 978-1-4351-6880-0

For information about custom editions, special sales, and premium and
corporate purchases, please contact Sterling Special Sales at
800-805-5489 or specialsales@sterlingpublishing.com.

Manufactured in Malaysia

4 6 8 10 9 7 5

sterlingpublishing.com

Cover design by Igor Satanovsky
Interior design by Sharon Jacobs

All images from iStock, except: agefotostock: © Sarvesh Joshi/Dinodia
Photo: 105; Dreamstime: xii, 11, 89; Shutterstock: 14

CHAKRAS
A Beginner's Guide to Healing

Use Your Body's
Energies
to Promote Health,
Healing, and
Happiness

Heidi E. Spear

FALL RIVER PRESS

New York

CONTENTS

Top 10 Benefits of Chakra Healing

1. Chakra healing relieves mental stress.

2. Chakra healing soothes an aching heart.

3. Chakra healing stabilizes your appetite.

4. If you're feeling weak, chakra healing gives you strength.

5. Chakra healing helps you cultivate intimate relationships.

6. Chakra healing strengthens your intuition and imagination.

7. Chakra healing complements treatments for depression and anxiety.

8. Chakra healing aids digestion.

9. Chakra healing helps you uncover what you are passionate about in all aspects of life.

10. Chakra healing supports you in creating exactly the life you desire.

Introduction

Overall well-being is always available to you, and there's an ancient secret to it. The ancient secret unlocks the most vital, mysterious, and intelligent healing power of the universe. The ancient secret is: you. You are the key to your overall well-being. You have all the elemental forces of the natural world within you, including the power to heal.

You have the capacity to heal while also seeking the expertise, guidance, and wisdom of teachers and trained medical professionals. As you enter your lifelong journey of health and vitality, reach out for support and advice. Tell your doctors and healers what you notice about yourself. Ask questions, and get answers. Work together, and increase your knowledge through experience and study. This book will support you on that quest.

The seven major chakras exist in you and affect you on physical, psychological, and spiritual levels. The chakras are bright, glowing energy centers that control the flow of life-force energy. Sometimes the chakras spin too slowly, sometimes too quickly, and sometimes just right. If they are spinning just right, energy travels freely to your physical, mental, and energetic bodies. This means you are firing on all cylinders. By learning about the chakras and how to balance them, you can live your life with ease, joy, clear-headedness, love, intimacy, health, security, and whatever else your heart desires. You will notice that chakras go in and out of balance, and you can learn from them and heal with them. As you balance the chakras, you become more connected to wisdom, joy, and the force of love and appreciation that connects you to everything. These good feelings go hand-in-hand with good health.

Chakra healing is a type of holistic healing, connecting mind, body, and spirit (or what you may call energy, Source, or God). The experience of chakra healing is colorful, creative, magical, surprising, restorative, and cleansing. It brings you home to who you truly are. If you are overweight, underweight, constipated, chronically tired, insecure, unable to complete tasks, depleted, anxious, and/or bored, these and many other conditions are not who you truly are. Who you truly are is radiant, self-confident, clear-thinking, compassionate, trusting, healthy, fun, and able to create the life you desire. You can shift from the other states into who you truly are as you get to know your chakras.

If you handle too much stress and neglect your body's needs, you become run down and subject to illness. Your body is intelligent and will compensate for deficiencies in various ways, keeping you as healthy as it can, as long as it can. However, you will not sustain mental or physical health long-term if the vital life-force energy doesn't flow through you in a balanced way. You need the chakras to be unblocked for health, youthfulness, joy, and creating the life you truly desire.

This book breaks down the ancient yogic and modern discoveries about the chakras. You will learn various options for balancing and supporting each and every chakra. You will learn how chakras affect you on very practical levels and about their relevance to the Law of Attraction: the law of the universe that explains how you attract what you want in your life. Your health and enjoyment of life is defined by each choice you make throughout the day. Every moment is a moment you can use to support your health.

Even with advances in modern medicine, your participation in your healing process is essential. Drugs and surgery can reduce and eliminate pain, and save your life, but without your cooperation the results may be ineffective or short-term. Patients are noticing that they have to play an active role in their healing process. Interest in yoga, meditation, and the chakra system continues to grow. Many of these practices can go very deep. One of the real benefits of chakra healing is if you want, you can heal deep wounds.

As you read this book, remember that you are unique. The way your physical, psychological, and energetic bodies are interacting with each other right now is unique. As you try out the exercises, go at your own pace. Make a commitment to honor and listen to yourself. You do not have to read this book chapter by chapter.

You can jump around to the sections that look interesting to you, and go from there. Have fun. Explore the chakras at your own pace. Follow your intuition. You've already begun.

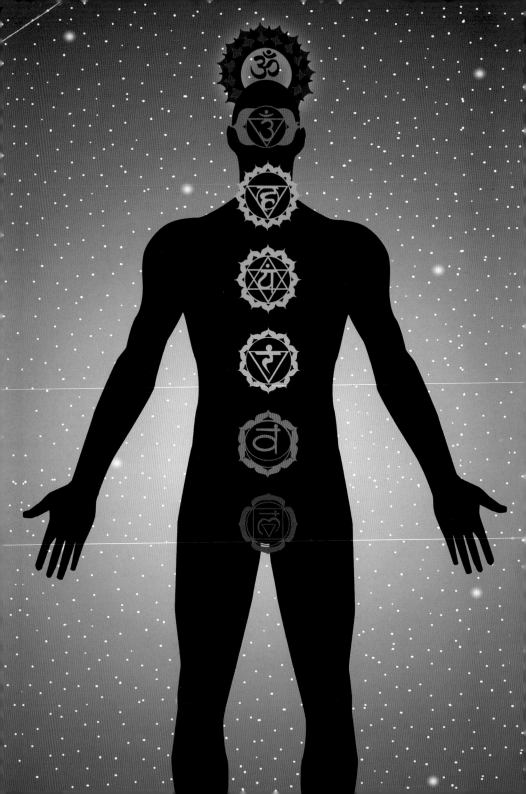

CHAPTER 1

What Are Chakras?

Chakras are spinning energy centers that directly influence your well-being and how consciously and happily you create your life's path. When all of the chakras are balanced you feel safe, creative, strong, and secure in yourself and in relationships. You are comfortable speaking your mind, and your thoughts come together with clarity and ease. You also feel connected to your intuition and the vital energy of the universe. At times, chakras become imbalanced, and there are ways to bring your deficient or excessive chakras into balance.

Your Renewable Energy Centers

Chakra is Sanskrit for *wheel* or *disc*, and the chakras are vortices of energy that spin as glowing wheels of light inside you. There are seven major chakras in the body. Each of them can be overactive or deficient, which means they are blocked and not in balance. At different points in the day, different days of the year, and different years of your life the chakras can become out of balance. Chakras can be out of balance since your time in the womb, or even earlier: in the yogic view, the karma you carry from your past lives is stored in the chakras. Throughout your life, what you experience on the outside (your environment, friends, and family) as well as what you experience inwardly (your thoughts and emotions) will affect your chakras and consequently your body and mind.

By becoming familiar with the physical and psychological signs and symptoms related to the functions of each chakra, you begin to understand how the chakras affect your mental, physical, and spiritual health. Then, you will know where to focus your healing energy. When the chakras are all spinning in balance, you will find it easier to be doing the things in your life that you want to do, with ease and joy. You will also be able to tap into your true desires and create the life that you truly want to live.

Each chakra's root is planted in the major current of energy that runs up and down the center of the spinal column. This line of energy is called the **sushumna nadi**. In between each of the chakras, along the sushumna, two other major currents of energy, **nadis**, cross back and forth. These are called the **ida** and **pingala nadis**. From the third eye the ida curves to the left, first, in a semicircular shape to cross the sushumna at the Throat Chakra. Then it curves in a semicircle to the right before crossing the sushumna and pingala at the Heart Chakra. The pingala nadi curves down the right side of the body, first, from the third eye and mirrors the pattern of the ida. There are different estimations of where the nadis meet with each criss-cross. One view is that the nadis cross in between the chakras, and those currents cause the chakras to spin, while the other view states that the ida and pingala cross at each chakra. Either way, the relevant point is that the chakras are affected by the flow of energy as it travels along the sushumna, ida, and pingala nadis.

The Body's Seven Major Chakras

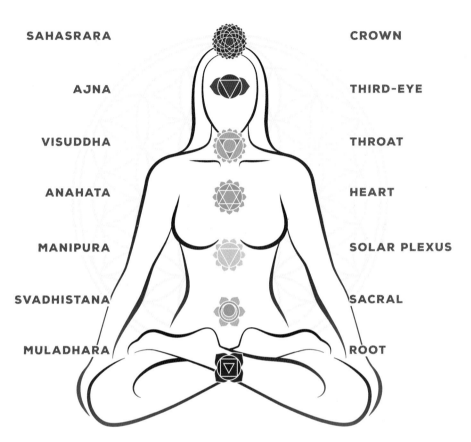

SAHASRARA — CROWN

AJNA — THIRD-EYE

VISUDDHA — THROAT

ANAHATA — HEART

MANIPURA — SOLAR PLEXUS

SVADHISTANA — SACRAL

MULADHARA — ROOT

A Bridge from Now to Eternity

The chakras are the bridge along which you can guide your awareness, up and down, to move the life-force energy of the earth and of the eternal oneness that connects all energy and all beings. The energy of the earth that rises up from your Root Chakra is called **Shakti** and the energy of pure consciousness that comes down through your Crown Chakra is called **Shiva**. As you work with the chakras, the goal is to unite Shiva and Shakti (life force and eternal consciousness). Shakti energy in the Tantrik view is called **Kundalini**—the same energy with another name. Visualizing where each chakra is located is an important part of how you will tap into their energies and correct imbalances.

Muladhara Chakra's Root Placement

The first chakra is called the *Root Chakra*, **Muladhara** in Sanskrit. The Root Chakra hooks into the base of the spine, in the area called the **perineum**. This is the area between the genitals and the anus. The Root Chakra's energy connects right to the earth's energy. You can draw energy upward to revitalize you, or send energy downward to ground yourself. To visualize where the Muladhara Chakra is, take a deep nourishing breath in through the nose, and imagine the breath travelling down into the perineum. While your attention is there, imagine a red glow energizing that area. Exhale through your nostrils and imagine any negative energy flowing out with the breath. Repeat this a few times, to get to know the location of your Muladhara Chakra.

> It is said that the life-force energy of Kundalini lies coiled as a serpent goddess at the base of the spine, wrapped three-and-a-half times around the Muladhara Chakra. As you awaken the Root Chakra, Kundalini energy rises up to unite with Shiva energy and transfers energy to each chakra on its way up to the Crown Chakra.

The Seat of Sweetness

To visualize the location of the second chakra, **Svadhistana,** turn your attention to your lower abdomen, below the navel. The root of the second chakra is said to be located in the first **lumbar vertebra** of the spine. Svadhistana is usually translated as *sweetness* (*svad*) or *one's own place* (*sva*). This chakra is associated with the pleasures of life: sexuality, creativity, and trust in intimate relationships. To lead your mind to where this chakra is, close your eyes, breathe in deeply through the nose, and expand the belly as you envision the breath flowing into the area below your navel. Hold the breath for a moment, picturing an orange glow while keeping your attention on this area of Svadhistana energy. Exhale slowly, drawing the belly in, expelling the air as you imagine unwanted negativity leaving the body through your nose. Repeat this a few times, strengthening your ability to visualize your Svadhistana Chakra. The Svadhistana Chakra is also called the *Sacral Chakra*.

Manipura

Manipura is the name of the third chakra, which is located in the solar plexus region of the body. This chakra is said to be rooted in area of the seventh and eighth **thoracic vertebrae**. Its name means *lustrous gem*, and the chakra is often depicted as glowing yellow. To become familiar with this chakra's location, place your hand on your front body between your navel and sternum. Inhale so that  your body expands into that hand, and as you inhale imagine you're inhaling a warm, yellow ribbon of light. Then, exhale releasing tension from the midsection. Repeat this visualization with breath a few times to sense the placement of your Manipura Chakra.

Anahata

The fourth chakra, **Anahata**, means *unstruck*. This is the Heart Chakra, located at the center of the chest, at the fourth thoracic vertebra. To visualize the placement of this chakra, use the three-part yogic breath. On the inhale, breathe deeply and expand the belly, and on the same inhale expand the rib cage and then the chest. As you expand the chest, imagine it filling up with a green glow. On the exhale, slowly let the breath go. Repeat this a few times, acknowledging the placement of the Heart Chakra.

Visuddha

The **Visuddha** Chakra is the fifth chakra, or *Throat Chakra*. *Visuddha* means *purification*. The Visuddha is the bridge from the Heart Chakra to the third eye. This chakra is located just above the collarbone, at the third **cervical vertebra**. To drop your awareness into the placement of the Visuddha Chakra, close your eyes and imagine you have just taken a large sip of clear blue water. As it goes down your throat, it washes over the Throat Chakra. Imagine this for a moment, clear blue water running effortlessly down the throat where the Visuddha Chakra spins.

Ajna

The Third-Eye Chakra is sometimes called the *Brow Chakra*. In Sanskrit, it's **Ajna**, *to perceive*. It is located in the space between the eyes and slightly higher than the brow line. To visualize this chakra, gently place the palms of your hands over your eyes, and pivot the hands so that the fingers of the left hand overlap the fingers of the right hand. Place your attention into that space where the hands overlap. Inhale and exhale a few times, imagining indigo-colored energy flowing into that space.

Sahasrara

Sahasrara, *thousandfold*, is the name of the seventh chakra, the Crown Chakra. It's located at the top of the head. To visualize this chakra, close your eyes, and allow your breath to come in and out of your body at its own pace. Imagine the glow of any or all of the following colors surrounding the top of your head on all sides: purple, white, and/or gold. Hold your lips in a gentle, easy smile, and continue for a few breaths to allow the glow to envelop your head.

> *Sahasrara* refers to the image of a lotus flower with one thousand petals. In nature, the lotus flower grows from the mud to blossom beautifully toward the sun. This is a metaphor for the human experience: while rooted deeply in the earth and *physical body*, you connect to the state of bliss and life-force energy that unites all things.

As you learn about the chakras and practice visualizing them, it will become second nature. Your relationship to your chakras will continue to grow. What might seem foreign now will seem natural soon enough.

Mirroring Nature

The basic elements of the living, natural world are listed differently in different cultures. In her writing on the chakras, Anodea Judith expands the typical four or five elemental list to seven elements: earth, water, fire, air, sound, light, and thought. Each element corresponds to principles that govern human life in the world, and each corresponds to a particular chakra. Anodea Judith's model is an invaluable tool for understanding how you are a mirror of the natural world and how the health of the chakras affects the flow of your life force.

Connection to Nature

You are not only a mirror of the natural world but also an intricate part of it. Do you often feel cut off from nature in your home, car, grocery store, or workplace? If so, you might be surprised to learn how the elements of the outside world are also within you.

- The **first chakra** is your connection to the earth: supportive, stable, grounding.

- The **second chakra** gives you the qualities of water: fluid, flowing, sensual.

- The third chakra is a billow for your internal fire: transformative heat, self-esteem, will.

- The **fourth chakra** is your relationship to air: holds and makes space, connection to others.

- The **fifth chakra** supports your sound: self-expression, communication.

- The **sixth chakra** is your wisdom light: enabling you to see clearly.

- The seventh chakra opens you up to pure consciousness: unity with all that is.

The elemental correspondences to each chakra are a reminder that you are not separate from the miracles and elements of the natural world. As strong, powerful, beautiful, and mysterious as they are, so are you.

Waste Less

The health of the planet, your habitat, depends on the way each person lives daily life. Each person's actions and reactions send energy out that causes ripples and effects everywhere. If you and your neighbors are not yet recycling, find out how you could do that in your area. Another easy way to reduce waste is to bring your own bags when you go the grocery store. There are lots of stylish eco-friendly bags to add color to your day, as well as bags that advertise causes you support. If you don't want to shop around for an eco-friendly bag, many grocery stores sell a selection right near the checkout lines. Certain styles fold up so you can put them in your purse or glove compartment, for easy access. You could even make your own bags, as a creative activity for the family. It's a great way to create less unnatural waste in the world.

The Beauty of Water

Instead of drinking tap or bottled water, see if you can find a natural spring near you. Getting water from a spring is a tangible reminder that water is a resource flowing from nature, it's not manufactured. You can buy glass bottles or jars to fill up at the spring, and then you have free water available any time of day. What's more, it's the healthiest water for you. Check out *www.findaspring.com* to locate a spring near you.

Water that flows from the spring carries the life-force energy straight from mother earth to your system. It's alive, so after you bring your water home from the spring, rotate the bottles a couple of times during the day to keep it moving a little. When it's bottled on a shelf for a while (in the stores, for example), the life in it slowly diminishes. Drinking and cooking with fresh spring water will allow you to get the most out of earth's natural resource to replenish, restore, and revitalize you. It's free, and it's the best for you.

Dr. Masaru Emoto performed a scientific study, freezing water samples from around the world and photographing the crystals. In many cities, the crystals from tap water were deformed or nonexistent, whereas water from pristine lakes formed intricate, symmetrical crystals. The photographs also show that affirming words, beautiful music, and prayers create exquisite crystals, while unkind words and cacophony leave water chaotic.

Water is something many people take for granted, but every new awareness makes a difference. Even if there are small ways you can limit your use of water, practice those small ways. Take a shower that is just a few minutes shorter than usual, turn off the faucet while brushing your teeth, and don't fill up an entire glass of water if you usually don't drink the whole thing.

Everything Is Connected

Knowing that you have all the powerful elements of the universe inside you connects you to the beauty, the wonder, and the ephemeral qualities you see outside. And because of that, for the benefit of your life, the lives of your children, the lives of people you don't even know, and the lives of everything on the planet that provides for you, it's essential to take responsibility for what you put outside. Your chakras need the energy from the sun, moon, water, and vegetation, so find ways by your actions and your intentions to support and honor the earth more.

Your Body as a Prism

The healing vital energy of the world can be found everywhere, even in waves of light. Each color of the rainbow vibrates at its own frequency in what you see as white light. A prism refracts the light. If you hold a prism up to natural light, the angles of the prism separate the vibrating waves, and the naked eye sees rainbows coming out of another side.

You can think of the body as working in a similar way. It's as though the universal healing white light gets refracted when it enters the body, and each color sustains a particular chakra. The most widely used modern model of the chakras is to associate them with the colors of the rainbow.

- The **Root Chakra** responds to the color red.

- The **Sacral Chakra** responds to the color orange.

- The Solar Plexus Chakra responds to the color yellow.

- The Heart Chakra responds to the color green.

- The **Throat Chakra** responds to the color blue.

- The **Third-Eye Chakra** responds to the color indigo.

- The **Crown Chakra** responds to violet, gold, and white.

Blocked chakras tend to balance in response to these colors. And there are modern clairvoyants whose experiences support this rainbow system. They see healthy chakras glowing as these colors. At times you will find reports of different colors associated with the chakras. This happens because chakras are energy centers, and ever changing. Some people may have a different experience from others.

Tantrik Chakra Model

The first Tantrik translation of the colors of the chakras was translated into English by Sir John Woodroffe, who published this and other texts under his pen name, Arthur Avalon. His famous translation of the chakras with extra notes was published in 1919 in *Serpent Power*. In it, he translates the detailed experience of meditation on the chakras as written by **Pūrṇānanda-Svāmī**, in 1577. In Pūrṇānanda-Svāmī's

Sat-Cakra-Nirupana, he wrote instructions on how to meditate on the chakras, and their symbolism. This type of information was usually only passed on in India orally and secretly from guru to disciple. It was and is considered sacred and holy because the energies of the earth and of consciousness that flow through the body are considered sacred. That Woodroffe could eventually get this material and receive help interpreting it meant that in the early twentieth century these sacred secrets could be revealed to a wider and English-speaking audience. This is one of the major sources for our understanding of chakra theory today.

The rainbow model (red, orange, yellow, green, blue, indigo, purple/white/gold) of the chakras and the model that Pūrṇānanda-Svāmī provides are guides to follow from those who have experienced awareness of the energy fields and watched the meditations work.

Pūrṇānanda-Svāmī gives very detailed images of the chakras for meditation. If you become more interested in the experiences of Pūrṇānanda-Svāmī and would like to read his detailed suggestions of meditations, Avalon's study will be of great use. To simplify, you can bring much-needed energy to the chakras by choosing a color to meditate on from his detailed descriptions. You could choose to focus on the major color in the **pericarp**, the vibrant center, or on the overall color that Pūrṇānanda-Svāmī saw. Above is a distillation of the major colors as Pūrṇānanda-Svāmī experienced them and passed them on.

MULADHARA

A lotus with a square yellow center and crimson petals.

SVADHISTANA

A vermillion color lotus with the water element in its white pericarp.

MANIPURA

A lotus the color of a rain cloud with a red fiery triangle in the center.

ANAHATA

A lotus the color of a Bandhuka flower with a smoky hexagonal mandala in its pericarp.

VISUDDHA

A ruddy-colored lotus, with a center like the spotless moon, white and pure.

AJNA

A lotus that is pure white like the moon.

SAHASRARA

A lotus that is white with red filaments, inside the pericarp is the golden sun.

Can I see colors emanating from chakras?

Chakra activity projects colors into your **aura**, or **auric field**. For some, it's easy to see auras in plain sight. Anyone can see auras in a **kirlian photograph**, a kind of energy photography. You can have your aura photographed, and on different days or after meditation, you could see a change in the colors of your auric field.

The strength of the chakras will respond to the energy around you, and you can help by putting yourself in supportive environments. You do this with all your choices: where you place yourself, whom you spend time with, what you think, what you eat, and if you meditate. Because the higher chakras are associated with colors of a higher vibration such as pure white light, spend some time outside by moonlight. The full moon is astonishingly luminous. Just as you spend time enjoying sunlight, spend time enjoying moonlight. Your higher chakras will be nourished by the interaction, and the effect will touch all the chakras.

Aura Colors

The auric field appears to have seven layers, each corresponding to one of the seven major chakras. Each layer is a three-dimensional oval shape surrounding the body, and they progress concentrically outward. The layer closest to the body appears a vibrant red when the Muladhara Chakra's energy is radiating in a balanced way, the second layer is orange and reflects the health of the Svadhistana Chakra, and so on, ending with the seventh layer that shows up as the color violet and corresponds to the Crown Chakra. So, the auric field looks like an egg-shaped rainbow enveloping the body, when all the chakras are in balance.

Chakras' Relationships to Internal Organs

Each chakra flowers out from the spine toward ductless glands of the endocrine system, affecting the production of hormones that run through the body. Each gland affects certain bodily functions, and therefore if you notice what's not functioning well you can trace it to a particular chakra or chakras. Knowing these relationships will help direct your healing practices.

- The **Muladhara Chakra** affects the **gonads**, and in some traditions the adrenals.

- The **Svadhistana Chakra** affects the **adrenals**, and in some traditions the **gonads**.

- The **Manipura Chakra** affects the cells in the pancreas called the islets of **Langerhans,** and **adrenals.**

- The **Anahata Chakra** affects the **thymus.**

- The **Visuddha Chakra** affects the **thyroid** and **parathyroid.**

- The **Ajna Chakra** affects the **pituitary** gland.

- The **Sahasrara Chakra** affects the **pineal gland.**

According to different systems, sometimes the pituitary and pineal glands are reversed in relation to the chakras, so that the pituitary is connected with Sahasrara and the pineal with Ajna. Alice Bailey and Charles Webster Leadbeater, both **Theosophists**, were the first to notice that energy from the chakras affects the endocrine and sympathetic nervous systems of the body. Their discoveries paved the way for today's continually unfolding understanding of how the chakras affect and respond to chemical and physical actions and reactions in the body.

CHAPTER 2

From East to West

Our knowledge of the existence and nature of chakras as energy centers comes from the yogic tradition in India. Yogis discovered chakras in deep states of meditation. In the early twentieth century, Englishman Sir John Woodroffe was the first to translate yogic texts on the chakras from Sanskrit into English. Woodroffe added extensive commentary to these translations. Once knowledge of chakras came to the West, Theosophists, in particular, began to explore the chakras and expand chakra theory toward where it stands today.

Sacred Eastern Wisdom

Chakra theory originates in the yogic tradition, where meditation on the chakras is used on the path of liberation. Before coming to the West, wisdom and training for chakra meditation was passed on only from guru to disciple, as sacred wisdom. The yogis experienced chakras as glowing brightly, connecting each person to the universal energy and to the strength and power of divine gods and goddesses.

Sir John Woodroffe, whose pen name is Arthur Avalon, was born in England. He studied at Oxford to become a lawyer, and practiced in India. With great interest in the Hindu philosophy, he studied and translated several Sanskrit texts into English. It is because of his interest in the chakras that the original texts of Pūrṇānanda-Svāmī, *Sat-Cakra-Nirupana* (1577), are available to this day.

Pūrṇānanda-Svāmī meditated on the chakras and saw them as glowing lotus flowers, with colored Sanskrit letters on the petals. Inside the pericarp of each flower are particular gods, goddesses, lotus flowers, weapons, and symbols. These images demonstrate the power of the energy in each chakra and give the advanced yogi a guide for meditating on each chakra. The goal of meditation on the chakras is liberation. It is a path of transcendence from physical form, with the aspiration to merge with the eternal oneness of the universe. It is held as sacred as a way of connecting to divine energy.

A foundation of the yogic philosophy is that human existence includes suffering. People are attached to their desires, and the attachment ultimately causes them to suffer. People try to avoid things that cause pain, and inevitably suffer. This is called "attachment and aversion," two habits that always leads to suffering. Yogis meditate to achieve liberation from suffering.

The translation of Pūrṇānanda-Svāmī's text offers great tips for experienced yogis who are regular meditators. Since the publication of his texts in English, clairvoyants, healers, and modern yogis have continued to explore the chakras, with the goal of understanding how they affect the body, mind, and spirit. Just as the yogis for thousands of years were interested in the nature of the mind–body–spirit connection, so yogis and seekers of today continue with the same inquiry.

Mainstream Chakra Study

The yogis were primarily interested in chakra meditation for liberation or **nirvana**. When the Westerners learned about the chakras, they became interested in how these energy centers might affect the physical body and the mind. Today, interest in chakra healing continues to grow. People are curious about how they can participate in their own healing, and they want to understand their own compositions. Books on the chakra system are now easily accessible, and it's easy to purchase crystals, meditation CDs and DVDs, bath salts, and other items to support your chakra-healing journey.

> If you want to explore chakra theory with well-known clairvoyants and healers, many have websites and give workshops. By searching online and reading their books, you can gather information to help you decide whose workshops you'd like to attend. Once there, you'll meet others who are interested in this exploration, and you may decide to keep in touch.

Thanks to multimedia, you can be led through chakra meditation in the comfort of your own home. Even if you are comfortable meditating on your own, being led by someone's voice can be supportive as part of your practice. Another benefit to following someone else's lead is that it will give you more ideas for your own meditation practice.

How Chakra Theory Evolved

The translations by Woodroffe are a first-hand account of a highly respected teacher's experience of the chakras. Pūrṇānanda-Svāmī's text was written centuries before the English took interest. His writing is poetic and descriptive, and Avalon's translations reveal the beauty and clarity of Pūrṇānanda-Svāmī's experience.

Woodroffe made many primary texts accessible, and later Charles Webster Leadbeater became a primary figure in the evolution of chakra theory. Best known for his books *The Inner Life* (1910) and *The Chakras* (1927), C. W. Leadbeater was a member of the school of mystical thought known as **Theosophy**. Theosophy was established as a school of thought in 1875, as a forum for exploring the mysteries of life. The theories they believe in adapt yogic philosophy and include reincarnation, karma, the power of thought to affect oneself and one's surroundings, and the existence of worlds of experience beyond the physical. Because these are foundations for them, it's no surprise that the mysterious chakras, which link physical and energetic existence, captured their interest.

Alice Bailey and Leadbeater both had interest in the chakras and were among the first to assert that chakra placement suggested a relationship between the chakras and the endocrine system. It makes sense that they would be interested to see what else they might discover about the body's energy centers, especially because Theosophists believe that human beings can actively participate in intellectual, spiritual, and physical evolution.

> The founder of the School of Theosophy, Madame Blatvatsky was trained in Tibet from 1868–1870, and in 1875 she brought her teachings to the world, calling it *Theosophy*. In 1884, Leadbeater joined Blatvatsky on a trip to India, to explore their ideas and ideals.

The interest of Theosophists in the yogic tradition has been catalytic in the popularization of chakra study. This type of popularization runs the risk of succumbing to adaptations that take the sacredness out of the tradition, and yet, that has not happened to chakra theory. The chakras connect you to whatever your belief is about your higher self, God, and universal energy. Whatever you believe in as the universal energy is sacred because it's worth appreciating and honoring. It is life force, it is your connection to your higher self and to all that is.

Recent Publications

Today, one of the most prolific and widely studied authors on the chakra system is Anodea Judith. Her pioneering work gives extensive information on the chakras and their relationship to psychology, particularly in her work *Eastern Body, Western Mind: Psychology and the Chakra System as a Path to the Self.* Her book *Wheels of Life: A User's Guide to the Chakra System* is a valuable source, published before chakra healing reached the public in the way it has now. Her books and DVDs illuminate the ins and outs of chakra healing with authority, expertise, and clarity. Please see Appendix B for a list of additional supportive and helpful resources.

Chakras and Yoga

The philosophy of yoga is the foundation for the practice of yoga postures. The purpose of yoga is to practice not getting caught up in the "monkey mind." The "monkey mind" metaphor refers to the way the mind can lead you up and down, and spin you around, like a trickster, hard to tame. The mind is like a monkey in that way. You don't want to be controlled by the monkey mind; you don't want to follow it around on all its escapades. So, the purpose of yoga is to practice and strengthen your ability to not get caught up in the monkey's antics. The purpose is to experience your Self as separate from the mind.

One way your monkey mind gets carried away is by weaving and creating stories that aren't true. Your mind finds ways to support your views on life, relationships, and work. Your mind will support patterns of your thoughts whether they are accurate and healthy for you or not. As you go through life, you will have experiences that challenge that worldview, showing you truth and reality. At those times, you can stick to your own view or see if the new information seems as though it more accurately reflects things as they are. Maybe it will, maybe it won't. Being able to see things clearly, just as they are, without adding interpretation or assumptions doesn't always come naturally. Naturally, the mind enjoys thinking. It enjoys forming judgments, plans, projections, and predictions. You don't always have to follow it wherever it goes.

This is not to say all planning should be avoided or all judgment is unnecessary. Of course, in day-to-day life, it's important to make plans. For example, if you are thinking about whether or not to take a vacation, you need to judge the best time and way to do so. And of course, in your job your thinking mind is a special asset. So, often in your life, using your mind is a valuable thing. It's just important for your well-being that you also learn when not to get caught up in it.

In particular, judging others and comparing yourself to them is not productive for you, and it also is usually based on false assumptions. Perhaps when you judge others, you put yourself above them to make you feel better about yourself. Or, other times, maybe you think someone else's life is so much easier, and you feel jealous. The key is to know when your judgments, plans, etc., are helpful and when they are defense mechanisms or based on assumptions that you don't know to be true.

> "Be kind, for everyone you meet is fighting a hard battle."
>
> —Plato

If you think that someone you know has an easier life than you, remember, it may not be true. Everyone has struggles and difficulties. Pay attention when you are with a friend, or when you talk to the person who helps you check out at the store. Decide to spend time being an extra good listener, keeping your ears and heart open to hear what someone else might reveal. If you are compassionate and open-hearted, you will hear that others also have their struggles.

Witness Consciousness

Not engaging with the monkey mind is also called developing **witness consciousness**. You are a witness of your life. You are not your emotions or your thought patterns. You are the witness to them. **Hatha yoga**, the physical practice of yoga, is a way to practice strengthening your witness consciousness. As you experience yoga postures, you might notice thoughts come up. They might be about what you ate for breakfast, or you might wonder if your friends are going to the movies with you this weekend. You notice the thoughts, and you let them go by without continuing to think about them. This also can happen with uncomfortable feelings. If you are in a yoga posture that is slightly uncomfortable, you might think you need to stop right away. That is just a thought, your body can handle holding the posture a little longer as long as you are being safe, breathing into it, and making sure you aren't feeling sharp pain. In these moments, when you're feeling slight discomfort and you don't allow yourself to succumb to it, you are strengthening witness consciousness. While you practice this during your physical practice, it strengthens your ability to do it at other times in your life when uncomfortable situations arise.

> The *Yoga Sutras* of *Patanjali* outline the philosophy of yoga. As translated by Sri Swami Satchidananda, the second sutra says, "the restraint of the modifications of the mind-stuff is yoga." This is another way of explaining witness consciousness.

If you're waiting in line at the grocery store, and you're becoming impatient, notice that impatience. And, as you notice it, you can first breathe and allow it to be there. Keep taking slow, deep breaths, allowing the impatience to be there. Then, you can decide to let it go. It's healthy for you to let impatience go. Take nice deep breaths in, and let impatience go out with your exhales.

It's better for the cardiovascular system to relax and not get uptight about waiting in line. If that means you are going to be late for an appointment, you can call the person to let her know. Or, if you want to be on time, you have the choice to leave the store without buying the groceries. You can come back later. You have choice. It might not have been your preference to leave without your groceries, but this is practice in being with what is, not always needing it to be the way you want. You can decide either to be okay with waiting in line, be frustrated waiting in line, or leave the store to be on time for your appointment. When frustration comes up, breathe, allow it to be there as you breathe deeply in, and exhale completely several times. Then, often it's your choice whether to stay in the situation or get out.

Bringing Energy Flow to the Chakra System

While doing the postures of yoga, you focus and control the breath. When you direct the breath, you direct **prana**, your life force. And, as you move through the postures you are helping to loosen tension and create space for prana to flow more easily throughout the body. That is why certain yoga postures are ideal for chakra healing: they can help release blocks by helping create space for energy to flow in places that may have been blocked. When you unblock energy flow, you create health.

Basic Goodness

One of the mind's functions is to create opposites and opposition. It tends toward categorizing something as good or bad, and then you might develop attachment or aversion to it. To support your practice of being with what is, without labeling or judging as good or bad, think of the basic goodness of the universe that is bigger than you. Especially if you're impatient in line or in traffic, expand your mind to think of the overall basic goodness to help remove you from your stress. Once you've stopped the flow of frustration, you create space for you to think clearly and make a choice rather than be immobile and heated in your frustration.

> "We should look further and more precisely at what we are, where we are, who we are, when we are, and how we are as human beings, so that we can take possession of our basic goodness. It is not really a possession, but nonetheless we deserve it."
>
> —Chögyam Trungpa Rinpoche

In the book *Shambhala: The Sacred Path of the Warrior*, Chögyam Trungpa Rinpoche explains that everyone and everything in nature has basic goodness. Each person, at his core, is good, and nature is good. Rinpoche explains he doesn't mean good as opposed to bad. On the path to true healing, it's important to practice seeing the world exactly as it is, without judging it as good or bad.

In the case of basic goodness, *good* refers to the genius way that the body, mind, spirit, and world work together: it is good in that it works. The sun shines, which is good because it works in harmony with the rest of the world. The sunshine nourishes life with vitamins and heat, helping plants, animals, and people to grow. It is good in the sense that it is part of a system that works. In the same way, your body, mind, and spirit also can function in harmony with the world. This is goodness. And, it is called *basic* because it is fundamental and foundational.

To learn who you truly are, what your heart truly desires in and for the world, and what you truly need, takes something other than fulfilling an instant desire. Chakra healing is healing on a very deep level: It's more than a cure, it's a healing process. And, it's likely that you will find that your heart's desires, your deep desires, are not about material things or fast satisfaction but about human connection, taking care of the world within and around you, and being seen for who you truly are.

Chakras and Life Force

The chakra system circulates energy, the same life-force energy that illuminates the sky and creates life on earth. When the chakras are blocked they are not giving and receiving life-force energy in a balanced way. They are not functioning properly. This correlates directly to your psychological and physical states. Each chakra creates, aggravates, and ameliorates certain psychological issues and physical symptoms, and by noticing how you are you can decide which chakras need healing work.

> Balancing all the chakras is better than focusing just on one chakra. All the chakras are connected, and the life-force energy needs to be able to travel all the way up and all the way down for your optimum health and vitality. For quick fixes, you can focus on one or two, but later take time to balance them all.

According to Anodea Judith, there are stages in which chakras develop. When you don't receive the energetic, emotional, and physical support you need, or if there is an energetic overload during those times of development, then certain chakras can be blocked even when you're in the womb. The energetic exchanges you receive as soon as you are conceived affect your subtle energy system, just as the nourishment you receive affects your physical development. Now that you are aware of your energy system, you can work to heal imbalances that perhaps you've had all of your life.

Feel Life Force

Are you familiar with feeling your life-force energy? If not, try this simple exercise. Hold your arms out to the sides and rapidly wiggle your fingers and shake your hands in the air. Shake and wave your hands. Count to thirty as you do this. Then suddenly stop. Notice what you feel. Do you feel a tingling? Do you feel vibration? That's life-force energy.

> **Are my chakras affected by people I work with?**
>
> Chakras always exchange information and energy outside of the body. For this reason, be aware of how you feel around others. People can deplete you without meaning to. If you feel like someone drains your energy, you might not be able to spend a lot of time with him. By the same token, you can be nourished by another's healing energy.

Spend more time evaluating your energy level. Spend time noticing how others make you feel. Who in your life fills you up? Who makes you feel tired? It's not always just what they say or how they say it, people's energy fields interact with yours. Your electromagnetic field can be scientifically measured. It's real.

Chakras and Meridians

The chakra system is connected to major lines of energy in the body, called **nadis**. The life force that flows through these is called prana, in Sanskrit. Prana is the same as the flow of energy of Chinese medicine called *chi* and in Japanese *qi*. If you practice tai chi or qi gong, you are accustomed to working with that energy.

Acupuncture

Chinese acupuncture is based on the desire to help chi flow freely throughout the body. The practice of acupuncture is to place tiny hair-thin needles on acupressure points to stimulate certain **meridians** that connect to different organs of the body. Meridians are energy channels that connect hands, feet, head, and all body parts together.

Acupuncture is a treatment that you receive repeatedly, even if for the same condition. Many people experience relief immediately, but because energy is always shifting and reacting to other energetic stimuli, acupuncture treatment is something that is scheduled on a regular basis to help continue to balance energy flow over time. The results of one treatment aren't usually permanent.

Chakras Correlation to Specific Meridians

In Paul Grilley's DVD on the chakras, he gives a straightforward list of which chakras control energy flow through which meridians. Grilley's list is based on the work of Dr. Hiroshi Motoyama. The correlations are shown in the following table, with the primary meridians being the ones most strongly affected by their corresponding chakras.

CHAKRAS AND CORRESPONDING MERIDIANS

CHAKRA	PRIMARY MERIDIANS	SECONDARY MERIDIANS
MULADHARA	kidney and urinary bladder	small intestine, liver, and triple heater
SVADHISTANA	kidney and urinary bladder	small intestine, liver, and triple heater
MANIPURA	stomach, spleen, liver, and gall bladder	large intestine and small intestine
ANAHATA	heart and small intestine	heart constrictor
VISUDDHA	lung and large intestine	heart constrictor
AJNA	governor vessel and conception vessel	urinary bladder and small intestine
SAHASRARA	governor vessel and conception vessel	urinary bladder and small intestine

From Paul Grilley, *Chakra Theory and Meditation*

The purpose of having this research available is to notice how different systems of thought can work together for overall healing. If you already work with the meridians, there might be ways that you can use this information to enhance your healing practices.

Alternative Treatment and Modern Medicine

The U.S. National Institutes of Health (NIH) is a government institute that since 1998 has shown interest in the healing power of **complementary** and **alternative healing practices** for health, including yoga, meditation, acupuncture, tai chi, and qi gong. The NIH is also interested in evaluating the effects of **whole systems of health**, including **Ayurveda**. All of these practices work with your energy body, addressing vital parts of you that **allopathic medicine**—the use of drugs and surgery—does not.

National Awareness

The NIH has a branch called National Center for Complementary and Alternative Medicine (NCCAM). NCCAM presents information as well as conducts and funds research on the efficacy of complementary and alternative medicine. The existence of this branch of the NIH is recognition that patients are very interested in complementary healing modalities, and doctors are interested in finding viable solutions to health concerns. Many people want to read scientific data before diving into another type of treatment, unless they've already tried everything allopathic and realize they need to be treated with other therapies. So, as NCCAM can provide scientific statistics, it will help inform people of the potential of these other forms of healing. To see what NCCAM is up to, visit *http://nccam.nih.gov.*

In 2005, Sara Lazar, a Harvard scientist, conducted a study on Insight Meditation practitioners. While leading their normal lives including work, family time, and other engagements, the participants meditated thirty to forty minutes per day. This was enough to positively alter their brain structures. The study showed increases in cortex—the part of the brain that supports cognitive and emotional processing.

While scientific research is still conducted to measure the results of CAM, in the meantime more and more people realize the importance of adding complementary modalities to their allopathic plans for health. Whether you add yoga, tai chi, massage, chakra healing, or meditation into your schedule, each of these modalities works with your energy body.

Chakras and Modern Medicine

As always, before embarking on any new activities, it's important to talk to a doctor who understands clearly the medications you are on and how you are doing with them. Let the doctor know what you are going to practice, in addition to what she prescribes. Chakra healing complements modern medicine well because it's not physically invasive and doesn't have the negative side effects that drugs do. One way to understand it is as a way of directing the effects of your yoga, meditation, and prayer. Many doctors are interested in learning about such therapies, particularly when they offer something supportive to your overall well-being.

How do I find a medical doctor who believes in CAM?

Doctors who recommend allopathic treatment as well as complementary and alternative therapies are called *integrative*. So, ask around or do web searches for an integrative doctor. The NCCAM site says, "Integrative medicine (also called integrated medicine) refers to a practice that combines both conventional and CAM treatments for which there is evidence of safety and effectiveness."

After learning about the chakra-healing journey, you may decide to find an integrative doctor as your primary care physician. A wonderful integrative doctor will feel absolutely comfortable recommending pain medication and other necessary allopathic treatments. He also will believe in your choice to add complementary support such as meditation, vitamins, and massage into your plan for healing. He can help you come up with a plan, suitable for where you are in your healing process. If he isn't familiar with the chakras, he will at least have heard of energy healing, and you can talk to him about it.

CHAPTER 3

Mapping the Mind-Body-Spirit Connection

Knowledge of the chakra system originates in ancient Indian culture and is rooted in yogic philosophy. For millennia, yogis and Hindus have relied on the description of the body that includes five **koshas** or *sheaths* as described in the **Upanishads** (the tenets of the Hindu religion). The koshas serve as a map to help navigate moment-to-moment experiences as you embark on chakra healing as an integrative mind-body-spirit approach to health.

You Are the Observer

Do you ever feel caught up in emotions, as though you're being swept away or spiraling down? Take just a moment now to remember what that feels like. Isn't it true that when you feel that way, no matter how caught up you are in those emotions, you still can observe your emotional state? For example, you might say, "I'm so emotional today," or "I'm so excited!" With those remarks, you are noticing, therefore you are separate from, your emotional state. So, even when they feel most consuming, emotions haven't gotten control of who you really are. Who you are is the observer: your true essence is constant and in equilibrium. The map of the koshas serves as one of the tools to help strengthen your ability to tap into that balanced center, from where healing energy flows.

> St. Francis of Assisi said, "what we are looking for is what is looking." In other words, when you search for comfort, joy, and well-being in other people, places, or things, you will eventually discover that the feeling of "home sweet home" is inside you, always available. You just need to be reminded of your way back to it.

The Larger Picture of Who You Are

If you are new to the chakras and to the Law of Attraction, then you might not realize that you are more in control of your life than you acknowledge. By becoming aware of your intentions, reactions, thoughts, words, actions, and the larger picture of who you are, you can begin to create the life you've imagined. Instead of focusing on what you don't have, or on things about you that you wish were different, start focusing on what you want and who you want to be. Then, you will move in your desired direction, and the universe will bring opportunities and people into your life to support you on this journey in unbelievable ways. This will happen because you are an energetic being: you are the same pulsing, creative energy that unites all life in the universe.

Each thought is a vibration that continues into the universe, and the universe begins to respond. The universe helps you create that reality: some realities take longer to manifest than others, and each time you have a thought you are either working with or against what you truly desire. Here's an example of how thought-as-energy travels. Has there ever been a day when you were thinking about calling a good friend whom you hadn't talked to in a while, and then she called you that night? Perhaps you said, "I was thinking of you today!" And maybe it felt just like coincidence. However, because you are open to each other's energy, it's just as likely that she received your thoughts across time and space and decided to call. Over time, if you keep your awareness on such coincidences, you will begin to see the pattern that your thoughts are energetic and you draw things to you and create the life you imagine.

In the movie *Avatar*, the natives of Pandora hook up to other creatures, each other, and ancestors with filaments that allow them to link up energetically and communicate through thoughts and feelings. As humans we can also do this. We just need to open to it, to be reminded how, and to practice: no extra filaments needed.

You are an energetic being with a physical form through which you enjoy and participate in the world. The koshas are the diagram, the explanation, of the five sheaths that make up your embodiment in the physical form. By moving your awareness through each sheath, you fully experience what it means to be alive. The five sheaths, or koshas, are: **annamaya** (food sheath), **pranamaya** (breath sheath), **manomaya** (mind sheath), **vijnanomya** (wisdom sheath), and **anandamaya** (bliss sheath). The common ending in these terms is *maya*, which means *illusion*. Each of these sheaths is an illusion because they are each impermanent, not eternal. In yogic terms, you are **Atman**: the soul, the eternal energy. And the sheaths are like the layers of an onion surrounding you. Along your energetic core are the chakras, the spinning energy vortices, whose functions affect your experience of each sheath.

Your Physical Body

In chakra healing, your relationship to your overall health is related to knowing how to nurture and nourish yourself. Your physical body is the part of you that is matter, that you can touch, and it is known as the *annamaya kosha*, or *food sheath*. This includes your skin, body parts, organs, and any other part of your body that benefits directly from your eating, drinking, and exercise habits. This is your physical form, and the health of your physical body will affect the other koshas because they are all interconnected.

To maintain a healthy body, you need to eat well, strengthen and move your muscles, maintain good posture, rest, and have fun. You should also pay attention to how your body feels and have regular checkups with a health-care professional. As you become more in touch with your own body and its needs, you will feel empowered toward your own healing. You will know when it's time to rest, when it's time to eat more greens, or when fruit is the answer. And, your body will begin to crave the right foods for you, so you and your body will become a team, working together and enjoying the benefits that come with taking care of your miraculous physical body.

A New Hobby

Need inspiration for more movement? Try a variety of ways to get your body moving, till you find one or more that light you up like a new hobby. You could practice a sport or martial art, play with a pet, sign up for group classes at a gym, take dance classes (or just dance around the room), or hoola hoop.

Trusting Your Gut Feeling

Your internal organs are affected by your lifestyle, emotions, and external energy, and they gather unspoken information to help you make assessments and decisions in your life. When you have a "gut feeling," you are accessing information you've gathered not just from your five senses, but from what's going on inside you. At those times, you are drawing from perception within, from energetic input that your body senses in the present moment and has held on to from past experiences.

Having a Heart-to-Heart

Scientific studies show that the heart is an organ of perception, like the mind. A significant portion of the heart is made up of the same neurons as those in the brain. In addition, the heart produces an electromagnetic field that radiates outside of the body. When heart fields collide, information is exchanged, and when two hearts are near each other and literally beat as one, the exchange of information and sense of connection reaches far beyond what words convey.

When two people are in love, their Heart Chakras give and receive each other's energy. When one of those people leaves, the Heart Chakra of the one left behind lacks that back-and-forth flow of energy, and the Heart Chakra gets imbalanced. In grief, the heart can weaken.

Even if you have not recently experienced heartache, the Heart Chakra can be out of balance based on your childhood environment or other factors. As you work on healing this center, you'll bring more love and heart-health into your life.

Beyond the Food Pyramid

Have you ever been to a nutritionist? If not, meeting with one is a great way to learn how to eat well. Many people in our culture want to eat well and don't know how. That's understandable. With all the commercials and brilliant marketing, it is very difficult to know what is nourishing and best for one's body over time. And, once it is imbalanced, or having an allergic reaction, your body won't necessarily crave what will be healthiest. Getting information from someone trained in nutrition is the best solution. One of the best reasons to see a nutritionist rather than try diets or go by product labels is that each person's body is different, and it changes over time, so seeing someone who has studied the latest information in nutrition is a gift to your body that will help you be healthy and nourished.

> The chakra system is connected to yogic philosophy, and the system of health that is the sister science to yoga is called *Ayurveda*. Ayurveda works with your constitution to give you a personalized plan for nourishing yourself inside and out.

Without seeing a nutritionist, there is an easy way to begin to change your habits. The basic and easy rule of thumb is to eat locally grown, organic whole foods. Eat vegetables and fruits that are in season, and buy them fresh. Whenever possible eat unprocessed foods in all the colors of the rainbow. Buy red, orange, yellow, green, blue, and purple foods; each has different vitamins for your body and also corresponds to your chakras. Each chakra is associated with a specific color, so bring those colors into your body through the foods you enjoy.

Taking care of your physical body is an important part of chakra healing because each chakra is connected to specific organs and functions of the body. It's a two-way street: healing the chakras will have a positive effect on your physical body, and taking care of your physical body helps support your chakras. So, use this as an excuse to take time out each day to do something that feels good to your body—your health depends on it. Give yourself some space, freedom, movement, massage, comfortable clothes, nourishing food, and think positive thoughts about yourself. Negative thoughts and emotions about your body affect your body. When the negative thoughts about your body and health arise, allow them to be there. Then, turn your attention to thinking about what you can do to take care of yourself, and take one step at a time in that direction. As you begin to take care, your body will respond in positive ways. And, according to chakra theory and experience, as you learn how to balance your chakras, you will boost your physical health beyond what the necessary food, exercise, and rest will do.

Energetic Movement

You can tell what your energy level feels like from day to day. You know if you're sluggish, if you're hyperactive, or if you're feeling productive with a sense of ease. That vital force of energy is *prana*, and the corresponding sheath is called the *pranamaya kosha*. The way for you to notice the movement of prana is your breath. Try the following exercise to begin to become acquainted with your breath:

> As you read this, notice your breath. Did it stop when you tried to notice it? Try noticing again, without controlling the breath. Let it flow in and out. Is it flowing slowly or quickly? Is it shallow or deep? Do your belly and chest expand and contract? To turn inward and really get a sense of how your breath is flowing, close your eyes and just watch the breath flow in and out a few times, without forcing it. Take a moment to try that. Just notice the breath.

Now you've watched your experience of the sheath that is your connection to universal life-force energy (the force of creation that helps plants and trees grow, and that brings you health and vitality). In yoga practice and in sports, you increase your body's ability to strengthen and avoid injury when you focus and control the breath. Professional teachers and trainers can tell you which movements to make on the inhale and which on the exhale so you're using the breath to support your practice. And if you experience strong emotions, slowing and deepening the breath can help settle difficult emotions and calm your thoughts when they begin to race. You can practice **pranayama**, ways of controlling the breath, to help you either rev up your energy or calm you down (see Chapter 11).

In relation to chakra healing, when you practice breath awareness and yogic breath control, you nourish the respiratory and circulatory systems, whose major organs are the lungs and heart. The lungs and heart reside in the chest, which is the area that receives the energy of the Annahata Chakra, the Heart Chakra. So, connecting to the breath and pranamaya kosha through pranayama is important for Heart-Chakra balancing.

Mind over Matter

The mind, *manomaya kosha*, refers to what you think of as *I* or *me*, your preferences, and what makes you unique in personality and thinking patterns. You are predominantly in the energy of this sheath when you are reading this book and interpreting the information in a way that makes sense to you. You are also primarily in this sheath when you are worried or obsessing over something. And, "mind over matter" proves to be true: what your mind thinks has an effect on your physical body, your *annamaya kosha*.

> In *Journey Into Healing*, Deepak Chopra, MD, writes, "we are the only creatures on earth who can change our biology by what we think and feel." It might seem impossible, but our physical form can change by our thoughts and feelings. Even neuropathways in the brain can be altered by focusing your attention on new thought patterns.

When your attention is mainly in the manomaya kosha, you are using your deduction, planning, and learning skills. These are positive ways to use the mind. Because the mind is active, though, sometimes the deducing and planning can actually get in the way of you fulfilling your highest potential and your deepest desires. In our culture, we are used to working hard to get what we want, and it's true that work is part of the equation. However, if you think and plan all the time, trying to control your and other's lives in ways that aren't possible, then this can lead to stress and no room for intuition or wonderfully unplanned solutions. And, mental stress and worry affect the entire body.

In particular the chakra that is related to this kosha is the Ajna, Brow, or Third-Eye Chakra. Overthinking overtakes the potential of this chakra to tap into intuition. Meditation in various forms helps to calm the mind, and allows you to tap into your intuition more often. Balancing the chakra that relates to the manomaya kosha will allow trusting and letting go—the essential effortless aspects of attracting the health and joyful life that is your birthright.

The Sage Within

Everyone has a *wisdom sheath, vijnanomya kosha*. No one has to travel far and wide to find wisdom or the secret to life, yet many do so because the life experience, dedication, and guidance of wise teachers and authors remind each person how to access universal, inner wisdom. You are sagacious. As you read this book and learn about your chakras and the Law of Attraction, you will begin to notice how quickly you pick this up because it's already known to you. Don't be discouraged if it takes practice to strengthen and trust in your relationship to your own wisdom.

> In his famous book for children and adults called *Le Petit Prince* (*The Little Prince*), Antoine de Saint-Exupéry writes, *"On ne voit bien qu'avec le coeur. L'essentiel est invisible pour les yeux."* In English, this means, "One cannot see rightly except with the heart. What is essential is invisible to the eyes."

One of the differences between this sheath and the manomaya kosha is that this sheath interprets the information from your organs of perception—your gut and heart. It's not with the manomaya kosha but with vijnanomya kosha that you interpret the signals from your internal organs.

The Brow Chakra is directly related to the vijnanomaya kosha. When the Brow Chakra is in balance you access the universal wisdom. Making decisions from this place, from a place of universal wisdom, will get you into alignment. What you think, feel, say, and do have the potential to be in sync and this is the recipe for living the life that best suits all your talents, skills, and desires. It's the way you'll live a fulfilled life, doing more of what you love and loving what you do. And, you'll be surprised by how things that seemed out of reach might fall into your lap.

The World of Bliss

The *bliss sheath*, *anandamaya kosha*, refers to the state beyond figuring things out and worrying, beyond input from the senses, beyond effort. The anandamaya kosha is often described as "the feeling of unity or oneness." It can feel as though you've dissolved into the universal energy. You feel as if you are the same energy that animates the whole universe: you are connected to the life in the trees, the wind, the stars, and the fireflies. It's a feeling of bliss that all is one, there is no separate "this" versus "that." You can experience this in yogic sleep (yoga nidra), meditation, savasana, or restorative yoga. You can also experience this in everyday activities: enjoying a walk in nature, laughing with a loved one, or playing with the bubbles as you wash your dishes.

Spending time experiencing your anandamaya kosha gives you perspective, so that when you're experiencing life through the other koshas you can step back and not take life too seriously. You'll be able to remember that you are connected to the universe in a way much greater than one choice or one setback. This gives you less fear and more freedom to fully experiment and experience life, and when you fear less you can create more.

You are not your emotions, and you are not your physical body, your breath, your thinking mind, or your wisdom—you *have* a body, breath, a mind, and wisdom. You are who notices what your senses pick up and how your mind interprets those sensations. You can notice what your mind is thinking, and you can decide where to focus your attention and even change your patterns of thinking and believing. But before working on your relationship to your thoughts, it's helpful to know this foundational map of the koshas because they will add more depth and understanding to your yoga and meditation practices.

CHAPTER 4

What Is Chakra Healing?

Chakra healing is much more than healing your physical body. By balancing the chakras, you open up to your fullest potential as a physical and energetic being, which means you have the ultimate potential for health, happiness, and creating the life you want to lead. You will experience ease, joy, and unexpected miracles. By picking up this book, you have shown that you already know, however deep inside, that it's possible to live a healthier, fulfilled life, and you are investigating ways to do it.

Healing on All Levels

According to chakra theory, when all the chakras are balanced, your body, mind, intuition, and the part of you that is eternal (soul, spirit, source energy, etc.) all work together. At these times, each chakra is functioning well: you sense the state of your body, you express your creative ideas, you have energy to follow through on commitments, your heart is open to receive with appropriate boundaries, you are authentic in your communication, you look clearly and objectively at your thought patterns and habits, and you listen to the quiet place inside.

When this happens, what you believe, think, say, and do line up, and you can manifest what you want in your life. You are in sync with your body, your mind, and source energy, which connects you to all life and the energy of the universe. It is through this, your connection to universal energy, that you are able to manifest your desires and work on deeply healing physical, mental, and emotional wounds.

What is universal energy?

Universal energy is the energy that creates life. The sun, water, and all living beings are made of energy. Therefore, all things communicate and affect each other. Your thoughts are energy, and they affect the path of your life and the make-up of your body, whose basic units are atoms, or energy.

It seems in this fast-paced world, it's common not to focus on health until something goes wrong. It seems normal to keep going and going until you feel an ache or pain, and then you visit a doctor. Until a physical sign affects the way you perform your daily activities, it's easy to ignore how you're feeling.

Part of Everyday Life

Maintaining good health is an ongoing practice, not something to wait to do until you're already showing physical symptoms of disease. Chakra healing can be done regularly, as part of your ongoing self-care practice, and this will be both a proactive and preventive way to take care of yourself and bring more joy into your life.

Find at least one way per day to do something for yourself. It might mean that you get up fifteen minutes early to linger with a cup of green tea, or maybe you will park your car further away from work to walk in the fresh air. Find something each day to give yourself some healthy "me" time.

Imprints in Your Energy Field

Disease first shows up in your energetic body, and so by working with your chakras you are helping prevent disease and deal with the root of where any present disease begins. If you've never thought about your subtle energy system, you're on the right track now.

Healing the energetic centers is the key to overall health because they are connected to everything else about you. If you only treat signs of disease in your physical body, the blocks and traumas that are stored in your energy body will eventually cause more physical disease. This is what chakra healing on all levels refers to: unblocking and balancing the flow of energy for the health of your body, mind, and spirit.

According to chakra theory, imprints of your karma from past lives are stored in the chakras. By working with the chakras you are not just clearing wounds you've accumulated since your birth in this life, you are also working with past lifetimes of karma. The body dies, and the energy system carries karma from one life to the next. Working on clearing the chakras is a way to keep evolving toward becoming a light in the world, and liberation or nirvana.

Getting to Know Yourself

The first step of chakra healing is to learn to become aware of how you are feeling physically, mentally, and emotionally moment to moment. Slow down during your day, and this will help you get used to paying attention to how you are. When you notice yourself dashing from one place to the next, losing your keys, or having ten different to-do lists, it's a perfect time to realize you must slow down. Take a deep breath. Pick up the to-do lists, and consolidate them.

On the other hand, if you are someone who doesn't feel rushed and busy, if you are instead feeling too static and bored, that is a good thing to notice as well, as you begin your chakra healing journey. The first step is learning to notice how you are feeling, not just physically, but also mentally and emotionally.

At least a few times per day, take a moment to pause and notice how you are feeling. Are you tired, worried, bored, or frustrated? Are you happy, grateful, productive, or content? At what points in the day does your state of mind shift, if at all? Make it a practice to begin to notice how you are feeling during your days and nights. How are you feeling right now? Notice. And, do not judge your feelings as good or bad. Just notice. For example, if you feel anxious during the day, there is no need to be discouraged, the first step is to notice without labeling it "bad" or "good." You'll come to see that labels aren't useful, and how you are feeling during the day affects your body. Noticing how you are feeling, in specific ways, will help illuminate how to proceed with chakra healing and will help you notice the benefits.

> "I've often heard the Dalai Lama say that having compassion for oneself is the basis for developing compassion for others. And this includes trusting oneself—trusting that we have what it takes to know ourselves thoroughly without feeling hopeless because of what we see."
>
> —Pema Chödrön

It's easy to get out of touch with yourself while focusing on the business of life. Family, work, and friends can occupy so much time that you might sacrifice your own needs. It's even likely that you aren't aware of your own needs because you feel too stuck or overwhelmed to pay attention and move forward.

High-Speed Living

Life is fast-paced, and in today's world it is especially easy to act and respond quickly to others. Texting, e-mailing, and mobile phones mean that information travels instantly, so things can get done fast and you can move onto the next to-do. The ability to multitask is often desired by employers, and this means that employees are mentally juggling several things at once. Accidents happen on the road because people are trying to drive and text. It's become a way of life to occupy the mind with more than one thing at a time. With this multitasking it's possible to occupy yourself with more and more and more distractions, and neglect yourself.

There are many possible reasons why you would get caught up in the fast-paced life. It's fun, it's stimulating, and the world has much to offer. In addition, consider whether or not you avoid looking honestly at yourself because you aren't sure what you would do with what you might find. There could be difficult feelings held inside, feelings held not only in your mind but also in the cells of your body. Your body holds memories. Looking at yourself, whether it's specifically at your mind or your body, can be intimidating. If a deep hurt is buried within, you've buried it as a self-preservation mechanism. So, when you go to unearth it, in this healing process, make sure you have support. Chakra healing supports your overall well-being, and it's best to do it while you are still working with your usual doctors, healers, and energy workers.

> Being in contact with a professional therapist or doctor, especially when you start a new healing process, is always a good idea. While the practices in this book can be done by yourself, when it comes to your health, always check in with professionally trained and reputable doctors, therapists, and energy healers as you progress.

With technology allowing you to be so connected to huge amounts of information in any second, it's important not to let the technology run you. You run the technology. So don't be afraid to turn off your computer for a few hours on a day when you're not working. Or don't answer your phone for a couple hours so you can hang out with your family or a friend. Give technology a break sometimes; it will be there when you come back to it.

The Hidden Sides of You

One important piece of chakra healing involves being willing to get to know yourself in the way you show up in the world—the sides of you that you might feel proud of as well as the sides of you that you might find unbearable to admit, the **shadow sides**. For healing to occur, it is important that you allow all sides of you to come to light, so you can work with them. In order to allow things to surface, keep an open mind, allow any judgments to gently float away. In the yogic tradition, this includes being open to seeing your good and bad karma, so you can make amends in the ways that are necessary to break free from your particular karmic patterns.

It might be hard two admit to your shadow sides, and so it might be hard for you to even know what they are. One way to notice your shadow sides is to reflect on times when someone does something that bothers you. Why does it bother you? Now, take some time and ask yourself if you ever do the same thing to others. You might not realize or think you do, but give it a few days or a week of awareness. Keep your eye out to see if you do that same thing that bothers you. Often others provide mirrors for us of our patterns, without us being aware enough to notice.

Now, dig deep and ask yourself, why do you do that thing you can't bear when you see it in someone else? What is it in you that causes you to do that? It's possible that you are protecting yourself in some way. As Rumi says in "The Guest House", welcome it in, be compassionate with it so that you won't repress it, again. What are you protecting yourself from? Ask yourself if you are ready to drop the fear and attachment to that pattern, and if not, what is holding you back?

What is
holding you
back?

Opening to Real Transformation

As you pause during the day and begin to notice how you are feeling, start noticing your reactions to what goes on around you. Those reactions belong to you, and you can change them. For example, if you are in a traffic jam, and you're getting uptight, angry, and frustrated, that is something you can change. You cannot change the traffic jam, you can change your reaction to it. And, it is your reaction, not the traffic jam, which negatively affects the health of your body and mind.

Breathe to Create Space

The way to change your reaction is first to notice it. That separates you from the feeling. Then, begin to breathe deeply in and exhale it all out. Breathe a few times, in and out, letting the frustration go, knowing it's not serving you to be frustrated. And, if you begin to worry that you are going to be late for an appointment, just let it go. There's nothing that worrying will do, even if you are going to be late. Make space and think about the bigger scheme of things: you have to be concerned about your health. In the moment, relax. Breathe deeply.

A traffic jam is an easy example of when you can notice your reaction as your own and practice changing it. When it's not a traffic jam in your path but another person who hurts or threatens you, you might have more trouble disengaging from your reactions. You may want to completely blame the other person for how you are feeling. In these circumstances, it is best to breathe when you feel your reaction come up. Take deep breaths, first. This will help dissipate the energy of your reaction so that you can deal with the situation in the most productive way and also cause less stress to your system.

Counteract the Effects of Stress

In addition to noticing your reactions, add more uplifting moments into your day. For example, after a long day of work, if you walk outside to get the mail, pause for a moment before going back inside. Take a few deep breaths and notice something beautiful in nature, or think about something you are grateful for. In the same way that being irritated in a traffic jam causes stress to your system, taking a few breaths with gratitude affects your health in a positive way.

> Worry is not preparation, though sometimes you may think it is. The next time your mind is occupied with worry, remember that worry doesn't prepare you for anything. Decide if there is something you can do that is productive about what you're worried about, or talk to someone for advice. Worry, in itself, blocks you; it's not productive.

Slowing down, noticing your reactivity, adding pauses to your life, and calming down: this is the catalyst for real transformation. You are on a journey of transforming patterns that you've been reinforcing all of your life. You are opening up to something better and more spacious, and it takes trust. It takes trust in yourself that you can do this, and trust that something good will come of this. It takes a belief that it is safe and okay for you to change.

You Are Intangible

As you begin to notice your reactions, you are separating yourself from them. You are the witness, and you are intangible. The real transformation begins when you begin to live from the place of your witness consciousness, instead of getting caught up in your reactions to others, to situations, and to limited beliefs about yourself.

At times, your reactions are defense mechanisms, and they come from the deep place within where fear resides. If you can observe those reactions, you will notice they aren't productive and they don't help you thrive. Your reactions are productive indicators for you on your path of wellness. Use them to see what in life gets you stuck. Then you will see which chakras to balance to help clear those blockages.

> In her poem "The Invitation", Oriah Mountain Dreamer juxtaposes a list of achievements of the physical world with the powerful journey to who you truly are. She writes, "It doesn't interest me/where or what or with whom/you have studied./I want to know/what sustains you/from the inside/when all else falls away."

When things happen in life that bother you, anger you, frustrate you, as the witness you can step back, look at the situation as it is, and breathe. Exploring the rough spots and the difficult emotions takes work and courage. At the same time, the healing process that you embark on can be creative, loving, and enjoyable.

Enjoying the Process

Being in the body can be a pleasurable experience. All of your senses have the capability to bring pleasure into your life: your eyes see the colors of a sunset and your sense of touch feels a soft breeze on your body. All it takes is a moment to experience the beauty of life around you and just "be."

In addition to appreciating the senses, taking care of your body can be enjoyable. The body wants to move, wants to be nourished, and wants to be healthy. Your life force wants to flow freely through you. If you haven't taken care of yourself for a while, at first it might seem difficult to start new habits. Then, in just a little bit of time you will start to notice a difference, you will feel the urge to keep taking good care because it will feel good. Taking care of yourself also can be fun: it's about finding the right activities for you and bringing an open-minded, positive outlook to the process. Soon you will feel a difference and the desire to keep up with your new habits.

Embark on a Mysterious Journey

Learning about the chakra system can be a mysterious and adventurous journey. You are learning about something that is not on the physical or mental plane. Exploring the chakras is a mysterious journey because it's energetic and it's experiential, just like a kiss. The magic of the first kiss is the energy that's exchanged, the energy that you feel inside, and the energy that arises in you when you think about physically connecting with someone you're attracted to. Experiencing that energy is transformational, whereas reading what someone else says about kissing isn't. The same goes for chakra healing and exploration. You can get guidance from reading the work of people with years of experience, but the only way for you to test the healing power of chakra exercises is for you to try it for yourself.

> Being intimate with someone you trust can be healing for the chakras. The trust between you strengthens Muladhara, the sexual intimacy supports Svadhistana, the passionate fire stokes Manipura, the love lights up Anahata, sound and communication support Visuddha, your intuitive connection strengthens Ajna, and the energy that rises up can connect you to Sahasrara-bliss.

It's best to have no expectations when you begin your chakra healing journey. Don't expect it to feel or be a certain way, stay open and allow it to be what it will be. That's when the magic happens. Alternate between time for study and stepping back to receive and allow the journey to unfold.

Creative Healing

Rather than thinking, "I *have* to heal my chakras for my health and happiness," think of chakra healing as a creative project. There are colors, sounds, stones, mantras, postures, and more for you to choose from. Instead of feeling overwhelmed by options, realize that you have choice.

You can try different practices at different times, and stick with the ones that feel they work best for you. The hardest part might just be setting aside the time to do it. Make space for this creative project that has the benefit of deep healing.

Creating New Relationships

As you begin this process and open to change, you might find your-self wanting to have people in your life who also are interested in the chakras, in overall well-being, in taking responsibility for their actions and reactions. Finding like-minded people will become easy. It's one of those mysteries you'll become accustomed to: once you start asking the universe for something or someone, in time the universe will provide.

Being in Your Own Way

After you put an intention out there, your job is to stay open, keep watching your reactions, notice if you get in your own way, and believe what you've asked for is coming. Oftentimes your own insecurities and assumptions stand in your way of attracting whom you would like into your life. Notice your insecurities, allow them to be there, and then let them pass. Believe you are worthy of such a friendship or partner. Working with the third chakra will help your self-esteem, the fourth chakra will help with your new connection, and the fifth will support you speaking authentically.

> **Why is it important to line up my beliefs with my desires?**
>
> According to the Law of Attraction, if you want something but believe that you won't get it, you're sending out conflicting vibrations. Your belief of not having and your desire for having are two different messages. If, instead, you feel you want something, and believe it's coming, you are sending out one vibration and the universe responds.

Chakra healing can only occur when you are open to change. When you really do want to heal, and when you really do want new relationships in your life that support you on this journey, you have to get out of your own way. In other words, your insecurities, doubts, fears, and judgments of what may come next will block you from continuing on the journey. Change, even positive change, requires courage. To allow it to come, do not stay in the place of fear; practice trusting.

Your Dream Partner

Have you spent time consciously asking for what you want in a partner, or do you just vaguely wish for the perfect partner without naming qualities? Don't be afraid to dream big. Take the time to think, specifically, about what you want. Write down the list, specifically, of 100 things you'd like about your partner. You won't attract what you want in life if you don't know what you want. In specific and authentic ways, write down what you want in a partner. And, then, be open to seeing what unfolds.

Everyday Magic

There is magic in your life every moment, it's up to you to choose whether to acknowledge it. The very fact that you are alive and breathing, that your heart beats and your breath flows involuntarily: this is magic. A flower grows on a vine and soon becomes a pumpkin: this is magic. And, as you open to the magic of yourself and your energy, you will notice in big and small ways that things come to you in a way that seems like magic. If being open to unexpected miracles seems neither possible nor reasonable, begin the chakra-healing journey. As you balance the chakras, over time, your view of what's possible in the world just might change.

The Gift of Imagination

Imagination is the best way to come up with new ideas for your life. Let your imagination go. There's no risk in imagining what you would like to do or have in your life. What have you wanted to do since you were young? Or, what have you heard others do recently that you wish you could do? Is there an adventure or a relaxation break you're interested in taking, even if not this year? Even if it seems like it would take a miracle for your dreams to happen, write your answers onto a sheet of paper. On another piece of paper, write down all the thoughts that are coming up, telling you reasons why you cannot have or do those things. Get the negative thoughts out of your system. Now, on the back of the first page that has your wish list, write down how you could literally make them happen. What steps would you need to take? Even if they seem unrealistic, write them down. When a negative thought comes up, write that on the other piece of paper that has your negative thoughts on it. At the end of this exercise, burn or throw away the negative thoughts and re-read the wish list. Keep that in your daily planner, or in your purse. Just let it ride along with you throughout your days. When you have the energy and time to work with it more, take it out again and start doing the steps. Until then, though, let it just hang out with you as you go about your daily life. Something magical might eventually happen.

Taking the time to let your imagination flow freely helps open you up to your dreams of what you want and need in your life. Each of us needs rest time, play time, and fulfillment. Allow your imagination to tell you what your heart desires. Acknowledge it, write it down, nurture it.

"Everything
you can imagine
is real."
–PABLO PICASSO

CHAPTER 5

Chakra Healing Benefits

Physical disturbances such as headaches, fatigue, and stomachaches are symptoms of disease that begin in your subtle energy body before manifesting as disease or pain in your physical body. If you only treat physical symptoms, those symptoms (and others) will return unless you address the imprints in your energy field. Those imprints can occur at birth, or even earlier. By healing your chakras, you are working on deep healing that lies beneath the show of physical pain.

Overall Well-Being

It's a tall order to ask for overall well-being. Healing the chakras can live up to that request, but it will require conscious effort from you. Have fun with it, be creative, and enjoy healing the chakras. In fact, an important part of this process is coming to it with the knowledge that this is something good for you and can be enjoyable. At the same time, healing the chakras will likely bring up difficult memories and emotions that you've been repressing or suppressing because they felt too big to deal with. As you enter on this journey of chakra healing, the potential is for overall well-being, and you will embark on a revealing process.

To heal on a deep level, you must care about what's happening in your subtle energy system. The subtle energy system works in tandem with your physical body and psychology, so unblocking energy flow can restore you on psychological, physical, and mental levels.

> Energy healer Annie B. Bond uses chakra healing to help those who have undergone chemotherapy. She notices that chemotherapy significantly reduces the energy in the chakras. After she performs a healing, "the pranic energy begins to spread out through organs and permeate bodily systems, bringing with it rejuvenating life force . . . One wonders how slow recovery would be without such a replenishing."

Alleviate Suffering

Chakra theory exists to help you navigate the journey of healing on all levels, and ultimately this means healing from all suffering. If you want to be free of suffering entirely, according to yoga philosophy you would transcend what the yogis call the cycle of **samsara** that includes birth, death, and rebirth.

Yogis believe you return lifetime after lifetime in physical form to work through your karma. Some karma affects your life in a way that will feel helpful to you, and some affects your life in a way that will make you feel uncomfortable. The sincerely beneficial, positive things you do for others and the world will come back to you in the same way. If you are dishonest or if you act in a way that is not harmonious in the world, when that karma comes back to you it will make you uncomfortable. In this view, what goes around comes around.

To get beyond this cycle is to transcend the cycle of samsara, not identify at all with a physical body or the pleasures and pain of the world, and merge with the oneness of the universal energy. There isn't an easy how-to-manual on that process of liberation, but the *Yoga Sutras* by Patanjali is a guide. Because of their relationship to prana, chakra meditation is a useful place to begin.

Authentic Self-Awareness

As you study your chakras and work to balance them, you will become more and more aware of who you truly are. You will notice yourself as an energetic being with unique gifts and wounds. You will look openly and with courage at where you close off in life, where you are open, and where you feel stuck. You will be able to see these habits in yourself and decide to practice letting them go.

> **If I don't believe in reincarnation, can I benefit from chakra healing?**
>
> You can use chakra healing with any belief system. Chakra healing gives you the opportunity to examine your patterns and health now, and learn which chakras correlate to your habits and symptoms. Then, by balancing the chakras that are out of balance, you can work on healing starting today.

As you uncover your habits and patterns, you will discover where you need to loosen up. In other words, you will learn where you can loosen your energetic grip on ways of being that really do not serve you. The easiest way is to begin to notice where your thoughts often go, what you focus on, who and what angers and upsets you, what brings you joy, what makes you tired, what gives you energy, what you wish for, and what you resent. As you sort out which things light you up in your life, you begin to acknowledge what your gifts are. And from there you can realize your **dharma**, how you can best contribute to the world. This is authentic self-awareness.

Your Dharma

Being truly open to seeing your own talents and natural passion in life requires courage, trust, and wisdom. All of these qualities can be worked on through chakra healing. It takes courage to follow a path that might go against what your family has taught you, or that you think you can't do. It takes trust that the universe will provide the support and abundance you need and desire. It takes wisdom to combine knowledge with intuition.

> There's wisdom in believing what you know deep inside about any situation, even if your mind tells you otherwise. The inner knowing is there. You might not want to hear it because it might mean something must change. Even if you choose not to take action, take time to hear what's going on inside.

It's likely that if you've not been following your inner knowing in relationships, work, or lifestyle, you might have illness because of it. To heal the illness you might have some important life transitions ahead of you as you work on following your inner knowing. And, following that wisdom will be your dharma.

Chakras and Your Life Path

Chakra healing can be a huge support as you discover and follow your dharma. When you do grounding practices for the Muladhara Chakra to keep it in balance, your body will feel grounded. When the body feels grounded, your mind calms down. As you move up the chakras and balance the Svadhistana Chakra, you enliven your ability to go with the flow. You might need to accept some upcoming change, and this helps you flow with it. Moving up to the Manipura, you stoke the fire of will, self-esteem, and stamina. Healing the Anahata will help you in your connections with others, perhaps they'll give advice and wisdom. A balanced Visuddha will help you stay true to yourself, when choices arise. The third eye will be your connection to your wisdom. And when you meditate on Sahasrara you'll experience the calm feeling of oneness that restores you on this journey.

Improving Relationships

Whether in partnership, companionship, marriage, friendship, or relationships with coworkers, working on chakra healing will help you in your relationships. You will:

- Feel more balanced, so you will be less needy and know you are supported.

- Be able to put things in perspective when conflicts arise.

- Become aware of which people in your life are not good for you.

- Attract the types of people you want in your life.

- Have the courage to initiate important conversations.

- Have a healthy sex drive.

- Become a good listener.

Chakra healing helps you in relationships because you will understand that you and others are energetic beings. You will understand that you have your own energetic blocks as does the other person. You will notice how your energy complements the energy of another, and how your energies mix in difficult ways. And with this knowledge, you can step back, take a breath, and have a conversation about what you are noticing.

Conscious Communication

There might be times in your life when another person repeatedly does something that hurts you. If this is a relationship worth keeping, it will be helpful to discuss the difficult situation. You can come to the conversation not blaming the other person and really wanting to explain that something isn't working for you. Then you can try to come up with a solution. There are certain techniques of conscious communication that you can practice. Following is an example of a situation that calls for conscious communication.

Julie has lunch with her friend Frederick once per week. Julie makes it a priority to be on time, so much so that she'd rather be early than late. Julie is this way with all of her lunch dates. She will judge whether or not traffic might be heavy or parking might be hard to find, so she will not be late. For Julie, being on time is her way of showing her friend that she respects him and values his time.

Frederick is late every time they have lunch. He is late by fifteen minutes. Each time he has an excuse to do with parking, hitting all the traffic lights, or having to wait too long in line at the bank before meeting Julie for lunch. As far as Frederick is concerned, he enjoys having lunch with Julie, he does his best to be right on time, and he doesn't realize being a few minutes late bothers Julie. Also, Frederick has other friends who are sometimes fifteen minutes late, and he isn't bothered by it.

For Julie, it's a real problem. On her own, she can own this reaction and do some work to try to temper it. But, she might be so upset she needs to talk to him about it and see if a change can happen. She could let Frederick know that when he is late for a lunch date, she feels angry; she imagines he doesn't respect that her time is precious, which makes her frustrated. She could say that she needs to feel like a priority when they make a lunch date, and her request is that he arrive on time or call if he is running late. For example, her conversation could follow a template like this:

- **When you . . .** (*state a very specific act*).

- **I feel . . .** (*identify your feelings, such as sad or angry*).

- **I imagine . . .** (*what you then think, or assume about the situation*).

- **Which causes in me . . .** (*explain what you feel because of what you assume*).

- **I need . . .** (*relate this to the need inside of you that you feel isn't being met*).

- **My request is . . .** (*state a request, as a request, to see if this could work for the other person*).

This kind of communication takes some practice. Because you need to be able to break down your reactions and speak them to the other person, this will likely take some thought. A good way to enter into a talk like that is to first ask the person if this is a good time to talk, and if not, then ask to set aside a time to talk so that it's not rushed or catching him off-guard. You want this to be a time when you both can listen to each other and have time to talk.

This approach to communication is based on the technique of conscious communication taught at Kripalu Center and the model of Nonviolent Communication (NVC) by Marshall B. Rosenburg, PhD. For more information about NVC go to: *www.cnvc.org*.

> Many times when there is hurt or anger between people, there has been a false assumption or misunderstanding that will likely remain unclear until there's a discussion. Being able to talk about uncomfortable situations often will illuminate where the misunderstanding lies.

Chakra healing can strengthen your courage to have a conversation, staying in the place of compassion and curiosity knowing that your interpretation and the other person's will likely be very different. It's important to come to the talk with tenderness, even if you're feeling hurt. And, if you are on the other end of such a conversation, try to really hear what the other person is saying. Try listening, without reacting, to what his experience is. And, you could work together to find a solution of how to stop the hurtful pattern. In relationships, listening is an invaluable skill to practice.

Intimacy

When you work with chakra healing, you will notice which chakras are blocked. Every chakra is important when you're in partnership with someone. Creating intimacy requires energy from all chakras: the trust in safety of the Muladhara, the sexual intimacy of the Svadhistana, the fire and passion of the Manipura, the tenderness of the Anahata, the openness of the Visuddha, the connection to each other on the level of intuition through the Ajna, and the connection to the bliss energy through the Sahasrara. When you are intimate with another person, sometimes the energy of their chakras can help awaken one of yours. Or, if you both are balanced in the same chakras, they can give and receive well to each other. If you both are blocked at the same chakra, the relationship may struggle until you realize where you are blocked and can talk about it and deal with it compassionately and patiently.

The Joy of Self-Care

Taking care of yourself can be a pleasure, and you deserve it. You already know you deserve to brush your teeth and take a shower. In fact, you deserve more self-care than that. Your body, mind, and spirit need you to pay attention. You will be more productive, a brighter light, and a support in the world if you take time out each day to take care of yourself.

Gradual Morning Movement

Get up early enough to have time to do a morning routine. At the very least, before jumping out of bed, take a moment to pause. Take a few breaths. Allow yourself to wake up in bed. Do a few easy, simple stretches. When you get out of bed, make sure you have time to eat a good breakfast, brush and floss your teeth, and step outside for a breath of fresh air before moving on with your busy day. It is healthy for you to enjoy yourself even as you start your day. It is said that discontent and too much seriousness block you from enlightened bliss and are signals that you are attached to your physical body and the cares of the world. Lightening up is good all around, for body, mind, and spirit. You still can participate in the world, and care about the state of affairs with more lightness and nonattachment to the outcomes. In other words, do your best work in the world without expectations of reward. Let the work itself be where you find contentment. Let it be the same with self-care. Enjoy taking care of yourself.

Eating the Rainbow

When grocery shopping, pick out foods in all the colors of the rainbow. If there's a food of a certain color and it's new to you, look for recipes online. Ask friends and coworkers if they have any favorite recipes for the season and swap. Take pleasure in trying new things, and seeing how many different colors you can eat in one day.

For the Good of All

When you take care of yourself, you're helping yourself and those around you. By being healthy you are a light for others, and a model of how good health can look and feel. As you become healthy, others will wonder how you did it. Taking pleasure in taking care of yourself allows others to see that it's possible and to feel all right doing the same. And, when you are healthy, you have the energy and ability to give back.

Ease, Safety, Joy, Trust, and Peace

The benefits of chakra healing, in sum, are that you can manage your life with more ease and less stress. This happens because life-force energy flows through your chakras in an appropriate way, and the energy spreads throughout your entire body. Energy affects psychological and physical functions, and because it's life-force energy it is good for you. It's the energy of creation, of transformation, of life.

Add a Sense of Ease to Your Day

Chakra healing has the potential to create more ease in your life. When you work with the chakras, you are following yogic and meditative practices that are designed to remove your mind from fixation on worries or stress. You are cultivating witness consciousness, whereby you'll see things just as they are without adding extra drama. By practicing creating less of a drama in your mind, you will create space to feel more ease around things as they come up. In addition you are bringing energy into the body with these healing practices, which can help feed parts of you that feel depleted or shut down. Having more energy can make your day easier.

Safety

Feeling safe is a basic need. If you don't feel secure or safe at home or supported by family or friends, your mind is occupied with that until you can make a change. This change could be a combination of needing to change your attitude, realizing in what ways you are safe, or if you aren't physically and emotionally safe, taking action and reaching out for guidance and help. If you are living in a safe home, and if you have food to sustain you and clothing to keep you warm, it's important to work on your Muladhara Chakra to help you feel safe in a world of uncertainty. The practices for the Muladhara Chakra are designed to help you feel grounded and connected to a feeling that all is well.

> Pema Chödrön, in *Comfortable with Uncertainty*, writes: "being able to lighten up is the key to feeling at home with your body, mind, and emotions, to feeling worthy to live on this planet." Here, she's addressing the issues of the Muladhara Chakra.

The main issues of the Muladhara Chakra are feeling safe and that you have a right to be alive. Pema Chödrön's books are resources that address those issues and many others. They are books you can turn to again and again for support and reminders about how to deal with the ups and downs of your life.

Joy

Accessing joy is a healthy part of life. When you feel lighter and joyful your body can function in its normal way without being tight from worry, or working extra hard to deal with the effects of stress. The way to joy through the chakra journey comes from the meditative and healing practices that you do, and the open attitude that you bring. Think of bringing a childlike curiosity, wonder, and innocence to the process.

> "We should feel that it's wonderful to be in this world. How wonderful it is to see red and yellow, blue and green, purple and black! All these colors are provided for us. We feel hot and cold; we taste sweet and sour. We have these sensations and we deserve them. They are good."
>
> —Chögyam Trungpa Rinpoche

An important addition to having the childlike wonder and joy is to feel like you deserve it. Not that you deserve it in an entitled way, as if you are better than others. Rather, you deserve it in the sense that it's okay to enjoy it, appreciate it, and take it in. In other words, you don't have to feel guilty for finding pleasure in life. It's healthy for your mind, body, and spirit to honor and have gratitude for life, breath, and what the earth provides. No one benefits if you are miserable.

Trust

A benefit of chakra healing is trusting. If you have life-force energy flowing appropriately through the chakras, your ability to trust will be healthy. This means you will trust more in your relationships, you will trust more in your abilities, and you will trust more in the basic good-ness of the universe. Trust also takes practice and belief. You have to practice your belief in other people, in yourself, in the basic goodness of the universe. The only way to gain more trust is by trying it out.

You won't be able to know if someone is trustworthy unless you give them the chance to show you. You won't know your abilities if you don't test them out. And, you won't know the basic goodness of the universe if you are always so sure the world is out to get you. These practices aren't easy. If you are used to not trusting, it won't be easy to turn it around. If that applies to you, the first step is to notice it. Then, you can add chakra healing to your modalities for healing this issue. In particular, the Muladhara Chakra deals with trust, in general, and balancing the Manipura, Anahata, and Visuddha will help you trust in yourself.

What happens if I send healing energy to the wrong chakra?

If you end up sending healing energy to a chakra that is already in balance, it will not have negative effects. All of the chakras will benefit from nourishing practices. All of the chakras affect each other, so sending healing energy to all will work well.

Chakra healing is a positive thing for your mind, body, and spirit. Enter it with gentleness and patience. It's essential for you to go gently and pay attention to how your body responds. Do not do anything that will cause you pain or seems too much for you. Gently and carefully cultivate this relationship with your energy system.

Peace

Finding peace comes first from within. If you feel as though you are constantly struggling, it's time to relax. At your very core, in stillness, there is peace. If you aren't used to accessing it, it will take some practice. Chakra healing helps bring peace to your life because you are allowing the life force to flow freely through the body's energy channels, supporting the body's endocrine system and **sympathetic nervous system**. When those are supported and they do not have to work overtime, then at appropriate times you can rest and your **parasympathetic nervous system** will become engaged. When your body is not in flight or fight mode, overworking the sympathetic nervous system, your body has time to restore itself. And as the body restores, you can feel at peace. If energy is flowing well through the body, it's much easier to feel peaceful than it is when energy is blocked.

CHAPTER 6

Chakras and Psychology

One of the most obvious ways to evaluate which chakras are imbalanced is to pay attention to how you're doing psychologically. The energy of certain psychological patterns has been traced to particular chakras. When you notice which patterns you're exhibiting in your life, you can work on balancing the energy of the corresponding chakra and the chakras directly above and below. When the chakras are functioning well, they will support your psychological equilibrium, your mental functioning, and your physical health.

Root Chakra: Security, Safety, and Stability

The issues of the Muladhara Chakra concern your basic needs. Do you have a safe home as well as money for food and clothes? If your basic needs are met, it's important to notice if you feel safe, secure, and stable. Your sense of security, safety, and stability comes from within, once you do have enough resources to live a comfortable life. At times when you truly do not have a home, food, or clothing then your thoughts will understandably be preoccupied with getting those for yourself. You instinctively need those basics.

At times when you have your needs met, then check to see if you still feel unstable in relationship to your basic necessities. If you still feel unstable, this could be a pattern imprinted in your energy field. A sense of real security comes from within, it's not about money. It's the belief that you have the right to be alive. It is in believing that you are worthy of loving and being loved. It stems from the recognition that your life isn't an accident or a mistake, and that you aren't a burden on the planet. You can shine and be seen, heard, and appreciated. And, you deserve to have money, a home, a car, and the pleasures that life offers. If you aren't secure in your right to exist, to be safe and content, then you will not feel stable, safe, and secure even with enough money. You will never feel safe until you address those deeper issues of your basic right to be alive and well. You can support yourself and strengthen such beliefs by working with the Muladhara Chakra.

> If you feel "spacey" or unable to focus, work on balancing your lower chakras. In particular, start with the energy center closest to earth: the Muladhara. Balancing the Root Chakra will help bring you out of the clouds and back down to earth.

Because all the chakras work together, if one isn't working well it will affect the others. If you're feeling unsafe and insecure, you will not have the energy for other aspects of your life such as being productive at work or be open to loving relationships. Dealing with the psychological issues of the first chakra will form a base support for all else in your life. When your Muladhara Chakra is balanced you are able to see tasks through to completion, you feel supported, and you feel safe in your day-to-day life.

Dealing with Anxiety

If you have feelings of anxiety, you can get help from the Muladhara Chakra. When you are anxious your mind will spin in circles of worry. You also might notice physical effects: your heart may beat faster, your breath may become shallow, and your belly may become upset. Chronic anxiety can lead to various physical symptoms and disease.

When you are anxious your energy is predominantly up in your mind. So, you want to bring your energy down. Doing something physical, energizing the body, will bring energy down from the mind into the body. If the weather permits, get outside to allow the earth's force to help ground you. Whether or not you can get outside, breathe in and out slowly, gently, and deeply, feeling your body expand to allow the air to rush inward on the inhale. Envision your connection to the earth, as you imagine your inhale going through your body into the ground. Create longer exhalation than inhalation to induce relaxation. If you are standing up, imagine your legs as though they have roots growing deeply into the earth. Know you are rooted and connected. If you want to sit down on the ground or floor, then you can imagine the energy coming down from your head out through the Muladhara Chakra into the earth. For several minutes, breathe and envision energy coming down into the body and flowing into the earth.

> Stomping your feet is a great way to ground. If you stomp outside, you leave the energy out there. Let it go. You can even stomp your feet outside each day after work, before entering your home. Even if you love your job, this will allow you not to bring work stress into the house.

If you recognize that anxiety is common in your life, add more physical activity into your day. If your tendency is to be thinking all of the time or if your job requires a lot of brain power, make sure you take some physical movement breaks. Literally move your body. This could mean putting on your iPod and dancing for a song (even at your desk), or while you're sitting down giving your face, arms, legs, and back a massage. At the very least you could stand up and take a walk down the hall or outside for a five-minute breath of air. Taking a five- or ten-minute break every hour or two during your day will not slow you down, it will help your productivity.

When you're taking a break to move, bring your awareness and attention into your body. If you're walking, feel your legs moving and standing on the ground; ground that energy. If you're doing a self-massage, notice how your muscles feel. And, don't worry that if you stop you won't be able to think again. Leave yourself a note about what you were doing, and when you return, your energy will be able to go back up into your mind and start working again. This is very healthy; it will give your mind a much-needed break, and help you practice grounding your energy so when anxiety arises you can ground yourself.

Attention Deficit/Hyperactivity Disorder (ADHD)

Chakra healing activities and therapy that focus on issues associated with the Muladhara Chakra could complement traditional treatments for Attention Deficit/Hyperactivity Disorder (ADHD). ADHD is characterized by restlessness, inability to focus, and impulsive behavior. The grounding quality of a balanced Muladhara Chakra that connects the body and mind to the earth could create a sense of comfort being still and focusing.

Creating Financial Abundance

You have the right to have money and to have success in any area of your life you choose. It's okay to have money, it's okay to be successful, and it's okay to work in a job you enjoy. If you have a deficient first chakra, you may be prone to fear that can affect your aspirations to acquire or hold onto what you need. You may associate different fears with accumulating what you want. On top of not believing you deserve it, it's possible you will be afraid of what might happen if you do become successful or have exactly what you want.

Fear can be a very useful part of your life. It will allow you to be cautious and examine risks and potential pitfalls as you make decisions in your life. If you stick in that zone, though, of fearing the potential pitfalls rather than moving ahead and giving new things a try, then you are being ruled by a deficiency in this chakra. When you work to unblock this chakra, you are unleashing your cosmic ability to bring your dreams to reality. The results of bringing new projects to fruition, entering new relationships, acquiring money, and improving your physical health become reality with the energy of this chakra.

Eating Well

If your Muladhara Chakra is underactive, you may notice you aren't eating enough and are losing weight. An excessive energetic response is overeating to help you feel grounded. It's true that eating can help ground you, so it's a valid physical response. In the long run, it's not healthy for your body to continue to eat to feel grounded. If you notice your eating habits aren't healthy for you, try Muladhara-balancing exercises and mentally check-in with yourself to see if you can address what makes you feel unsafe.

Clinging

If you notice you have clinging patterns, your Root Chakra could be acting excessively to compensate for its imbalance. To try to feel more stable, you cling to people and possessions. Clinging behavior will cause people to pull away, which will leave you feeling more ungrounded. If you notice yourself acting this way, it's a sign of an unbalanced Root Chakra.

Sacral Chakra: Creating and Adapting to Change

The health of your second chakra, Svadhistana, shows up in your emotional stability, sexuality, creativity, attitude toward pleasure, and relationship to going with the flow of life. Being able to enjoy dancing, having sex, creating, and trying new experiences all relate to the second chakra. If you feel guilty when you think about taking pleasure in life, if no new activities interest you, or if you can't enjoy the sensations in your body (including massage or dancing) then it's likely that energy isn't flowing steadily through the second chakra.

What is a healthy relationship to pleasure?

A healthy relationship to pleasure is when you can enjoy yourself and feel satisfied afterward. For example, you can enjoy going dancing for a few hours, and also you could live without it. It means that your ability to feel emotionally balanced isn't dependent on that pleasurable activity, and it's not your way of avoiding reality.

As one of the lower chakras, Svadhistana is associated with feeling stable. Being able to go with the flow or explore something new with creativity is also related to how secure you feel. If you aren't feeling as though you are basically safe, supported, and allowed to be as you are, then trying new things will be incredibly difficult if at all possible. When your second chakra is balanced, you enjoy taking pleasure in life, you can tap into your creative juices, and you have a healthy relationship to your sexuality.

Addiction and Repression

Addiction is associated with an unbalanced second chakra. If you don't have a healthy relationship to pleasure, it can turn into addiction. In this case, perhaps you feel as though you can't get enough of what you have been denied or what you think you shouldn't do. So you are compelled to desire it, to have it, or experience it over and over. This can show up as obsessive behavior, and reinforce itself in a guilt-filled indulgent pattern of behavior. Guilt shows up in this case because you are denied something pleasurable, and then it can become exacerbated when you allow yourself to have it. Addiction can be a sign that the second chakra is reacting excessively.

On the other hand, if you are completely withdrawn from pleasure, creativity, and sensation, then the chakra is deficient. Both are blocked conditions, it's just that the exercises you choose to unblock the chakra will differ based on whether you're dealing with an excessive or deficient chakra.

Sweetness

A literal translation of *Svadhistana* is *sweetness*, and when this chakra is balanced you feel at ease enjoying life's pleasures. You relax when taking a hot bath. You smile when eating ice cream. You intentionally rub the flannel sheet against your cheek when pulling up the covers. You experience intimacy with your sexual partners. These all are moments that are pleasurable, and your enjoyment helps balance your Sacral Chakra.

Solar Plexus: Self-Esteem, Willpower, Transformation

The third chakra, Manipura, is your personal power center. When you're feeling secure about what you have to offer, when you can turn challenges into opportunities, and when you feel good about offering your ideas to others energy is flowing well through the third chakra.

A common quality that challenges this chakra's flow is shame. If you deal with issues around shame, bringing energy to this chakra will be a helpful piece of your practice. If you avoid confrontation, or if you isolate yourself from the world, working with this chakra could be very supportive for you.

Depression and Chronic Fatigue

Depression and chronic fatigue can be symptoms of a weak third chakra. A functioning third chakra is associated with an appropriate amount of energy and enthusiasm for moving forward in life; a deficient chakra shows less will for living, doing, and participating. In those cases, energy moves sluggishly through this chakra, which isn't supportive of its element: fire.

A healthy dose of fire is essential, but pay attention to see if you have an excessive third chakra. Are you secure sharing the spotlight and tasks, or are you demanding and overbearing? If the answer is the latter, you could be compensating for a weak third chakra. Knowing the difference will help you tailor your healing process.

If you experience depression, working on bringing more energy to this chakra can help. Sometimes, be aware that perhaps you need rest. If you've been overdoing it, the body and mind could use solid downtime. Exhaustion can be the result of numerous things, so when your body calls for rest allow yourself time to rest. Especially if you know you're dealing with a lot and juggling a lot in your life, of course you will need time to recharge. If you find that your need for sleep hinders your day-to-day activities, that's when you should talk to someone about it, and also try the energizing Manipura activities. You also may need a combination of both restorative and energizing activities in your day. You can stoke your Manipura fire, as well as make sure you're giving your body and mind the rest they call for.

Depression can also be associated with the Heart Chakra. Because a deficient Anahata Chakra can cause you to feel isolated and alone, depression can follow. Bringing energy to both the Manipura and Anahata could be very helpful complements to your other treatments for depression.

Anger

A lot of anger reveals an excessive third chakra. Other symptoms are being judgmental, impatient, and controlling. If these are qualities you relate to, an important part of your practice will be the methods that balance an overactive third chakra.

Motivation for Your Healing Journey

When energy flows well through the third chakra it will help you with your entire healing process. Willpower will help you stick to your practices, good self-esteem will remind you that you're worth it, and the transformative energy will help you literally transform. Take good care of this chakra, as you do with all of them, because it will help you push through the sluggish doldrums that you may sometimes feel. And, when energy flows freely here, it will help you initiate projects or changes in your life you've been wanting.

Heart Chakra: Expansive

The Heart Chakra is tender and sensitive. It perceives the energy of others, and gathers information. If your Heart Chakra is blocked, it not only prevents you from giving love, it stops you from feeling love. In this case, the Heart Chakra is protected in its closed-off state, and it cannot receive.

Heart Connection

When your heart is open to receive the energy of another living being, information is exchanged that goes beyond what words can convey. You may never be able to put it into words, and it wouldn't matter. There is a felt sense of communication between two friends, family members, and lovers when the heart space is open that doesn't need to be expressed in any other way. You may feel it as warmth, you may feel it as joy, you may feel it as support. However it feels in your physical body, you know that your hearts are communicating with each other and exchanging nourishing energy.

Having an open heart can feel risky. Anodea Judith explains that when love is rejected, it can cause a person to "dis-integrate." In other words, instead of the connected feeling that the person wanted to share, rejection can cause an intensely uncomfortable feeling of separateness. The Heart Chakra may close. It's a risk, arguably well worth taking.

In instances when the Heart Chakra shuts down, you can reopen it with healing practices just as you can open all of the chakras. Though the heart is sensitive, it is also strong. It can recover from heartache if you nurture it.

True Love

Love at the Heart Chakra is different from the sexual love felt in the second chakra. Love at the Heart Chakra is unconditional, it doesn't have to be between lovers, and it lifts your spirit. There's acceptance, support, joy, respect, and true care between people whose Heart Chakras are both open to each other. It's a feeling of peace and harmony like no other, and it continues to create good feelings such as spaciousness, acceptance, and ease. An important aspect of this type of love is also self-love, self-acceptance.

Like any other chakra, the Heart Chakra can be excessive. If you are so vehemently expressing your love and not pausing or relaxing, you cannot take in love. In this case, it would help to use chakra healing to transfer the excessive energy into other chakras, leaving space in the Heart Chakra to receive.

Throat Chakra: Authentically You

The Visuddha Chakra is the energy behind self-expression. This is the chakra that allows you to express your true feelings, wants, and needs. While you need the proper functioning of all the chakras, when Vissudha is imbalanced you will have trouble with relationships socially and professionally. This chakra relates to your communication skills.

Learning to Ask for Support

Others won't know what you need or how things are really going for you if you are unable to tell them. At work, this could lead you to burn out, if you are unable to clearly and appropriately ask for the help you need. In relationships, those who love you will not know what makes you feel supported, what hurts you, and how to work together, if you avoid having the hard conversations. If you are unable to express your truth, you could become resentful of others and frustrated. Understandably, from their perspective, if they don't know what you really want or need, how could they support you? In your efforts not to rock the boat, others will not have the benefit of your viewpoint. The effect is that you may choose to leave relationships or jobs rather than have the conversations that could actually make things much better.

> One way to energize your Throat Chakra is to hum or sing more often. If you don't want to sing in front of others, sing in the shower or sing in the car. If someone drives by and notices, you might inspire her to do the same.

Just as speaking your truth will allow others to support you, it will allow you to support them. When you are supported and heard, you can focus your energy on the tasks at hand rather than losing energy to emotions or blocks that come up because you're not saying what needs to be said.

Listen Carefully

If you talk often, rapidly, or loudly, your Throat Chakra might be excessive. One of the ways to calm your energy down is to set an intention to listen more often and more carefully. Reassure yourself that you will get your turn to talk, if not today, then next time. With an excessive Throat Chakra, you might feel you need to keep talking to be heard to feel connected. Know that listening will help you feel connected.

If you truly listen to another person, you are witnessing something sacred, a connection between two people. It's a miracle to be in these bodies with these abilities to talk, listen, understand, and respond.

And, we all have our own language. Even if you speak to someone who speaks the same literal language, often the same words will land differently for different people. When listening to someone, truly listen.

Forging the Path of Your Life

Some say that creativity is linked to this chakra instead of the second chakra. Creativity at the Throat Chakra refers to the way you can contribute to the creation of your path in life based on your ability to express yourself. You create your life by being able to tell people your gifts and talents, by contributing to conversations, and by helping to solve problems. If you're standing on the sidelines because your Throat Chakra is weak, others may not notice you or realize how much you have to offer. Self-expression is key to your own development and to being able to use your talents in the world.

Contributing to Evolution

When the Throat Chakra is balanced, you are able to stand in your truth. You are unafraid to communicate what you think, you listen to other people when they respond, and you are open to hearing other points of view. Together, you can solve problems, support each other, and enjoy life. If your chakra is excessive, you might be overly talkative and self-righteous, causing another person to shut down. If your Throat Chakra is deficient, you will likely be soft-spoken and unable to stand up for what you need. The goal is to be an honest, effective communicator with a compassionate and authentic voice and ear.

The Third Eye: Seeing Beyond the Physical

This chakra is your connection to the wisdom beyond your five physical senses. It's beyond your gut feelings that get input from outside stimuli; this is your connection to wisdom. This is the energetic center of your ability to telepathically send thoughts and images to others, including your animal friends.

Wisdom

Knowledge generated here is a different kind of knowing from what your mind or body know. This is your connection to wisdom of the ages. Here, messages come to you that you know to be true deep inside. When this chakra is balanced you are making choices that are aligned with who you truly are. You don't settle for less than what you deserve. What you deserve is kindness, respect, love, and all the support you need. For this chakra to truly be in balance, the other chakras must be, too, which means that you'll be giving and receiving energy appropriately at the other levels. In other words, your sense of what you truly deserve will be coming from a rational, grounded, compassionate, and mindful place. Then you will feel deep trust in the wisdom of the universe and make decisions from that place. You will trust that as you follow what you know to be true, with integrity and self-inquiry, you will be supported.

Logic

If you always make choices based solely on logic, then your Third-Eye Chakra will not have much energy flowing through it. If you are not open to the possibility that something great can happen without you controlling every moment, without you figuring it all out first, then you will be limiting yourself to what you know or what you logically think is possible. There's so much out there that you might not yet know about. Can you be open to seeing what could unfold beyond your imagination?

> "There are more things in heaven and earth, Horatio, than are dreamt of in your philosophy."
>
> —Hamlet

With a balanced Third-Eye Chakra, you will use your mind for all that it can give you. In this way, you will strengthen your knowledge with study and discernment. At the same time, you will be open to wisdom and gifts that can come to you when you step back, quiet the mind, and receive.

With this chakra, watch out for living in illusion. Illusion in this case could mean that you hold onto false beliefs about yourself and others, things you believe you've "sensed" without seeing if reality supports that belief. If you notice you hold on to certain judgments or beliefs that aren't serving your relationships, bring energy down from this chakra.

This chakra is where studies merge with intuition. When this chakra is functioning well, you are shining brightly in the world. You are confident that at this moment you are acting based on knowledge and your sense of what you know to be true. It might feel like you have to take some risks in life, and you will wisely decide in which ways a risk is worth it. With the grounding from Muladhara, the fluidity of Svadhistana, the power of Manipura, the openness of Anahata, the authenticity of Visuddha, you are well-equipped to handle what you decide to do.

Nightmares and Obsession

Because this is a center for creativity and imagination, an excessive amount of energy in this center could cause nightmares and obsessions. Those are effects of an imagination in overdrive. If you notice you are prone to nightmares, or fantasies that become obsessions, then chakra healing practices to bring energy down from this chakra will help diffuse that energy.

The Crown Chakra: Unity

This is your connection to the blissful energy that you notice in the glory of a colorful sunset. Here is your connection to the energy of pure consciousness, the intelligence of the universe, the feeling that all is one. Having a well-balanced Crown Chakra helps strengthen your witness consciousness. You'll have an easier time not getting drawn into life's drama or attached to things you really don't need.

Inner Peacefulness

When you have energy flowing freely through this chakra you have a sense of inner peace. You're not thinking about other people's opinions of you. You're not worried about your physical survival. You're not dreaming that things would be other than they are. Your personality is magnetic because you're fully alive. You are experiencing health mentally, physically, and spiritually. You have an understanding of boundaries so that you aren't oppressive, overbearing, or manipulative. You understand that you are a separate being in your body, needing to take care of your health and life, and you balance this with your understanding that we are all one.

Bipolar Disorder

In Liz Simpson's *The Book of Chakra Healing* she lists bipolar disorder as a symptom of a Crown Chakra that spins too quickly. Of course, seeing a medical doctor is of utmost importance if you have this condition. In addition, chakra-healing practices to bring energy down into the body would be very supportive. Practice grounding chakra exercises daily.

Exhaustion

While exhaustion could use the help of all chakras, constant exhaustion and the inability to make decisions could indicate a deficient Crown Chakra. If you aren't connecting to the energy that exists beyond your physical body, if you feel limited to just what your own body and mind can produce, you may be prone to exhaustion.

CHAPTER 7

Chakras and Physical Healing

Healthy chakras support physical health. A good rule of thumb is if you have physical pain or dysfunction in your body, work on the chakra nearest to that area. Low back pain and leg pain, for example, would correspond to your Root and Sacral Chakras. To heal chakras and the physical body, complementary healing modalities using visualizations, crystals, and color work with vibrations to strengthen chakras. These techniques allow you to use your own creativity and intuition. As always, if you are new to these therapies, collaborate with a trained healer.

Chakras and the Endocrine System

Energy from the chakras affects the glands of the endocrine system, which initiate essential biochemical processes. If you notice you have an imbalance in your physical body that relates to any gland in the endocrine system, then you can trace that function to a specific chakra. Working on that chakra will then balance the energy flow to that gland and support its proper function.

Sex Hormones

The endocrine system's glands that are closest to the earth are the gonads. These are responsible for the production of the hormones that are responsible for the secondary physical characteristics associated with male and female and fertility. The hormones are testosterone, progesterone, and estrogen. If you have troubles from improper secretion and functions of these hormones, work on your lower chakras. The first and second chakras' energies support the gonads.

Fight-or-Flight Response

The adrenals balance the body's response to stress, including regulating your metabolism and supporting your immune system. The adrenals get activated in the "flight-or-fight" response, regulating the hormones adrenaline, cortisol, and aldosterone. If you are often in the "flight or fight" response, your body doesn't have time to revitalize and nourish itself. Balancing the lower chakras will help ground you and bring you out of this condition that is meant just for times when you really need it.

If, for example, you're in fight-or-flight more often than relaxation, take the time to figure out why. Is it based mainly on external factors? Is it predominantly psychological? Look into the causes and work on ameliorating them. In addition, find ways to add relaxation into your life. In relaxation, your body recovers from the work, thinking, and moving that you do all day. Relaxation is restorative, and helps the body perform its functions.

In addition to relaxation, balancing the lowest three chakras can help get you out of flight-or-fight response. For example, if you're in flight or fight often because you're experiencing a lot of change, bringing energy to the Muladhara will help stabilize and ground you. Working on the Svadhistana will help you relax around the changes, and be more fluid. And, the Manipura will give you fire and courage to feel self-confident as you ride these waves of change. Energizing these chakras, because of their location, will send energy to the adrenals to support them while you're dealing with so much change. A combination of energizing your chakras and getting enough rest will help your body stay healthier in stressful times.

> Stress includes environmental stress (i.e., pollution), emotional stress, mental stress, and stress from being exposed to anything you're allergic to (including food). It also includes life changes. Even if it's a promotion, or anything you consider a "good" life change, several big changes at once can compromise your health. Pay attention to your body, nurturing it every chance you get.

If you're under stress for a period of time, it can cause your adrenals to work overtime and need some support. Stress will have a domino effect, causing other glands of the endocrine system to overwork. Energizing all of the chakras will support the function of the gonads and adrenals, which work together with all the glands in the endocrine system.

Sleep and Metabolism

Studies show that when you're getting enough sleep, particularly in the rapid eye movement (REM) state, your ability to problem solve and come up with creative ideas increases. Getting enough sleep is also linked to maintaining a healthy weight. If you are sleep-deprived, your body doesn't function at its optimum level. Your endocrine system will be taxed, so your metabolism will be affected. You will not absorb vitamins in the way you need to, nor will you burn calories at an appropriate rate. Getting enough sleep will help your body restore and rejuvenate, bringing your metabolism into balance.

A wonderful way to add more deep relaxation into your life, to get all the benefits of good sleep, is to practice **yoga nidra**, yogic sleep. Yoga nidra is a deep relaxation technique that also can help with insomnia, the inability to sleep. There are several CDs you can purchase that are guided yoga nidra experiences.

To experience yoga nidra, play a guided CD, lie down in a comfortable position, listen, and let go. It's best if you try to stay awake so you can consciously follow what you're hearing, unless you're doing it for insomnia. In that case, of course, the goal is to fall asleep. Even if you fall asleep, you will still receive the benefits of yoga nidra. Doing an hour of yoga nidra is as restorative as almost a full night of sleep.

Is weight loss related to sleeping?

Two hormones in your body relate to hunger. Ghrelin tells you you're hungry, leptin tells you you're full. Sleeping seven to nine hours per night regulates those hormones and your hunger. If you only get four to seven hours of sleep, your ghrelin levels will be higher than your leptin levels, and you will likely gain weight from overeating.

Yoga nidra refers to the state you will experience that is between wakefulness and being sound asleep. In this state you become deeply relaxed, at the level of each kosha. In some guided yoga nidra, you are guided to set deep intentions. Anytime you give energy to your intentions, they are set further in motion. Setting intentions in yoga nidra is powerful because you're in a meditative state, free from other distractions.

Manipura and the Pancreas

The islets of Langerhans cells in the pancreas are responsible for secreting insulin, which metabolizes sugar. Dysfunction here can result in diabetes. Because of its location in the body, the third chakra's energy flowers out toward the pancreas. A blocked third chakra could affect the functions of your pancreas over time.

Anahata and Immunity

The center of the sternum is where the Heart Chakra flowers out. In that region is the thymus, which produces T-cells that recognize when something foreign is in the body. Loss of function of the thymus hinders the body's ability to fight infection. The Heart Chakra's energy radiates outward toward this gland in the endocrine system.

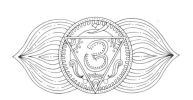

Visuddha and the Thyroid

The Throat Chakra flowers out toward the thyroid. Troubles with the thyroid include hyperthyroidism, hypothyroidism, weight problems, sore throat, and difficulty swallowing. If you have a thyroid condition, pay attention to the Throat Chakra when you do your healing practices.

Ajna and Sahasrara at the Command Center

The upper two chakras are both near the brain, near the pituitary and the pineal glands. The pituitary gland is thought to control and regulate the function of all of the glands. The pineal gland secretes melatonin in response to darkness; it helps regulate your sleeping schedule. If you're having trouble sleeping, gently massage the top of your head and then the third eye. Bring awareness to those areas. Do this for several minutes, imagining relaxation and serenity floating from your fingertips deep into your mind.

If you don't necessarily understand the exact connection between the chakras and the endocrine system, it's okay because much about the endocrine system is yet to be discovered. What's important is that if you have troubles with any functions of your endocrine system, chakra theory can complement your other treatments.

The endocrine system, like all systems of the body, is complicated. Science can explain certain functions, though it doesn't yet claim to understand everything about how the endocrine system works. Because there are so many unknowns about the mind and body, supplementing allopathic treatments with your own visualizations, intentions, and attention can speed up and increase healing.

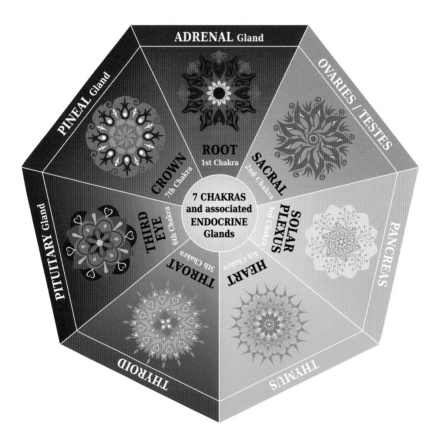

Chakras and Crystal Healing

Crystals come from the earth and are believed to have certain healing qualities. When you place the crystals on your body, your intentions help the energy of the crystals enter into your body. The healing energy vibrates into your physical body and stimulates the chakras.

Cleansing Crystals

Before using your crystals, it's important to cleanse them of negative energy. You can cleanse them by leaving them out overnight in the light of a full moon. The energy of the moon is said to clear them, returning them to their own pure vibration. There are other ways to cleanse crystals of negative energy:

- Go to a fresh spring, and bathe your crystal with the points facing downward.

- Create a salt solution using sea salt and water. Only use sea salt and cool water. Place the crystal, point down, and leave it to cleanse in the solution overnight.

- Bury your crystal in a jar of dry sea salt, dried herbs, or outside in the earth overnight.

- "Smudge" your crystals by burning sage leaves and clearing the air around the crystals with the smoke from the burning sage. You can buy sage already bundled specifically for smudging, and one bundle can be used several times.

Use glass or ceramic containers to cleanse your crystals. And before cleansing crystals in water, make sure your crystals aren't water soluble or else they will dissolve. As you cleanse your crystals, imagine white light flooding through them. Send them love from your heart and fill them with an intention, such as, "I intend for this crystal to cultivate easeful healing for my highest good." It's always best to use the word "ease" and "easefully" when you set intentions for healing.

Choosing Crystals for Each Chakra

Books and charts differ about which crystals will help heal each chakra. You can cultivate your own relationship to crystals, and find which ones you can connect with. There are some standards with each chakra that follow the rainbow as a guide: red for Muladhara, orange for Svadhistana, yellow for Manipura, green or pink for Anahata, blue for Visuddha, indigo for Ajna, and a white/clear or amethyst crystal for Sahasrara.

Allow yourself to be creative with the crystals. Find out what particular crystals are known for, and match them up to what you might need at each chakra. Because each person is different, there is not a prescription that will suit everyone. As a starting point, though, the rainbow guide will work well.

The colors of the rainbow associated with each chakra will help bolster a deficient chakra. If you have an excessive chakra, rather than using a crystal to enhance that chakra, try using a crystal at the chakras below or above the excessive one to help diffuse the excess energy.

Crystal healing potential is activated by the mind's intention. Just like all else on earth, crystals vibrate at certain frequencies. When placed near the chakra you want to balance, with your or your healer's intention, the crystal increases the healing vibration. Crystals amplify the energy you send through them and draw out negative energies from the body.

Once crystals have been cleansed, keep them in a nice pouch on your altar, or in another special place (see "Creating an Altar," page 171). If you keep them in a place where you can see them, then every time you see them you can be reminded of the natural beauty and healing energy that comes from the earth.

Placement of Crystals

One of the ways to use crystals for healing is to place one in your non-dominant hand. Meditate on the crystal, its healing power, and the intention you want to infuse in it. Hold the crystal in your hand, and then move your hand toward the area of your body for healing to occur. Hold it there, with the crystal against your body, and meditate on its healing energy. On each exhale, envision the crystal drawing negative energy out. On each inhale, imagine the body absorbing the crystal's healing energy.

You can also use one of the meditations from this book that is appropriate to that chakra. If you want to do this lying down, you can lay the crystals on your body and meditate with them there while you lie down. Some say that the less you touch the crystals the better, that way their energy remains purely their own. Others say as long as you keep your energy positive and on your healing, then your own hands and energy will enhance the crystal's effects. Try it both ways and see which way works best for you.

After you've finished using the crystals for this visualization, take some time for the healing effects to integrate. Give yourself a few moments, at least, before resuming other activities. Allow the effects to sink in.

You could also use crystal healing after another chakra healing practice. For example, you could start your chakra healing session with a yoga sequence, and then follow it up with crystal healing. Or, while you do your yoga sequence you could take a few sips of your crystal essence.

Is there another way I can use crystal energy for healing?

You can create an "essence" with quartz. Water will copy the crystal's vibration. To create an essence, place spring water in a glass container, and have crystals surrounding it with the points facing the water. After a few hours, use it in your bath water or sip it a few times per day. It will last two to three days.

If you create an essence, or elixir, it has the vibrational quality of the crystal. To preserve your essence for more than a couple of days, place it in a dark glass bottle and add the same amount of vodka as liquid, as a preservative. Keep the bottle out of sunlight and out of contact with other bottles.

Crystals Matched with Chakras

There are many kinds of crystals to choose from. Here are some examples of crystals you can use at each chakra, following the rainbow as your guide.

With these suggestions as your guide, you will find crystals of different shapes and sizes. It doesn't matter which one you choose. Choose what you feel attracted to, and don't forget to cleanse it before each use.

CHAKRA	CRYSTAL
Root	Bloodstone
Sacral	Carnelian
Solar Plexus	Citrine
Heart	Rose Quartz or Jade
Throat	Lapiz Lazuli or Turquoise
Third-Eye	Amethyst
Crown	Clear Quartz or Moonstone

Color Therapy

Working with a similar principle as crystal healing, color therapy uses the vibrational quality of color to resonate with your chakras. You can use the color associated with a particular chakra to add energy to the deficient chakras. Color therapy is used in various ways today. It comes from ancient wisdom and modern exploration and investigation. If you decide to use color therapy, and want to deepen your knowledge, see the work of Theophilus Gimbel.

Deciding What to Wear

One way to increase the energy of a particular chakra is to wear the color of that chakra. For example, if you have a meeting in the afternoon and you want to increase your willpower, your self-esteem, and your fire, wear something yellow—the color associated with the Manipura Chakra. Notice, in the chakras where you feel weak, is there a lack of that color in your life: in your wardrobe, room, or jewelry?

Taking in the Colors of the Natural World

Notice the myriad ways in nature that color appears, and use the vibration of the light from those natural objects to affect you. For example, for nourishing your heart take a walk in the green, spring grass. For groundedness in the winter, buy yourself a red poinsettia. To heighten your connection to spirit, keep purple lavender by your bedside. Take time to look at these objects, and be mindful of what you surround yourself with in your home and office. Your body perceives the vibrations, even if you aren't looking.

There's never a lack of inspiration from nature when it comes to color. Flowers come in spectacular shapes and colors, and the colors of animals, plants, and the sky are innumerable. Taking in the vibrations of color will stimulate your body if you aren't completely energetically closing yourself off.

The smell of lavender is known for its relaxing and soothing effects. It helps with depression, anxiety, and insomnia. What's more, lavender is a blueish-purple color that is often associated with the Ajna Chakra. And this chakra is often associated with the pineal gland, where melatonin is produced to help induce relaxation for sleep.

Colored Water

A way to perform color therapy on yourself is to pour pure spring water in a glass bottle that is the color you desire. Set the bottle in the sunlight so that the water absorbs the vibration of the color. Then, throughout the day, take sips of that water.

Because as an adult, your body is around 70 percent water, you absorb the vibrations around you just as water does. When you drink water that has a particular vibrational frequency, your body will copy that vibrational frequency. If you are new to color therapy, start slowly with this practice. Anytime you begin a new energetic practice, take it slowly. Don't overdo. Your body is intelligent and sensitive. Overloading your system by taking on your practice too quickly will not lead to the opening or expansion that you hope for. With patience and a regular practice, change will occur.

Reiki and the Chakras

Reiki is a healing modality during which a trained practitioner, called a Master or Teacher, acts as a vessel to transmit the life-force energy to your body. Reiki can be performed on you when you are fully clothed. A Master can also do Reiki for you from a distance. If you become trained in Reiki, you can use it to charge anything with positive energy, or to heal or cleanse the chakras.

When someone is trained as a Reiki Master, he is given attunements, which attune him to the energy of the universe. During these attunements, energy moves up and down the chakras. First, it goes from the Crown down to the Root, and then back up again. It can bring life into lifeless chakras, bringing new levels of awareness and sensitivity into your life.

CHAPTER 8

Meditation and Visualization

A requisite skill of healing your chakras is meditation and visualization. Observe the mind and learn to focus on an image, color, sound, your breath, or nothing at all. If you haven't intentionally meditated before, you might think, "I can't meditate." Let that thought go. That's your first lesson in meditation: let the thought drift by. In meditation the goal is always the same: as the potentially distracting thoughts come up, let them go by. A common metaphor is: your thoughts are clouds drifting across the sky.

Learning to Meditate

Meditation can be the most wonderful experience of your life because it's when you experience life right here, right now. You will allow your attention to be on the quiet and basic goodness of the present moment. Worries about the past, present, or future are not your concern when you meditate. There are several ways to be in meditation, and you can come to it with no expectations or pressure on yourself. It's not something to "do," it's a way to be.

> Planning, like many things, is good in moderation. When meditating, you are not planning. You are simply being. A little less planning in life makes space for unexpected miracles and creative ideas to enter. Too much planning crowds your life and mind, leaving no space for the promise of something better than you could have imagined.

You may have the idea that to meditate, you must sit in a particular position on the floor, with your legs crossed, and do something to attain a state of bliss and enlightenment. Fortunately, meditation isn't about these things. You are meditating when you don't get caught up in doing, planning, judging, and worrying. Meditating is when you can just be.

Create a Silent Space

When the time comes for meditation, make sure that you've turned your telephone's ringer off. Go to a place in your house where you can close a door and not be bothered. If there are others in your home, let them know you'd like not to be disturbed for the amount of time you've set aside. It's very important that you really set aside quiet time and let others know, so they can support you by leaving you alone.

Once you've become accustomed to meditating, you could set up a special place for meditation away from clutter in your home where you can keep your props—pillow, cushions, blocks, and/or a blanket. Enjoy making your meditation time separate from anything else you do. Sometimes it's easiest to do it first thing in the morning when no one's awake, or before going to bed when others are asleep. As a morning practice, it's a great way to start your day.

Finding Your Seat

Once you are ready, find a comfortable, seated position. If you can be comfortable in a cross-legged position, then sit on the floor with your legs crossed. Place a cushion underneath your tailbone. Position the cushion comfortably so you keep the natural curve in the small of your back, the **lumbar spine**. If, when you cross your legs, your knees are higher than your hips, then sit on more pillows or yoga blocks so your hips are higher than your knees. Or, instead of raising your seat, place blocks or cushions underneath your upper legs so they are supported and can relax. Another option is to sit upright in a chair. If, when you sit in the chair, your feet do not touch the floor, rest them on blocks, shoeboxes, telephone books, or anything that you can put on the floor that is comfortable for your feet to rest on. When sitting in the chair, do not cross your legs. Now that you are comfortably seated, make sure you will be warm enough. Wrap a blanket around your shoulders to stay warm.

Check Your Posture

Once you have found your seated position, feel the sitting bones solidly supported. Gently sit up straight. Don't strain, and do keep the curve in your lumbar spine. Bring your chin down slightly so that the top of your head is parallel to the ceiling: this allows the top of your spine, the cervical vertebrae, to rest in a neutral position. Inhale and shrug your shoulders up, and on the exhale gently roll them back and down. Resume normal breathing, and allow your arms to hang with your hands in your lap or on your thighs. Your palms can be open in the "receiving" position, or faced down in the "introspective" position. Take a deep inhale and long exhale to begin to come into the practice of meditation.

Focus on the Breath

Notice if there's any tension in your jaw. Allow the teeth to part slightly at the back of the mouth to help release tension. Gently close your eyes, and notice the breath go in and out. Just notice the breath without controlling it. As distracting thoughts come to mind, acknowledge them as thoughts, and return your focus to the breath. Notice how your body expands on the inhale, contracts on the exhale. And, again, each time a concern comes up, acknowledge it, and if it helps to think the word "thinking" to label it, do that. Then let it pass. *Voilà!* You are meditating. Do not try to stop the thoughts from coming. Instead, allow whatever comes up to come up, and then allow it to drift by without hanging on or fueling that thought by engaging with it.

> **Must I sit completely still to meditate?**
>
> The urge to scratch or move is another opportunity to watch and let go. Notice it, without moving, and return to the breath. Allow the discomfort to be there, and breathe. Practicing this will strengthen your ability in life to deal with uncomfortable situations. If you must move, do it with care, then return focus to the breath.

Like Riding a Bike

Once you've started mediating, it's like riding a bike. Your breath is the bike, the vehicle that carries you through life. Your thoughts are the road that will go up and down, take turns this way and that. Focusing on the breath, you can ride along the road without getting stuck or caught up in concern as you encounter twists and turns. The thoughts will come and go, just like hills come and go. If in meditation you get tripped up by a thought, it's okay. Get back on the bike by turning your attention to your breath. Some days it might be easier to ride the thoughts than other days. That's one thing that keeps it fresh, the terrain is unpredictable, and with your breath, you are well-equipped to handle the ride.

Don't Let This Moment Pass You By

How often are you barely able to concentrate on what you're doing because of all the to-dos in your life, and all the thoughts weighing on your mind? You now have a good reason to start slowing down, taking a pause throughout your day, and giving yourself "me" time. The good reason is your overall well-being. If you continue to go, go, go, whether physically, mentally, or both, then it's likely that you don't take time to be in the moment as often as your body needs. When you're going on autopilot with so much thinking, doing, and moving your body gets out of balance. You might notice this in a variety of ways: weight loss or gain, mental or emotional fatigue, depression, lack of motivation, feeling overwhelmed, getting easily irritated, losing your keys, or losing sleep. All of these are signs that you body isn't functioning in the way it works best, and according to chakra theory your chakras will be out of balance. The first step in helping your body back to health and balancing the chakras is learning to drop into the present moment, to stop thinking, doing, and going. Allow yourself to be.

Present-Moment Awareness

Present-moment awareness brings witness consciousness into your daily life, allowing you to practice seeing life as it is. By holding your attention to the present moment, without stories, judgment, worries, and planning, you begin to awaken to the basic goodness of the moment. The more you practice this, the easier it is to come back to this state at different points in your day, and moment-by-moment get out of a stressful mindset. With intentional practice, living in the present moment will sometimes happen without you intentionally trying.

Being in the present moment is wonderful for your overall health. When your mind isn't in a state of stress, then your body can focus on its proper functions rather than overworking to cope with stress.

Present-moment awareness is useful in situations that might not be associated with pleasure. For example, at times when you need to bring up a difficult conversation, your skills of present-moment awareness can help you listen and respond to what is actually being said. Learning NVC, nonviolent communication, by Marshall B. Rosenburg can be a relationship-saving tool.

You will likely find it easier to start practicing present-moment awareness at times when you are doing something that can make you feel content. For example, going for a walk, playing with your dog, or baking cookies are activities ripe with opportunities to notice basic goodness. When doing these activities, sights, smells, and touch can bring you into the sensational pleasures of being alive.

Body Scan

Another way to get into the present moment is to do a body scan. It's often nice to have it guided for you, and you can find CDs that lead a body-scan meditation. It's also effective to do it yourself. The idea is to sit or lie down and place your attention on one body part at a time. Then, relax that body part by inhaling and exhaling, imagining the breath travelling to that area. Here's an example of a body scan.

Lie down on your back, with your legs outstretched comfortably on the floor. Place a pillow or cushion underneath your knees. Do not put a pillow underneath your head. Cover yourself with a blanket if you think you might get cold, as your body temperature will drop as you relax deeply.

Once you are comfortably lying down, take a slow, deep inhale through your nose and exhale through your mouth. Let go. Feel yourself supported by the ground, by mother earth. You are held, you can let go. Pay attention to your breath flowing in and out for a few breaths.

Then turn your attention to your right foot. Notice your toes, relax the entire foot. Relax the right ankle. Feel your entire right leg. Relax the right leg. Notice the right side of your torso. Relax the right side of your torso. Relax the right shoulder. Relax the top of the right arm, relax the forearm. Relax the right hand, including the right fingers. Relax the entire right arm.

Notice your left foot. Relax the toes, relax the entire left foot. Relax the ankle. Feel your left leg. Relax the entire left leg. Draw your awareness to the left side of your torso. Relax the left side of your torso. Relax the left shoulder. Relax the top of the left arm, relax the forearm. Relax the entire left arm.

Relax the lower back. Relax the middle of your back. Relax the shoulder blades. Relax the neck. Relax the jaw. Relax the tongue. Relax the eyelids. Relax the temples. Relax the brow. Relax the entire head.

The body scan is a way to become present to your body and to feel grounded. It helps you recognize that the ground literally supports you, and you can let go and release. The practice is also good for tuning in to how you are, which becomes so important to chakra healing since deficiencies or excesses in the chakras manifest in the physical body.

Do What You Love

A wonderful way to get into the present moment is to do things that you love, and to love what you do. If you enjoy swimming, knitting, horseback riding, hiking, reading, singing, dancing, or painting, make time for it in your life. And, as you do the activity, be present to it. Leave your stresses and worries behind when you do it, and really enjoy what you're doing.

Engage the Senses

If you're painting, notice the feel of the brush gliding along the paper and how the colorful paint streaks on the page. If you're dancing, let the music pulse through your body. Connect your senses to the activities you choose, and allow yourself to have a good time. Bring this kind of enjoyment to whatever you can in your life. Even in washing the dishes, see if you can appreciate the feel of warm water and sudsy bubbles on your hands. Each time you enjoy a moment rather than dread it, you are cultivating present-moment awareness and contributing positively to your overall well-being.

Share Your Joy with Others

In your everyday connections, be open about your good feelings about life. Without bragging, and from a genuine place of seeing the good in the moment, tell people what you notice. For those who are interested, eventually, they will also start noticing the good things in life. And, this kind of energy resonates in your energy bodies. Their energy and your energy affect the health of the chakras.

Getting Outside

Nature is the perfect route to present-moment awareness. By stepping outdoors you surround yourself with nature's life force, which is the same energy that runs inside of you.

Find activities to do that you would enjoy outside. Investigate what kinds of outdoor options there are where you live. There is so much variety in nature that you won't get bored even if you take regular walks along the same streets. The sky looks different at sunrise, midday, sunset, midnight, and the hours in between.

> Walking barefoot outside is healthy for you. Breathing fresh air, getting vitamin D from the sunshine, and spending time in water is natural and good. In addition, many believe that standing barefoot on the earth can heal ailments. The intelligent energy of the earth can travel to places in your body that need healing energy.

Take a Break

Take a break from television on the weekend to go outside and watch cloud formations, find shadows cast by the sun, or stand in the rain and hear it bounce off your umbrella. At night, look for constellations if the sky is clear. If you live in the city, you can still enjoy the different feeling of the earth when the sky is dark. When the moon is getting fuller, sit outside and bathe in the moonlight in the same way you bathe in the sun. Connecting to the life force of nature strengthens the life force in you.

Labyrinths

A labyrinth is constructed as one continuous path that begins at its mouth and curves back and forth according to an ancient pattern, leading to its center. A labyrinth is not a maze, which presents obstacles along the path. In a labyrinth, when you follow the path, you will make it to the center. You can't miss it. Typically labyrinths are created in the seven-circuit pattern, though other patterns exist.

Walking Meditation

Labyrinths are used for mediation and spiritual inquiry, which is why they are often found at churches, synagogues, and retreats. Sometimes the creators of a labyrinth will invite a **dowser** to help locate the ideal energetic spot for a labyrinth. Other times people will just find a peaceful place to create this sacred symbol. As you walk the labyrinth, you feel the supportive earth at your feet and see the expansive sky above your head. The labyrinth invites you into a walking meditation.

You will find labyrinths of different sizes, in various locations, and constructed with a variety of materials: rocks, tiles, string, clay, plants, lights, paint, etc. As you walk different labyrinths you get to experience the natural energy of the different settings of each individual labyrinth.

Even if you walk the same labyrinth over and over, your experience each time could be different. The labyrinth itself might look different, even in subtle ways, depending on how the sunlight hits the path or how its surrounding environment changes throughout the year. Take note of it, notice how each day is new, each day is a gift. You also could have different experiences based on your intention for walking the labyrinth. Here are some examples of suggested ways to context your labyrinth walk.

- **Ask a question:** Meditate on a question you feel stuck on and open your heart for guidance. On the way in toward the center pray to release what's keeping you stuck. Once you are in the center, pray for guidance. On the way out, open to receive.

- **Cultivate gratitude:** With each step you take, say "I'm grateful" with sincerity.

- **Walking meditation:** Focus on taking very slow steps. As thoughts come up, let them go.

- **Honor others:** Hold in your heart loved ones who are living or not and send them your energy.

- **Dance:** Dance or skip along the path.

Once you've decided the context for your walk, approach the labyrinth. Stand at the mouth and pause. This is the beginning of your walk. Walk the labyrinth at whatever pace feels comfortable to you. It's okay to pass others walking the labyrinth if you want to walk faster than they do. Walk the labyrinth to the center. Once in the center, pause. Reflect. Do what comes naturally in the center, and stay there as long as you wish. Then, follow the path out the same way you came in. After you exit the labyrinth, it is customary to turn toward it and offer gratitude.

The Labyrinth as a Mirror

After walking the labyrinth, you may want to sit down to journal or just take some time to integrate what you experienced. Often, the attitude you bring into the labyrinth mirrors the attitude you bring to the rest of your life. It's a useful mirror in that way. If you walked in a rushed manner, do you notice that you are often rushing in your life? If you are constantly anxious as the labyrinth twists and turns, do you also notice you have a lot of anxiety outside of the labyrinth? If you are completely focused on trying to figure out the path as you walk it, do you find that in your life you have trouble allowing a situation to unfold without being under your control? And, as you change your attitude toward the labyrinth over time, perhaps you will change parts of your attitude toward life.

The History of Labyrinths

The origin of the labyrinth is somewhat shrouded in mystery. The word likely originated in reference to dancing, when the term *labyrinthine* referred to a dance pattern in the Neolithic period. The first known **petroglyphs** (rock carvings) of what appear to be labyrinths are from the Bronze Age. Evidence supports the conclusion that by the second century BCE the word *labyrinth* referred to the concept that we know now: the unicursal path that folds back and forth, leading from the mouth to the center and out again, with no intersections and no dead ends.

Where can I find a labyrinth?

Labyrinths can be indoors or outside. Often they can be found on the grounds of religious, spiritual, or meditation centers. You can search for labyrinth locations online. You also can draw your own labyrinth and "walk" it with your fingertip, or create your own larger labyrinth by getting creative with various materials. You can create a temporary or permanent labyrinth.

Chakra Meditation in a Labyrinth

Walking the labyrinth in a simple way that feels comfortable to you is a great way to start. Thoughts will come up, things will happen, and you can learn valuable information from what happens when you walk a labyrinth open to what it will reveal. You could also meditate on the chakras as you walk the labyrinth. You could do a meditation on each chakra in relation to its element (see Chapter 1). Begin with a visualization of the placement of the Root Chakra and sense your connection to the earth as you enter the labyrinth. After several breaths on the first chakra, move your awareness up to the second chakra, focusing on water. Next, move up to the third chakra, and so on, arriving at the seventh chakra when you reach the center.

Another suggestion is to meditate on the chakra in relationship to which loop of the circuit you are on. When you enter a seven-circuit pattern, you enter at the third circuit (if you count the walls from the edge, you will see you enter in three paths from the edge). Then, you'll be at the second, first, fourth, seventh, sixth, fifth, and center. You can meditate on the color associated with that chakra, you could repeat the seed sound of that chakra, or you could meditate on the element associated with that chakra. All of these techniques will bring awareness and energy to the chakras.

Haiku

The rules of writing haiku were constructed in the Japanese language, which is very different from the English language. It is customary to hear that haiku must be written in three lines with five syllables in the first and last lines and seven syllables in the second line. However, as time has gone by, people who write haiku in English have tended to think that the number of syllables per line isn't what matters.

Haiku in English

To write a haiku in English, concentrate more on simply capturing a fleeting moment, evoking a beautiful image of the ephemeral quality of life. You can ignore rules about the number of syllables so that instead you can focus on the thought behind why those rules were made, which was to create simplicity and beauty.

A haiku often captures a moment in nature, and typically includes a word that lets the reader know what season it is. For example, the word *daffodils* would indicate spring. When you start writing haiku in English usually it's best to use two or three syllables in the first line, five in the second, and three in the last line. Three lines are common. It also helps to read several haiku first, so you can get a sense for how they feel.

It's traditional in Japanese haiku to use a **kireji** or a *cutting* word. This word is used to show juxtaposition between two ideas in the haiku, or to signal the end of one of the images. In English, it's typically done with a punctuation mark, like a dash or period, since our language works differently.

The beauty of the haiku is worth replicating into English even if there's a language barrier when it comes to the rules. Writing and reading haiku are meditative practices and help bring you into the present moment.

Haiku at the End of Life

In Japanese and yogic cultures spiritual masters compose a haiku on their deathbed as a teaching to leave behind for their students. The belief is that if you are able to connect to a place of peace inside while you live your life, then you will be able to find that peace of mind as you die. The ability to compose a haiku when facing death shows a sense of equilibrium in the face of leaving this life. And, beautiful haiku have been left behind by revered masters, capturing the seasons of nature and of life. Starting to practice writing haiku long before dying is key because you strengthen your ability to be in that space of present-moment awareness, which then you can access at the end of life.

CHAPTER 9

How to Take Care of Your Spine

The health of your spine is important to your overall functioning. Your spine holds your body up, so you can sit and stand tall. It also protects your spinal cord, which is made up of millions of nerves that transmit messages from your brain to all the parts of your body. The nerves make it possible for you to feel sensation, perform biological functions, and move. In addition, the spine houses the main energy channel of your body that connects the chakras.

The Backbone of Your Body

Made up of thirty-three vertebrae (four coccyx, five sacral, five lumbar, twelve thoracic, and seven cervical), the spine begins at the sacrum, and extends up to the base of the skull. The vertebrae are stacked one on top of another, with a cushion-like disc in between each one to act as a shock absorber. Each vertebra has a hole through which the spinal cord passes, so that the spinal cord is protected by bone.

> The terms "slipped" or "herniated" disc describe when a disc is pushed out from its snug place in the spine. When it's pushed out it's not cushioning the vertebrae, and it could be putting pressure on nerves in the spinal column. This can affect your ability to function and to feel sensation. It also can cause a lot of pain.

When you look at the spine from the side, it forms an "s" curve. If you feel the curve of your own spine, you will notice that the lumbar spine curves forward, the thoracic spine curves backward, and the cervical spine curves forward. The "s" shape helps the spine support your body weight and withstand various kind of stress.

Nerve Ganglia

The nerves that run up and down the spinal column also branch out into nerve roots through the sides of the vertebra and form **ganglia**, masses of nerve tissue. There are seven major ganglia, and each **ganglion** is situated in the place of one of the chakras. Because every ganglion is near one of the chakras, if the nerves in the spine are harmed, this could affect the functioning of your energy centers.

Protecting Your Spine

One of the best ways to protect your spine is to be mindful. Through-out your day, pause and notice how you are sitting and how your back is feeling. Don't stay in one position for hours on end; get up and move. Move slowly at first, and do easy stretches and movements to lubricate the spine. When you start off with slow movements in the body, your body knows to secrete synovial fluid to the joints.

The Six Movements of the Spine

You can move your spine in six different ways. When you practice slowly doing the six movements of the spine, you are warming up the spine. After you have been still for a long time, for example after sleeping the whole night through, your spine could use a warm-up before you start your day.

Cat and Cow Spinal Movement

Two movements of the spine can be done with the cat and cow pose. To do the cat and cow spinal movement, come onto your hands and knees. For cat pose, exhale, and round your back so that your belly button rises up toward the spine, your tailbone tilts downward, and your head comes down between your arms. On the inhale, come into cow pose. Arch your back so that your belly dips toward the floor, your shoulder blades come toward each other, your eyes look forward, and your tail-bone lifts. Do cat and cow pose three times, coordinating them with the inhale and exhale.

Lateral Angle Pose

Two of the movements of the spine create a sideways "c" curve of the spine. Sit in a comfortable position with your legs crossed on the floor. Alternatively, stack two blocks on top of each other, and sit on top of them with your legs crossed in front of you, or have your legs bent underneath you in a kneeling position. Place your left hand on your left hip. Inhale your right arm up, then exhale and gently lean to the left.

Pause. Inhale, come back to center. Gently place your hands on your thighs, and pause. Place your right hand on your right hip. Inhale your left arm up. Exhale and gently lean to the right. Inhale back to center.

Twisting

The last two movements of the spine can be performed by a gentle twist. Before you twist, it's important to first elongate. To do this, inhale and imagine that there is a string from the top of your head to the ceiling, and it's pulling you up slowly against the pull of gravity. Always do this before entering into a twist when you are standing or sitting.

> With every inhale and exhale, imagine prana flowing into your spine and the areas of your body that are opening up as a result of the six movements. Notice how it feels first thing in the morning to give your spine these ten or fifteen minutes of attention.

To enter into a lying-down twist, lie down on your back, with your knees bent so that your feet are flat on the floor. Extend your arms out to the sides at 90 degree angles from your torso, so you are in a "t" position. Inhale, and on the exhale let your knees drop to the left. Inhale back to center. Exhale, let your knees drop to the right. Inhale back to center. Do this a few more times, and if it's comfortable for you, then turn your head in the opposite direction of your knees each time. Don't forget to inhale and exhale with each movement.

Standing that Supports the Spine

Standing is something you do so often you may never even think about it. However, when you stand, gravity pulls you down as your spine holds you up. The spine has the "s" curve to help it bear weight, so making sure you are standing well will help the spine do its job.

Standing on Both Feet

Some people when standing for a long time will lean their weight on one leg or the other. Take a moment to try that, and notice that your spine isn't in alignment. Because of this crooked posture, your spine isn't in its optimal position for weight bearing. Also, if you stay in certain postures habitually, you are training certain muscles to elongate while other muscles become shortened. Any adjustments like these throw off your posture and also become physical habits that are not healthy for your spine.

When standing, stand on both feet at once. Or, have a block handy, and stand with one foot on the ground, and one foot resting on the block. Be sure to alternate which foot is on the block.

Walking Mindfully

Notice if when you walk you sway your hips, bounce, or take very small steps. Notice if you place your feet parallel to each other or pointed inward or outward. You may want to see a physical therapist and have your walk evaluated, as a preventative measure. By becoming more mindful of your gait, you can protect your spine.

Take Bigger Steps

If you take small, quick steps when you walk, try taking longer steps. Keep your spine straight up and down as you walk, and swing your arms. When you step with your left foot, your right arm swings forward, and vice versa. This helps with balance and helps you flow as you move.

Strengthen Your Abdomen

As you walk up and down stairs and on dangerous terrain, hold your abdomen in. The benefit is that you will strengthen those muscles and protect your spine. It's important to know both how to strengthen your abdomen and how to allow it to relax.

A good way to practice relaxing your belly is to sit up and place your hands on your belly. Inhale, and feel your belly expand into your hands. Exhale and feel your belly pull back toward your spine. Now, breathe naturally, keep your hands on the belly, and allow the belly to relax.

Practice relaxing your belly and strengthening it, every day. You can practice contracting your abodomen for ten counts and relaxing your abdomen for ten counts while in the car, sitting at your desk, and walking through the grocery store. Here's one way to strengthen your abdomen muscles:

1. Lie on your back, with your knees bent and your feet flat on the floor.

2. Place your hands on your belly just beneath your belly button.

3. Contract the muscles from the perineum up to the belly button.

4. Hold for ten seconds while still breathing in and out.

5. Release, and feel your belly relax.

Practice this a few times in a row. Over time, work up to doing ten repetitions in a row.

Relax the Belly

Just as important as strengthening your abdomen muscles is practicing relaxing the abdomen muscles. While strong abdomen muscles will protect the spine, a soft belly will ease nervous tension and help with overall relaxation. Practice engaging the abdomen for support and releasing the abdomen for relaxation.

Protecting the Spine in the Car

Getting in and out of the car, sitting for long periods of time, and holding your legs in one position without much movement all are part of driving around. There are ways to support the health of your spine while driving.

Getting Into the Car

To get into your car, turn so that your back is toward the seat. Engage the abdomen and push your hips back so you slowly sit down into the chair. Once you are in the chair, then pivot your body so that your back is against the back of the car seat and your feet are toward the pedals. Have a back roll (you can buy one at a back-care store) or roll up a towel. Put this roll in the natural curve of your lumbar spine. Lean back. You want to feel as though your spine is supported, with its natural curves. When you have the back roll in the correct spot, you will notice the difference.

Good Posture in the Driver's Seat

Once you're seated and your back feels supported, place your hands on the steering wheel. Make sure you don't have to reach very far away, and instead of putting your hands at 10 and 2, put them lower down so that your arms can relax. When you have to hold your arms out way in front of you and up higher, your shoulders are tense.

Move Your Body While Driving

If you're driving for more than fifteen minutes, practice some slight pelvic tilts while driving. In other words, do the cat and cow movements, perhaps less exaggerated than what you can do on your yoga mat. Also, while paying close attention to driving, take one hand off the wheel at a time and wiggle the fingers and shake the arm a little.

> Enjoy movement in the car. Turn on the radio or pop in a CD, and make small movements to the music. Moving body parts and singing in the car is a great way to keep energy flowing in your body.

Movement like this gets the prana flowing, and breaks up the physical and mental monotony of driving. It also brings warmth and blood flow to the muscles. Keeping the muscles flexible is good for the spine because everything is connected, and if the muscles get too tight or too accustomed to a certain position, they could pull on the spine and bring it out of alignment.

Getting Out of the Car

To get out of the car, do the reverse of how you got in. First, pivot so that your legs can hang outside the car door. Then, engage your abdominal muscles, place your feet on the ground, and stand up. You'll notice that getting out of the car this way helps keep your spine in alignment. With all the times you may get in and out of a car, it will make a difference to your body if you modify how you do it.

Sitting at a Desk

Today, with laptops, iPads, netbooks, and ebooks there are various options for how you will read, do your work, and stay connected. It's easy to get sucked into e-mail, Internet surfing, paper writing, and shopping online. Begin to get into the habit of paying attention to your body's needs and not getting trapped in a seated position for hours on end without a physical break. It's worth taking short breaks because your physical condition will affect your mental condition and ability to focus and stay refreshed during a long workday or project.

How to Sit at a Desk

When you sit at a desk, your feet should be on the floor or on a block so that your legs are bent at the knees in a 90-degree angle. Your spine should be in a neutral position with the natural curves supported. Use a back roll at your lumbar spine so you can lean back and relax if you'll be sitting off and on for a while. Your arms should hang at your sides, and ideally have arm rests to rest on. Your arms should bend at the elbow in a 90-degree angle as you type. Your keyboard should be separate from the monitor so that the keyboard can be in a place where your forearms are perpendicular to your torso when you type. The monitor should be high enough so it is at eye-level. You can prop it on a shoebox or yoga block if it's not high enough. Feel that this seated posture, like yoga postures, is steady and comfortable.

Taking Breaks

Even when you have good posture at your desk, take breaks to roll your shoulders up and back. Gently turn your head to look side to side. And, even rub your hands together to generate heat and prana, and then palm your eyes with your cupped hands and breathe deeply to relax. Stand up at least every half hour, and move your limbs before sitting back down.

You can also use this time to check in with any one of your chakras or all of them. Taking a break at work will help you stay productive throughout your day:

- Keep crystals in your desk, and when you notice a certain deficiency that you want to boost, hold the crystal in your hand for a few moments and visualize its energizing power.

- Make color-infused water the night before and sip the colored water throughout your day at work.

- Bring an object into work that is the color of the chakra you are working on. Throughout your day, look at the object and take in the color's vibrations.

- Have photographs with you of loved ones, to keep your Heart Chakra strong.

Healing the chakras is something that can be so useful throughout your day, so you can bring the tools with you into work. For example, if you're feeling spacey at work, do something for your Root Chakra to help ground you. If you notice you're becoming agitated, judgmental, or critical, see if you can get outside for some air and space. Breathe into the Heart Chakra. Make space around what's happening, and ground your excess energy into the earth.

What can I do in the afternoon, when I feel tired at work?

First of all, see if going outside and getting fresh air will help. Second, do a simple visualization of all the chakras, balancing out stagnant energy. Start with the Root Chakra, and just envision the glowing red color. Visualize each chakra with its corresponding color, and after you get to the crown, pause and see if you feel better.

Get creative, use chakra healing to help you whether at home or at work. And, don't feel chained to your desk. If you get up to take breaks, you, your coworkers, and your employer will benefit. You can keep yourself healthier and happier by taking breaks from sitting at your desk.

Lying Down

There might be various times in the day that you lie down. Maybe you lie down on the couch to watch TV, maybe you lie on the floor to play with your dog, and maybe you lie in a chair to take a nap. You also lie down at night to sleep. Notice how your spine is positioned when you lie down.

On the Couch

If you are watching television while lying on your back on the couch, check your posture. You want your spine supported so that no part is straining. Make sure something is supporting your head/neck and your lumbar spine. Also, do not stay in a position where your head is twisted or bent in an unnatural position. Line yourself up with the television in a way that allows your spine to be in good alignment.

If the television is placed so that you are lying on your side on the couch, make sure that your head is supported. You also may want a pillow between your knees. And, if you can, lean back on the back of the couch, and make sure you feel that the curves of your spine are supported. And get up at least every half hour to move your body. Or, even at every commercial break, get up for a little stretch.

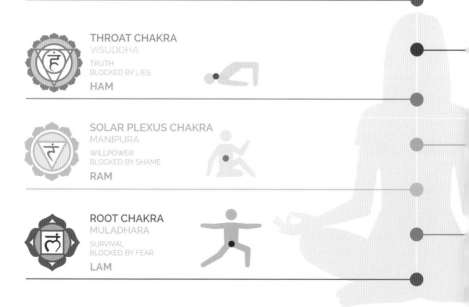

CROWN CHAKRA
SAHASRARA
COSMIC ENERGY
BLOCKED BY ATTACHMENT
SILENCE

THROAT CHAKRA
VISUDDHA
TRUTH
BLOCKED BY LIES
HAM

SOLAR PLEXUS CHAKRA
MANIPURA
WILLPOWER
BLOCKED BY SHAME
RAM

ROOT CHAKRA
MULADHARA
SURVIVAL
BLOCKED BY FEAR
LAM

Lying in Bed

If you sleep on your back in bed, it might feel good for you to put a pillow or two under your knees. You don't need a high pillow for underneath your head. Check to make sure that the natural curve in your neck is supported.

Make sure that the pillow doesn't make your head tilt too far up or too far down. These adjustments might sound minor, but imagine what happens if all night your spine is in an unnatural position versus if it's in the position it was designed for. It's so much healthier for the tendons and muscles that attach to the spine if they can be in their natural, relaxed state, too.

> Have fun with your pets and also be mindful of your spine. Don't make fast, sudden twists or turns or jolt yourself. You can have fun, roll around, and play while still being mindful.

ENERGY POINTS OF THE SUBTLE BODY

 THIRD EYE CHAKRA
AJNA
INTUITION
BLOCKED BY ILLUSION
OM

 HEART CHAKRA
ANAHATA
LOVE
BLOCKED BY GRIEF
YAM

 SACRAL CHAKRA
SVADHISTHANA
PLEASURE
BLOCKED BY GUILT
VAM

Your Posture and Your Chakras

How you carry yourself affects and is affected by your chakras. If the energy of a chakra is too strong, it can push on your bones and organs. If the energy of a chakra is too weak, your body may slightly collapse or sink in at those parts. In the same way, if you physically tax your body it can affect the energy flow to and from the chakras. For the health of the chakras, you want to have a tall, even spine while maintaining the natural curves. Imagine this while walking down the street, going up stairs, practicing yoga postures, etc.

The Effects of Slouching

If you slouch a lot, you are potentially caving in on your solar plexus, heart, and throat. By caving in on your solar plexus, you are diminishing your self-esteem, your will to accomplish and transform, and your fiery energy. By crowding your heart you are closing off to giving and receiving love. You are also diminishing your ability to accurately perceive what is going on around you. Your heart can interpret energetic input, and if you're slouching you are not open to receive. When you shield your Throat Chakra, you are compromising your communication. This has to do with your ability to listen as well as your ability to speak your truth. Slouching can have this affect on your energy centers and then have physical repercussions, too.

When you crowd your Manipura Chakra, maybe your digestion will not work so well. When you close off energy to your heart chakra, all kinds of disease can result from a heart closed off to love. Love is what connects you to everything else in the world, from healing energy to relationships to creating the life you desire. When your throat doesn't get the energy it needs, your thyroid can become compromised, leading to metabolic complications.

To allow these chakras to receive and transmit energy, hold yourself up. Support your spine, and pay attention to your posture. Also, take some time to ask yourself, what is going on in your life energetically or emotionally that might be making you want to slouch over and protect these chakras. See if there are in fact external forces that you should stop exposing yourself to, so you feel safe enough to sit up tall.

CHAPTER 10

The Chakras and Yoga

Yoga is a way of life, with eight limbs as the path of practice. Many people are introduced to yoga through sequences of physical postures. The physical practice is one of the eight limbs that help you delve into the experience of yoga. Sanskrit for "union," yoga is the sense of your wholeness, your body, mind, and connection to all of life. The eight limbs can enhance your experience of chakra healing. The ancient philosophy of yoga encourages practice of all the limbs, which purify the mind and body for chakra meditation.

The Yoga Experience

Hatha yoga is a physical practice. One of its benefits is that it helps prana flow throughout the body. Sometimes in your practice, you will want to initiate poses to get the life force flowing. Other times, if you allow it to, your body will create its own sequence of postures guided by prana. Practicing postures is one way to cultivate witness consciousness. It's the practice of not getting attached or reacting to sensations based only on what your mind thinks, separate from your felt experience. As you do hatha yoga, you cultivate the ability to witness what happens in your mind without attaching and reaction to its ups and downs. Eventually, the mind may become still and you will experience easeful states of awareness beyond the thinking mind.

The Eight Limbs of Yoga

The eight limbs of yoga are, according to Pūrṇānanda-Svāmī, a precursor to starting the chakra-healing journey. According to Pūrṇānanda-Svāmī, one must first practice the limbs of yoga to purify her nature, then receive the sacred teachings on Liberation from her guru. For the modern yogi, who may not have a guru, you have access to the sutras and the information about chakra meditation that used to be passed from guru to disciple, plus Western explorations and adaptations for your lifestyle.

The eight limbs of yoga are described in the *Yoga Sutras*, by Patanjali. Sutra means "thread," and each sutra is a thread of wisdom to guide you on the path of yoga. These sutras, written thousands of years ago, continue to serve as the foundation for yoga practice.

Yamas

The first limb of yoga is the list of **yamas**. Yamas are suggested observances that apply to your attitude in relationship to the world. The yamas are provided as ways to live your life mindfully and skillfully, creating more ease and conscious creation of your life's path.

You might recognize the yamas based on your own religious or cultural background. You may also recognize them as good guidelines based on experience you have already had in your lifetime. Most, if not all of the yamas and niyamas, will not come as a surprise to you as guidelines for living a healthy life, beneficial to you and in harmony with others.

Ahimsa

Ahimsa (*nonviolence*) means avoiding violence to others and yourself. This refers to thoughts, words, and actions. It suggests you avoid harming other people, beings, and the earth. To practice this yama, it must come from a sincere place. In other words, truly, you aim to have no harmful thoughts toward yourself or others. This includes psychological as well as physical violence. Of course, in everyday life harmful thoughts may come up. You may be harsh on yourself, on your children, or on a colleague. As these harmful thoughts come up, observe them. Observe how they make you feel. Without judging yourself on top of having the harmful thoughts, just watch them. Hold them in compassion, then think of how you might lessen the frequency of harmful thoughts. Sending energy to your heart chakra is one way to strengthen your connection to compassion.

Satya

Satya, or *honesty*, is the practice of truthfulness. Line up your thoughts, emotions, words, and actions so that you are acting with integrity. Practice satya with ahimsa, nonviolence. Be careful with your truths. Speak them, and practice doing so with skill. Satya also includes truthfulness to yourself. Sometimes it's hard to bear your own truths, and yet on this path you must practice. If you cannot be true to yourself, you may also be out of integrity with others.

Asteya

Asteya (*non-stealing*) means not taking what it not freely given. Focus your mind, heart, and actions on your own path, without desiring or taking what belongs to someone else.

Bramacharya

Bramacharya means *appropriate use of energy*, including sexual energy. Sometimes yogis explain bramacharya only in relationship to sexual energy, but all energy is worth using with mindfulness. Your sexual energy is a powerful energy. You can channel it to good use in your life, and when used appropriately it can build strong intimate relationships. It can also cause problems if used inappropriately. It is linked to other yamas like asteya and satya. For example, if you desire intimacy with someone else's partner or someone who is not interested in you, then cultivating bramacharya is appropriate.

Thinking of bramacharya as skillful use of all energy, you can imagine how it would be an important practice for thriving, for your relationships. An exercise you could do is to write down all the things you do for three to five days. Look at where and how you spend your energy. Are there ways you would want to spend it differently? Would you be able to make some time for more movement? Where could you fit in some "me" time? Are you giving too much energy to others—might you need to cut out a social engagement so you can balance your checkbook? Just observe, and make choices that will help you thrive. Sometimes a social engagement is more important than balancing your checkbook, sometimes it's not. You will decide.

Aparigraha

Aparigraha, or *non-grasping*, is the practice of not being greedy. Take what you earn and what you need and leave some for others to have enough, too. Don't take advantage; when you are given something, practice being satisfied.

As you go through your life, in work, in personal relationships, and in relationship to your own path, keep the yamas in mind and notice your experience of them. Especially if these are new to you, pick one at a time and really work with it. Don't take these definitions of them only literally, see how they apply to your life in ways that might not be mentioned here. And remember these are guidelines for you, to help you live a healthy life and create what you want. They aren't meant as rules to be followed for the sake of trying to adhere to a strict way of life. You can actually create more flow and freedom in your life when you are using your energy in harmonious and healthy ways, and these are guides for how to do that.

Niyamas

Niyamas are suggestions for how to take care of yourself, nurturing and respecting your body, mind, and spirit. Your interest in chakra healing shows that you are interested in your well-being. These niyamas are observances designed to support your overall well-being.

Saucha

Saucha (*purity*) refers to purity and cleanliness on the outside and inside. Keeping clean on the outside for you might include **dinacharya**, the Ayurvedic way of taking care of your senses each day. It refers to saying clean and keeping your body in physically good shape. On the inside, keep the internal systems of the body clean, which can include making sure that your diet is appropriate for your body type and your system. Everyone is different, and if you eat right for your type, then your system will stay clean and work well. Also work on having a pure mind, which following the yamas will help.

Santosha

Santosha, or *contentment*, suggests you learn to be content with how things are in your life. When you experience difficulties in life, cultivating contentment will help make it a growing experience.

Tapas

Tapas (*discipline*) refers to the fire in you. *Tapas* suggests using your fiery energy for discipline in your life. *Tapas* literally means *heat*. Discipline yourself with your practices. Eat well and in moderation, and commit to the practices you choose for chakra healing.

Svadyaya

Svadyaya, or *self-study*, means to practice self-inquiry. Cultivating witness consciousness helps you witness how you act, react, and live in your life. Are you practicing the yamas and niyamas? Where are your gifts? What are your limitations? Your everyday life is full of opportunities to witness how you are, which will help you along your path for overall well-being. Svadyaya also refers to your Self, as in your Self that is your true nature, your higher Self. Beyond all the thinking and doing, get to know your true nature. Through the yamas, niyamas, and eight limbs of yoga there's lots of room for self-study. And, as you go on the journey of chakra healing, you'll notice that self-study helps you know where to focus healing energy.

Ishvara Pranidana

Ishvara Pranidana, or *turning it over to the divine*, means acknowledging the force at work that is greater than your fears and limitations. Trusting and celebrating God, divinity, spirit, or the intelligence of universal energy is the suggestion of this niyama. When things happen that were not in your plan, relax. Relax and believe that all will be well.

Are the yamas and niyamas like the Ten Commandments?

The yamas and niyamas are not commandments, they are guidelines for **sadhus** on the yogic path. Following them will also lead to good health. The yamas and niyamas are a set of guidelines for living in a way that is supportive of you and others in the world.

Whether or not you intend to practice yoga, the yamas and niyamas are a valid way to think about the mark you are leaving as you walk through life. They can help you make changes in your life for the better. Being aware and intentional about how you treat yourself and others will help you be more content, enjoy better health, and notice where you want to be putting your energy in life. These yamas and niyamas are also good for the health of your energy system, cultivating qualities in you that support the chakras. The table, opposite, shows correlations between the yamas and niyamas and the chakras.

Practicing the yamas and niyamas will nurture the chakras. When you practice Aparigraha you are strengthening your belief that you have enough, that you are provided with what you need. You are safe and secure, and these are the issues of the Root Chakra. Saucha also supports your Root Chakra. Purity of your bodily systems, including skin and muscles, supports the Muladhara energy.

YAMAS, NIYAMAS, AND CHAKRAS

CHAKRA	QUALITY	YAMA	NIYAMA
ROOT	Non-Grasping and Cleanliness	Aparigraha	Saucha
SACRAL	Appropriate Use of Energy and Contentment	Bramacharya	Santosha
SOLAR PLEXUS	Manage Inner Fire	⸺	Tapas
HEART	Nonviolence	Ahimsa	⸺
THROAT	Integrity	Satya	⸺
THIRD-EYE	Self-study	⸺	Svadyaya
CROWN	Connection to Divine	⸺	Ishvara Pranidana

Bramacharya and Santosha support the Sacral Chakra whose issues are around energy and emotions. Tapas supports your Solar Plexus Chakra. Satya supports the Throat Chakra; speaking your truth and being in integrity strengthens this energy center.

Ahimsa supports the heart: nonviolence to yourself and others cultivates the kind of love that emanates from here. Svadyaya brings energy to the third eye. At the third eye you are connecting to your wisdom, combining what you learn through study and what you know with intuition. Ishvara Pranidana is the energy of the Crown Chakra, your connection in the universal intelligence that creates life and vitality.

Asana

Asana is the third limb in Patanjali's model. *Asana* is the word for the yoga postures in a Hatha yoga practice. Asana practice both connects you to your physical body and helps you transcend it. It's related to the Root Chakra because of its ability to help you ground, and an asana practice can be used for the health of all the chakras. Different postures help balance different chakras.

> The remaining limbs of the eight limbs of yoga—Asana, Pranayama, Pratyahara, Dharana, Dhyana, and Samadhi—link to the five koshas. Asana corresponds to the Annamaya kosha, Pranayama to the kosha of the same name, Pratyahara to the Manomaya kosha, Dharana to the Vijnanomaya kosha, and Dhyana and Samadhi to the Anandamaya kosha.

In each posture, your body is supported by the earth. Any part of you that touches the earth during your yoga practice connects you to the earth's grounding and healing energy. Notice that where you connect to the ground there is stability and a flow of energy. Place your awareness on that connection; take it in.

Pranayama

Pranayama is breath control. There are various ways to do Pranayama, and all are ways of working with your prana. The breath is your connection to moving prana around your body. Pranayama is very effective for drawing energy toward the chakras, then upward toward the Crown Chakra. Depending on the technique you use, breath control can be used in various ways including to cool you down, heat you up, relax you, or energize you.

Pratyahara

Pratyahara is the withdrawal of the senses. It refers to not becoming attached to external objects, allowing for inward reflection. This happens during meditation, when you purposefully practice not clinging to sight, sound, physical sensation, or thought. The reason for Pratyahara is to practice the separation between your will and the senses' cravings. This way, you have choice about when and why you do things and you aren't controlled by desire.

Dharana

Dharana is focus on a single object. Practicing focusing on a single object helps you learn to still the mind. When the mind is still, then you can be single-minded in your explorations on the path of yoga and/or the path of healing.

Dhyana

Dhyana is worshipping the divine. It is being able to recognize illusion in the world versus reality. It is connecting to the knowing beyond what the senses perceive and experience.

Samadhi

Samadhi, or *bliss*, is the goal of practice. It is when you cannot distinguish yourself as "I" or "Me." You are not caught up in the thoughts of the conscious mind, and you experience of oneness with all that is. The thinking mind is at rest, and you experience bliss.

The goal of practicing all of the limbs of yoga is to achieve Samadhi. Bliss. In ancient tradition this meant to transcend the body. To bring this into our own lives, it is about experiencing the bliss of the physical body as well as the energy and bliss bodies.

Muladhara Chakra and Hatha Yoga

You can balance your Muladhara Chakra with *Hatha yoga*, the physical practice of yoga. Through the practice of the postures, bring awareness into your physical body. With breath awareness, envision prana flowing to specific areas of the body—nourishing the tissues and organs, strengthening, soothing muscles and joints. During Hatha yoga, you bring life and health into the physical body and feel your connection to the living, supportive earth. When you feel ungrounded, bring energy to the Muladhara Chakra through Hatha yoga to feel grounded, safe, and connected.

> When practicing Hatha yoga, listen carefully to your body. If you feel sharp pain, slowly lessen the intensity or come out of the posture. If you feel just a little discomfort, not sharp pain, take deep breaths and envision your breath going into that area. This can dislodge a block and allow prana to flow, a wonderful benefit of yoga.

Svadhistana Chakra and Tantra Yoga

Tantra yoga is a specific practice that includes meditation on the chakras and the importance of awakening the Kundalini energy to unite with divine consciousness, Shiva. Tantra yoga also supports enjoying and being present with the sweetness of being alive in the physical body. Tantra is often associated with sexuality, with the idea that if you practice Tantra it will improve your experience of sex. Because of its regard for enjoying the sweetness in life, it relates to the Svadhistana Chakra. One of the forms of meditation that Tantra teaches is **Japa**, repeating a mantra using malas.

Malas and Meditation

Adding malas to your meditation practice can help focus your mind and allow you to pray in increments of the number 108, a sacred number in the yogic tradition as well as other traditions. Mala beads are made of various materials such as wood, gemstones, and crystals. You can choose a set of malas based on the energy associated with each crystal, and be sure to cleanse the crystals before your first use.

Malas are sacred objects; as you infuse them with blessings and prayers they hold that vibration. They are strung as a loop of 108 beads, and you can wear them around your neck as protection and a reminder of your dedication to your practice.

To practice Japa:

1. Get in a comfortable position for meditation, in a quiet spot.

2. Choose a mantra.

3. Start with the bead next to the "guru" bead, which is the bead at the knot. Hold the first bead in between your thumb and middle finger. Move the beads between those two fingers, and at each bead repeat the mantra you've chosen.

4. When you've passed each bead through your fingers and you arrive at the guru bead, you've done 108 repetitions. Do not cross over or use the guru bead. Instead, you can do another round by passing the beads between your fingers in the other direction.

5. After you've completed your Japa meditation for the number of rounds you've chosen, take a few moments to stop and integrate the experience. Allow the effects of the Japa to resonate within you.

To practice Japa you can chant or repeat "**om**" at each bead, or you can choose a longer mantra. There are many Sanskrit mantras with specific intentions such as healing, prosperity, and surrender. You can also pick a line from a prayer from any religious or cultural tradition that works for you and connects you to the divine. A prayer that is considered the prayer of all prayers in Sanskrit is *Om mani padme hum*, which has been translated to mean in *the jewel of the lotus*. This is a metaphorical translation. The lotus is the sacred flower of the yogic tradition, and each of the chakras appears in the shape of a lotus flower, with a divine god or goddess inside on yet another lotus. *Om mani padme hum* isn't literally translatable; the phrase is said to contain all the teachings of the Buddha.

Chanting, speaking, or thinking a mantra creates a vibration. The energy of that vibration creates healing for you and affects others. In 1993, a study in Washington, D.C., researched the effect of several people meditating from June 7 to July 30. The rate of violent crime significantly dropped. See the movie *What the Bleep Do We Know?!* and *www.istpp.org/crime_prevention*.

When you repeat a mantra, the meaning and vibration of the words have healing power. The second chakra is associated with emotions, which can pull you away from a feeling of equilibrium and focus. Repeating a mantra helps you become one-pointed in focus as you focus on repeating the mantra and moving the beads through your fingers. This type of focus is also one of the niyamas: Dharana. The second chakra is also associated with sweetness, and practicing Japa can connect you to the sweetness of whatever you are meditating on.

Manipura Chakra and Karma Yoga

Karma yoga is yoga of service. It means that you surrender the fruits of your efforts. Your contentment in the work or preparation is not based on the outcome. You are content doing the work and preparation for the benefit of others. If it's not well-received, maybe right now that particular type of work is not needed in the world, and you can ask to do something for someone that is helpful if you want to be sure it will be well-received. Practice not basing your self-esteem on the praise of others. The Manipura Chakra is connected to self-esteem.

Experience the joy of service and giving without concern for any personal gain. Using the strength in Manipura Chakra and releasing your need for others' approval and compensation will help you (and Manipura) shine.

Anahata Chakra and Bhakti Yoga

Bhakti yoga is yoga of devotion, devotion to the divine. When you practice this type of yoga, you are opening your Heart Chakra. One way to practice Bhakti yoga is to chant. You can do a call-and-response chant, where a leader chants and the audience responds. This type of chant happens at **kirtans**, and also in other traditions such as in Christian churches and Jewish synagogues. Also, you can chant or sing devotional lyrics on your own, or with your iPod or CD. In Bhakti yoga, typically you will choose an element or incarnation of the divine to honor, and focus on it for your highest good and development. When you do this, you are cultivating and energizing the love in your heart center.

Visuddha Chakra and Mantra

Mantra refers to the actual phrase or word that you will repeat multiple times, and it refers to the act of repeating that phrase or word multiple times. To practice Mantra, you choose a mantra and repeat it, either with malas or just as many times as you decide.

You can use Mantra with other forms of yoga. For example, you could choose a mantra at the start of your Hatha yoga practice and repeat it throughout your practice. Choose anything that will express the state of being that you wish to experience. If you were to choose the mantra, "I am healthy," then you would repeat this mantra in your mind as you go through your yoga practice. During the practice, if another thought comes to mind, such as, "I don't have any more energy," you can allow that thought to float by, and then refocus on the mantra "I am healthy." Notice the difference between the focus on "I don't have energy," or "I am healthy." Because the mind and body are connected, the thoughts you choose to hold onto will affect how you're feeling. You could also practice a mantra in the car, on your way to work. Some Sanskrit mantras are:

- *Lokha Samasta Sukino Bhavantu*
  (may all beings everywhere know peace)

- *Om nama shivaya*
  (I surrender to Shiva—the energy of universal consciousness)

- *Om mani padme hum*
  (the mantra that encompasses all teachings of Buddha)

Of course, there are many other mantras, and you can use your own from other cultures and traditions. Choose something that feels authentic, that truly speaks to what you want to cultivate and express.

> **Are there rules for making up a mantra?**
>
> When you create a mantra, keep it simple. And, create it in the present tense as though it is already so. For example, instead of saying, "I will be relaxed," say "I am relaxed." And, as you say it, put belief in it. Believe and say, "I am relaxed," as your mantra.

Mantra meditation is associated with the Throat Chakra, which is the energy of communication. This is the energy center for lining up what you believe and what you express. As you practice mantra, you strengthen your Throat Chakra, especially if you practice aloud. Use your voice, listen to your voice. Enjoy and appreciate your right to speak and be heard.

Ajna Chakra and Jnana Yoga

Jnana yoga is the yogic path of study and is often associated with Vedanta. *Vedanta* often refers to the *Upanishads*, ancient texts on the philosophy of yoga. The Vedanta path speaks of our human existence as having three layers, a variation of five sheaths as explored in Sankhya yoga philosophy (based on the yoga sutras). According to Vedanta the three layers are the **physical body**, the **subtle body**, and the **causal body**. You will hear yogis talk both of this type of discrimination of the body as well as the system of the five koshas.

The causal body refers to the Anandamaya kosha, relating to the energy that links you to the divine energy. The connection is made through the strength of the Crown Chakra. The subtle energy body contains the Vijnanomaya kosha, the Manomaya kosha, and the Pranamaya kosha. These are connected to the Third-Eye, Throat, and Heart Chakras. The physical body is the Annamaya kosha, which is primarily connected to the issues of the Solar Plexus, Sacral, and Root Chakras.

When you explore these different states of your existence, you are practicing Jnana yoga: self-study. This is also practicing the niyama Svadyaya. Jnana yoga is connected to the third eye, which can see all aspects of the self: physical, subtle, and causal.

Sahasrara Chakra and Raja Yoga

Raja yoga is thought of as *the* path of yoga. It is the term used for following the yoga sutras as outlined by Patanjali. It's practicing yoga for development of witness consciousness.

> "For thousands of years the Yogis have probed the mysteries of the mind and consciousness and we may well discover that some of their findings are applicable to our own search as well."
>
> —Sri Swami Satchidananda

Raja yoga refers to having an interest in understanding the nature of the mind and finding a way to be still and calm, not tossed about by the fickle nature of the mind. It is a practice of connecting to your higher self, following the path of yoga to achieve liberation. The practice of Raja yoga correlates to the Crown Chakra, the energy center that opens up to divine consciousness.

CHAPTER 11

Pranayama and the Chakras

Pranayama is the practice of noticing, controlling, and using the breath to help guide prana through the body. Breathing techniques help balance the chakras and can be used in various everyday situations to calm you down, energize you, and cheer you up. Pranayama is an ancient practice with many benefits for modern life. And perhaps the best part is, it's free and always available. You don't have to buy any props, and you can do it wherever you are.

The Healing Power of Breath

Breathing is your connection to life force. Scientifically, it brings oxygen in and allows carbon dioxide out. In relation to your vital energy, you can use the breath to control where prana flows. You can also use breath to influence your physical and mind states, with numerous applications. Related to healing the chakras, you can direct your breath to each chakra and up the central energy channel of the body, increasing your life force and bringing healing energy to the entire body.

What Is Pranayama?

Pranayama is one of the eight limbs of yoga, and it consists of various techniques of inhaling, retaining, and exhaling your breath. The word *Pranayama* can be broken into its two parts: *prana*, "life force"; and *yama*, "to restrain" or "hold back."

> *Yama* in *Pranayama* is the same word as *yama* for the *yamas* and *niyamas*. For yamas and niyamas, *yama* is explained as the practices to do in the world, to help distinguish it from the niyamas, which are practices focused inwardly. Both, though, can also be seen as "restraints." As you discipline yourself with those practices, you restrain and exhibit mindfulness.

Pranayama exercises vary in their difficulty, intensity, and purpose. For some you add the movement of arms and legs, for others you sit still and quietly, and for some you make sound. As with any practice, start slow or with few repetitions to allow your body to become acclimated. Over time, you can increase repetitions and level of difficulty.

Physical Pain and the Brain

Pain is the body's way of sounding alarms to alert you that it believes it's in danger. Your body has sensors all through it, and these sensors look out for potential and actual danger. When your body has deemed that danger is sufficient, the sensors send a message to the brain so that you will feel pain. Studies show that pain is complicated. It's not always present for all injuries, and for others it's excruciating. Also, for the same surgical procedures or injuries, different people experience different levels of pain.

The prevailing explanation is that psychological factors contribute to pain. The context of the injury makes a difference. For example, sometimes you won't feel pain in your body until you see the injury. Or, if you're angry at your younger brother and he pushes you into the wall, you might feel more pain because of your emotions.

How you contextualize the situation psychologically affects how you experience the pain. Did someone intentionally hurt you? How are you feeling, generally, in your life outside of this situation? Do you have support for taking care of this injury? If you have difficult situations in your life, it could increase the experience of pain. In addition, not understanding what's going on in the body can increase pain. The bottom line is that fear, uncertainty, and other disturbing emotions in and around the injury can cause more pain.

The brain also needs to receive sensory input that the threat of danger is gone for the pain to subside. The book *Explain Pain* gives the example that one of the most common pains on the planet is a toothache, and yet there are times when a patient calls to make an emergency appointment and the pain is gone when he gets to the dentist's office. The conclusion is that the brain is satisfied that the patient did the right thing, before the dentist did anything. The brain felt it was safe to stop giving the alert signal.

Pranayama and Pain

Physically, people may hold their breath or stop breathing when in pain. The brain will identify this as more cause for alarm. Pranayama can help. The appropriate breathing exercises will help calm the body, calm the mind, and allow healing energy to move to those places where your brain is telling you there's a problem. This encourages the brain to receive signals to calm down, feel safe, and soften or stop sending the alert.

> "Where the mind goes, the prana follows."
>
> —Thirumoolar, South Indian saint

The way that breath helps is twofold. First of all, it creates space in the body. Where the body is tense, more pain and feelings of discomfort can occur. By creating space, emotionally and physically, you create the conditions for ease, peace, and calm in mind and body. The second way that breath helps with pain is that it promotes healing. Remember that the body has nadis running through it, channels that carry prana. Pranayama will purify those nadis, unblocking areas that are blocked off from carrying energy. When the channels are clear, prana can move to areas where the body needs it. This allows your body to heal itself, as it's open and receiving healing life force. The body wants to be well and is designed to heal, so by relaxing and creating space the body can do its work. With the same premise, Pranayama unblocks chakras, sending energy to support those beaming wheels of light.

Visualizations and Breath

Visualization is an integral part of Pranayama. Depending on the specific Pranayama that you choose to do, you will coordinate your breath with visualizations of where you want the breath and healing energy to travel. You have at your disposal a free and invaluable self-healing tool: You can direct healing energy to wherever you feel pain or discomfort in the body. And, you can use it to help calm your overactive mind, too. Sometimes the hardest part is just to remember to do it. Visualizations strengthen the Ajna Chakra, in particular, whose energy connects you to imagination and seeing areas of yourself and existence that the biology of the eye cannot.

Why Practice Pranayama?

Practicing Pranayama has numerous positive effects, including supporting the body through postures, reducing pain, healing the body, and helping you avoid getting trapped by the mind-stuff as it comes up. There are several types of Pranayama, each with its own benefits.

Dirgha Breath

Pronounced "deer-gha," Dirgha is also called the *yogic breath*. It's a breath you can use throughout your asana practice and life. It's deep breathing, focusing on expanding the torso to allow as much breath as possible to fill the lungs. The purpose of this breath is to focus your attention, to bring your awareness to the present moment. It's a perfect way to become present for meditation or asana, to separate this moment from the hustle and bustle of your day. You can also do it first thing in the morning, each day, to transition from whatever you experienced in sleep to a new place from which to start your day.

Can anyone do breathing exercises?

Breathing exercises can be wonderful for anyone because you control your pace and movement. For every exercise, though, there are circumstances under which you should not do Pranayama. Notice guidelines for when certain breathing practices are not recommended. And, as always, monitor the effects for you. The benefits of Pranayama are numerous, as long as you stay mindful.

In relationship to the chakras, because Dirgha is a long and slow breath, you can envision the breath passing along each one of the chakras. It is great for doing a visualization check-in with each chakra.

Ujjayi, Calming Ocean Sound

To practice Ujjayi Pranayama, you slightly constrict the back of your throat as you breathe in and out. This will cause a sound that will resonate in your ears like the tides of the ocean as they go out to sea and come back to land, spilling across the sand. Ujjayi is a calming breath, and the sound is another tool to help you focus the mind. As you breathe in and out, in Dirgha, add this sound to each inhale and exhale. Ujjayi is also described as sounding like Darth Vadar, the character from the *Star Wars* films.

Nadi Shodhana for Equilibrium

Nadi Shodhana is known as the *channel purifying breath*. When you alternate the flow of breath from one side to the other, you are balancing and purifying the flow of energy through the ida and pingala nadis as well as the flow to alternate sides of the brain. Each side of the brain is associated with certain functions. The right side is connected to creative and intuitive functioning, and the left side is associated with logical and rational thought. When you alternate the flow of energy from one side to the other, you are balancing them so that one isn't feeling quite as dominant over the other. This kind of breathing has a balancing and calming effect on your entire system.

Anuloma Viloma

Anuloma Viloma is *alternate nostril breathing*. It is similar to Nadi Shodhana because you alternate nostrils, and the addition for Anuloma Viloma is that you practice retention. In the retention there is time to notice and direct energy while increasing inward focus.

Kapalabhati as Raising Energy

Kapalabhati stokes your inner fire. It's a way of raising your energy. You can do Kapalabhati if you're feeling sluggish and need a boost. You can also do it during your asana practice to add more fire to your practice. It's best to wait to do Kapalabhati for two hours after a light meal or four hours after a heavy meal.

> Kapalabhati is not recommended for women who are pregnant or for people with uncontrolled high blood pressure. It is also not intended for people who have recently had surgery, especially anywhere in the torso. You can control how vigorously you do the practice, so always be mindful of how your body handles the movement and flow of air.

Kapalabhati is primarily associated with the Manipura Chakra. When you do this breathing exercise, you engage muscles in the area of the solar plexus with a forceful exhale, then you allow the air to flow in on a passive inhale. The Manipura Chakra is strengthened with the increase in movement, energy, and heat.

When to Use Pranayama

Different breathing exercises are useful at different times in your day or practice. You can practice Pranayama in the car, in your bedroom, as part of a yoga practice, at your desk, at the post office, or even at the airport. The practices are meant to support your daily life, so they don't have to be confined to practice in a yoga class or in the privacy of your meditation space.

Dirgha Breaks

Practicing Dirgha breath can support you throughout your day. It's a Pranayama you can do without drawing attention to yourself. Whether you're at work, standing in line, or taking a walk, you can practice this deep breathing technique to bring more vitality and a sense of calm to your life. And, the more often you practice, the more it will become second nature in times of stress.

Pranayama is an important addition to asana practice. Whether you use Dirgha to keep the breath steady or Kapalabhati at times to increase the energy, Pranayama helps keep the mind steady.

Nadi Shodhana to Switch Gears

Nadi Shodhana is a great way to switch gears. If you are transitioning from a hectic schedule to your yoga practice, Nadi Shodhana is a great way to transition.

> Nadi Shodhana is said to help with the symptoms of menopause. Symptoms such as hot flashes, difficulty sleeping, and mood swings can be tempered with Nadi Shodhana because it's designed to help create balance. Practicing for ten to fifteen minutes at a time once or twice a day could alleviate menopausal symptoms.

Nadi Shodhana is also a great breath to use when you are making decisions. Because many people form habits of making decisions using one of the hemispheres of the brain, by using Nadi Shodhana first you can make decisions from a more balanced mindset. You will be using both your logical and intuitive faculties as you consider the choices.

Kapalabhati for Energy

A great time to practice Kapalabhati is when you are watching television. Watching TV can be a sluggish experience, and you could sit there for hours and hours in the same position. During commercial breaks, sit or stand up and practice Kapalabhati. It's a great way to engage your internal fire and get energy flowing at a time when you are otherwise sedentary.

Kapalabhati works well as a break from sitting at the computer, too. Whether you are working or just checking e-mails, take breaks for this Pranayama that will energize you and strengthen your metabolism. It's a perfect addition to any lifestyle that calls for extended amounts of sitting still, staring at a computer screen.

How to Practice Pranayama

Pranayama is a powerful, ancient practice of directing energy in the body. Enjoy being creative about when and where you practice Pranayama to bring more health and vitality into your life. How you practice, the actual methods, are specific and simple once you've practiced them.

> Dirgha can help with low back pain. Sit or lie down with a rolled-up towel placed comfortably in the natural curve of your spine. If you lie down, also try placing a pillow underneath your knees. As you inhale deeply, envision breath travelling with healing energy to the place where your back hurts. Exhale, let go, relax. Repeat.

DIRGHA PRANAYAMA PRACTICE

1. Sit or lie down in a comfortable position, with your spine supported.

2. Close your eyes or fix your gaze softly on a still object.

3. Inhale, expanding the belly area in three dimensions. Envision the breath going deep into the belly. As you do this, imagine that lower part of your entire torso expanding in three dimensions—the side and back body, as well as the front.

4. Keep inhaling, and imagine the torso expanding at the level of the rib cage.

5. Continue to inhale expanding the chest in front and behind to the shoulder blades.

6. Finally, as you exhale, allow the chest, rib cage, then belly to soften.

Dirgha Pranayama is a deep, long inhale and slow exhale. You can repeat it several times. The inhale physically starts in the area of the Svadhistana Chakra and physically continues up to the Throat Chakra, though you can envision it going up to your Ajna Chakra. To practice chakra visualization with Dirgha, as you inhale and expand the belly, envision the breath travelling down to feed the lotus at the Root Chakra. As you continue to expand the torso on the inhale, envision the location of each chakra along the way, up to the Ajna Chakra. To keep your awareness on the calming effects of being in your physical body, do not envision the breath going up to the Crown Chakra. Keep the visualizations between the Muladhara and Ajna for embodiment.

Dirgha breath is also useful during your entire asana practice. Keep the breath steady and deep, helping prana release blocks in the body and sustain your energy.

NADI SHODHANA PRACTICE

1. Find a comfortable seated position. Make sure your spine is upright, no slouching.

2. Do a few moments of Dirgha to center yourself.

3. Hold your hand in Vishnu Mudra. To do this keep your thumb, ring finger, and pinky extended, while your pointer and middle fingers are bent down toward your palm.

4. With eyes closed use your right thumb to close your right nostril. Exhale through your left nostril.

5. With your right thumb still holding your right nostril closed, inhale through the left nostril.

6. Use the ring finger of your right hand to close your left nostril.

7. Exhale through the right nostril.

8. Inhale through the right nostril. And, repeat the process from Step 4.

As you practice rounds of Nadi Shodhana, begin to extend the length of the inhale and the exhale. Do this comfortably to induce relaxation and to balance the hemispheres of the brain. When you've completed the rounds you want to do, take several moments to be still and notice the effects of the practice.

ANULOMA VILOMA

1. Sit in a comfortable seated position.

2. Practice Nadi Shodhana for a few rounds.

3. To start Anuloma Viloma, retain the breath between the inhale and the exhale.

4. As you get more comfortable, hold the breath longer between the inhale and exhale, and just observe what happens in your body.

5. Repeat the cycles of Anuloma Viloma for up to fifteen minutes to receive balancing benefits of the practice. Then, after you are finished, pause and notice the effects.

After doing any of the breathing exercises, pause and notice. Allow the body to adjust from the Pranayama back to normal breathing. When you do this, you also allow the effects to sink in. Keep the breathing practices meditative. Do not strain.

KAPALABHATI PRACTICE

1. Get into a comfortable seated or standing position.

2. Practice a few rounds of Dirgha breath.

3. Inhale deeply.

4. Forcefully contract the abdomen muscles toward the spine, swiftly pushing the air out.

5. Relax the muscles, passively allowing the air to rush back into your body.

6. Repeat at a moderate pace, forcefully pressing air out, passively allowing it back in.

7. As you become experienced, you can do this in rapid succession.

8. After 15 rapid contractions of your abdomen and passive inhalations, allow a long inhale and exhale. Relax while your breath returns to normal.

9. Repeat 15 rounds three times, if you body will allow it. Increase the repetitions to 30 per round, when you are comfortable and used to Kapalabhati.

Before practicing Kapalabhati and all of the breathing exercises, be sure that your nasal passages are clear. Have some tissues nearby, just in case. And, it's best not to practice Pranayama if you have a cold or upper respiratory infection.

Restoring the Chakras

To restore the chakras with Pranayama, combine Dirgha breath with visualization to send the breath where you want it to go. To assist your visualization, place a hand on the body part you want to heal. Breathe deeply and envision the breath travelling to where your hand is placed. At the same time, imagine healing energy emanating from your hand to that spot. Here are guidelines for how to match up chakras with Pranayama.

CHAKRAS AND PRANAYAMA

CHAKRAS	PRANAYAMA	EFFECT
Root and Sacral	Dirgha	Grounding
Manipura	Kapalabhati	Stimulating
Heart	Dirgha with Ujjayi	Soothing
Throat	Dirgha with Ujjayi	Stimulating
Third-Eye	Nadi Shodhana	Balancing

As you practice Pranayama, over time it will become second nature. You will be able to use your breath to help you reduce stress, elevate your energy, sustain focus, and support your chakras.

CHAPTER 12

Gentle Yoga Practice for Chakra Balancing

In addition to learning to associate with the seer who sees beyond the fabrications of the mind, one of the primary reasons for the physical postures of yoga is to prepare the body for meditation and stillness. The physical practices open more space in the body, allowing prana to flow and support the chakras. If you intend to be still for a while in meditation, adding physical movement to your day helps counteract the effects of sitting still, which can create stiffness and unhealthy holding patterns in the muscles.

Why Do a Physical Practice?

The chakras help direct life-force energy to the various parts of your mind, body, and spirit. When they are balanced, energy flows through you in a way that makes you alert, creative, productive, compassionate, physically healthy, kind, centered, and emotionally stable. A gentle yoga practice with mindful attention on your body and mind will help you get to know your particular patterns in life. You'll notice where you tend to get blocked or tripped up on your path to the fullest expression of who you are.

Energy Becomes Physical Reality

Physical disease starts with something foreign, unsupportive, and obtrusive to the healthy joyful natural state of the life-force energy in you. The negative imprint in the energy field sustains and grows with your own thoughts, feelings, emotions, choices, and actions. Your energy field also responds to other people's energy and to environmental factors that you're exposed to (such as allergens, pollutants, and bacteria). When you notice negative energy around you or within you, and you try to pretend it's not there, you resist it, or you add to it; that taxes you. Instead of supporting your health, negativity diminishes it. Your mind, body, and chakras work to try to get you back to equilibrium. Your natural state is equilibrium and health, so your body and mind try as they might to be in balance. While working to compensate for the effects of the negative energy, your body may fail to perform its usual essential functions like proper digestion or hormone secretion that you need for immunity. In addition, the negative energetic imprint affects your physical body and can cause headaches, migraine, ulcers, tumors, and more. What once begins as energy becomes manifest in physical reality.

> If you become ill or develop a serious physical limitation or emergency, it's not your fault. It's part of the journey of life. When disease shows up, care for yourself. And if there is something you can do to try to prevent it from happening again, see it as a chance to grow and learn on a soul level.

One way to help prevent major disease and to calm chronic conditions is to keep prana flowing freely. And, an important part of freeing up space for prana to flow is to cultivate a healthy physical practice for your body. Based on your dosha, your health, the season, and your chakras, you can learn which yoga postures will balance your constitution and keep energy pathways clear in the body.

Physical Movement Shifts Energy

Moving your body supports the flow of life-force energy within you. For example, when you do Pranayama, you are using your physical body to control the flow of air in and out. The physical movements that you perform to control the air flow are also controlling the flow of prana. Where the breath goes, prana goes.

When you practice Hatha yoga, with conscious breath awareness, you will notice that movements such as twists, elongations, and bends allow energy to travel through the body in a way that is revitalizing, rejuvenating, and restorative. When your physical body moves, the energy will shift within you. Your mental state will change based on the postures and Pranayama that you do.

> If you are having trouble changing your mindset or your mood just with will, move your body. Do a few physical postures, dance to a song on your iPod, or do several rounds of an appropriate Pranayama. Your mood will shift, even if just a bit, if you let go and allow.

Because physical movement shifts energy, physical movement supports the chakras. You can use your body as a tool to help move the energy around—from the chakras that are overloaded to the chakras that are deficient. And, at the same time, the postures nourish your body helping it to become youthful, limber, and in proper alignment.

What You Need

Before starting any physical practice, talk it over with your doctors and healers. Know the state of your body and get advice about which postures could be good for you and which to avoid. Especially when pregnant or dealing with uncontrolled high blood pressure, back injuries, and recent surgery, you will want the advice of your doctors, therapists, and healers. Practice patience and mindfulness when you come to yoga. The postures may seem a little more challenging than you think, and you may not be able to do as much as you hope, at first. Part of the practice for you is being okay with where you are now. It can help you accept where you are if you acknowledge the very fact that, right now, you are taking care of yourself. Making time to take care of yourself is the first step, which many people don't even get to.

If you practice acceptance of where you are now and you don't push it, in time you will see your body will respond well. If you do push yourself past your body's limit, you could end up with injury, setbacks, and frustration. It's essential to get into the postures properly and safely. Then, with breath and focus, explore your edge. Your body knows what it needs, and it will be different for each person. It will be different for you, too, day-to-day. Listen to the wisdom of your body. See if you can enjoy that each day is new, and each day is an opportunity for a fresh start.

What to Wear

Wear comfortable clothes. When trying on clothes for a very gentle yoga practice, you want to make sure that you can do easy twists, lie down, sit up, and bend forward comfortably while feeling covered in a way that's comfortable for you.

Practice with bare feet to prevent sliding, and wear layers of clothes so if you get uncomfortably warm you can remove a layer. You may start out wearing a long-sleeved top or sweatshirt, and then after warming up you would want to have on just a T-shirt or tank top. The idea is that you can move freely, comfortably, and safely.

Depending on your dosha, you will know if you tend to be cold or if you are someone who tends to be too hot. Support yourself; take care of yourself. It's important for your physical practice. If you are always cold during your practice, your body won't move as well as it could. It could be stiff, dry, and brittle. You could feel anxious and unable to relax. If you are too hot and you wear too many layers in your yoga practice, you could get competitive, agitated, and dehydrated. Make the yoga practice healthy for you, not aggravating to your mind, body, and spirit.

Props to Have on Hand

There are a few props to have with you to assist your body as you go through the poses. Having props helps you make the postures "steady and sweet," which makes the physical practice effective. Here is a list of what you will need:

- Yoga mat

- Blanket

- Strap or tie

- Two blocks

- At least one cushion

- Optional: chair

Once you have these props, they will last you a very long time. It's worth the time and financial investment to buy products specifically to support you in this practice. The yoga mat will help you do the postures with less chance of slipping. It also protects your bare feet from the dust or dirt that might be on the rug or floor. A blanket is so versatile and can be used early in the practice to support your seat, your limbs, or the natural curves of your spine. At the end of your practice the blanket will keep you warm during savasana, the final pose: relaxation pose or corpse pose. A strap or tie acts as an extension of your arms, helping you do things you wouldn't be able to do otherwise. Blocks can also be used to add length to your arms, and in other ways they help you safely and easefully do postures you couldn't otherwise do. Cushions are supportive for your body, at the very least during centering and meditation, and can also be used as support for your body, especially in luxurious restorative postures. And, finally, a chair is useful if you are unable to sit on the floor, have back issues, or are not too flexible. It helps you modify postures. Modifying postures allows you to do the postures in a way that will help prana flow in your body, when your body isn't flexible.

Enhance Your Practice

To receive continued benefit from your practice, enhance your practice with books, DVDs, and CDs on the yoga and chakra topics that interest you. Continue to gain knowledge. If you hear of a yoga teacher in your area whom others recommend, try a class. Continue to expand your experience to find out what works for you.

Warm Up

Anytime you do anything physical, whether it's taking a walk outside or doing a physical yoga practice, you need to warm up the body. Whether you do the following sequence all the way through or just choose to focus on one chakra, always warm up first. Be intentional about the healing benefits you are about to receive: take time to center yourself and transition from your other activities into this practice.

Centering for Chakra Healing Sequence

Sit in a comfortable, seated position with your legs crossed. This posture is *sukasana*. Place a cushion or a folded blanket under your **sitz bones** (sitting bones); this helps you sit up tall while maintaining the natural curves in your spine. Gently place your hands in your lap. Close your eyes. Relax your forehead, eyes, jaw, and tongue. Scan all the way down your body, relaxing each body part, as you breathe in and out naturally.

After scanning the body, simply watch the breath as it flows in and out. Do this for a few breaths. Then, begin Dirgha Pranayama. Allow the belly, ribs, and chest to expand in three dimensions as you inhale. As you exhale, allow the chest, ribs, and belly to relax. Continue Dirgha Pranayama for several breaths. Then, return to the natural breath, and open your eyes.

Preparing the Body for a Gentle Sequence

While in sukasana place your hands palms down on your thighs. Gently exhale as you round the spine so that the bottom of your pelvis tilts forward and the crown of your head comes forward. Then inhale as you smoothly arch the spine by tilting the top of your pelvis forward, pressing your chest forward, and carefully tilting your head back. Repeat this sequence gently three to four times.

Come back to neutral. Raise both arms up overhead, pull your abdomen in, gently elongate the spine, and slowly twist your torso to the left. Lower your arms, placing your right hand on your left knee and your left hand down to the earth beside or behind you. Inhale and exhale in this position. Then, inhale the arms up and repeat this twist by turning to the other side. Inhale and exhale while twisted to the other side. Gently return to center. Bring your hands into your lap. Close your eyes. Breathe naturally for a few breaths. Then, repeat this twist twice on each side.

If sitting on the floor is uncomfortable, you can do the twist while sitting on a chair.

Come into a steady and stable standing posture, mountain pose: tadasana. Stand with your feet hip-width distance apart. Feel the balls of your feet and the heels rooting into the earth. Engage the muscles in your thighs while keeping the knees slightly and softly bent. Stand with your pelvis in a neutral position. Place your hands on your hips, inhale and imagine growing taller in the spine. Exhale and gently roll your shoulders up and back. Gaze forward, with the top of your head parallel to the ceiling, breathe naturally, and stand strong in tadasana with your fingertips extending down toward the earth.

Bring your right hand to your hip. On the inhale, raise the left arm out to the side and continue to raise it up in the air. On the exhale, lean slightly to the right side so that you create a slight arc in your torso. Inhale and exhale a few gentle breaths in this position. Gently inhale your left arm back up toward the center, bringing your whole torso into alignment. Exhale, release both arms to your sides. Repeat this on the other side. Pause and notice the effects.

Lightly jump several times in place, relaxing any part of you that doesn't need to be engaged as you jump. Let the arms hang, let the tongue and jaw be relaxed. Keep breathing and jumping for three minutes, going at different paces. Jump and pause between jumps, then jump up and down without pausing. Open your mouth and let out a sound, "aaaahhhhhhhhhhhh," as you do this—bouncing the tension out of the body, warming it up.

Come to stillness. Notice if you feel any sensation as you stand still for a few breaths. Then, look down at your feet and wiggle your toes. Wiggle them, and keep breathing. Add to your wiggling toes, wiggling fingers. Wiggle fingers and toes for a few breaths. Then, pause. Observe how you feel.

Finally, rotate your ankles one at a time, in one direction then the other. Do this nine times for each ankle. Rotate your wrists nine times, then pause.

The following sections are instructions for a gentle Hatha yoga sequence to balance all the chakras, one at a time. Doing the entire sequence will allow you to focus on each chakra and have a complete practice. If you do not have time for a full practice, and want to work on just one or a few of the chakras, always begin the practice with a warm up. And, end your practice with savasana.

For savasana, lie on your back with your legs straight on the floor. Place a cushion underneath your knees to help the low back relax. Allow your arms to relax along your sides. Slightly tilt your chin toward your chest, so the neck is long and relaxed. Relax your forehead, your eyes, your tongue, and your jaw. Let your whole body go, and lie in savasana for several minutes. When you are ready to get up, slowly roll to one side and press yourself up into a seated position. Notice how you feel. Then, slowly transition into your day.

Yoga for the Root Chakra

Lie on your back on the floor. Relax. Feel yourself sinking into the support of the earth. Inhale, and on the exhale, bend your knees and draw them into your chest. Hold onto your calves or knees with your hands as you breathe in and out. Know that your colon is massaged as your belly presses into your thighs. Breathe in and out, noticing how the back of your body is supported by the earth and how this position brings attention into your physical body.

From here, come into happy baby pose. Draw your knees apart and back toward your shoulders. Hold your right foot with your right hand and your left foot with your left hand, and lift your feet into the air with each knee bent at a 90 degree angle. The tops of your thighs are angled out from your torso, your knees are bent, and your feet are pointing toward the ceiling. Hold happy baby pose and take seven slow,

deep breaths. Visualize deep red energy coming up from the earth into your low back, which is solidly on the ground. Visualize the earth's energy swirling into your Root Chakra through your back. Rock your body side to side, if that feels soothing. Feel your back body grounding into the earth, and bring a gentle smile to your face.

After several breaths, release this pose by hugging the legs into the chest, and roll over onto your right side in fetal position. Relax in fetal position, visualizing your Root Chakra as a glowing red lotus. Feel the support of the earth beneath you.

Gently sit up. Feel your sitz bones against the earth, or put the cushion under your sitz bones if that's more comfortable. Come into bound angle pose: baddha konasana. Bring the soles of your feet together so that the knees are pointed outward, away from the body. If your thighs do not rest comfortably on or very near the earth, use blocks to support your thighs while you are seated on a cushion or a blanket.

Hold your feet in your hands. Breathe naturally, as you gently massage your feet while in bound angle. As you massage your feet be

aware that you are touching acupressure points, sending prana throughout your body. And, you are grounding yourself by bringing attention to your feet. After you've massaged your feet for a few moments, stop and hold your feet. As you inhale and exhale a few times, send warmth and healing red energy from your hands to your feet and feel the glow rise up your legs to your Root Chakra. With a tall spine, inhale and pull in your abdomen to protect your spine. On the exhale, initiating the movement from the hips, gently lean forward, leading with the chest. Lean forward no more than 45 degrees. Hold this posture for a few deep breaths in and out.

Release this posture by sitting up, releasing your hold on your feet, bending your knees up toward the chest, and slowly rolling yourself down onto your back. Do any small movements that your body is asking for as a counter movement to baddha konasana. Then, move onto the next section for the Sacral Chakra.

Yoga for the Sacral Chakra

Roll onto your belly. Turn your head to one side, and take a few breaths. Enjoy the support of the earth. Come into boat pose. Place your arms down along your sides. Place your forehead or chin on the floor. Or fold your hands under your forehead as in the following figure. Inhale and press your pelvis into the earth. Pressing your pelvis into the earth, exhale and while keeping your pelvis grounded point the toes of your left foot toward the back of the room so that your left leg begins to lift off the floor. Press your pelvis into the earth, hold the left leg slightly off the floor as you inhale. Exhale, release the leg back down. Inhale, holding your pelvis to the floor. Exhale and point the toes of your right food toward the back of the room so that your right leg begins to lift off the floor. Press your pelvis into the earth, hold the right leg slightly off the floor as you inhale. Exhale, release the leg back down. Turn your head to one side, take a few relaxing breaths.

Place your forehead or chin on the floor. Pull your abdomen in, root your pelvis into the earth, and as you inhale, reach both feet toward the

back of the room so that both legs are slightly off the ground. As you breathe in and out, press your pelvis against the earth, hold your abdomen in, and gently raise your arms slightly off the ground with palms facing down while they stay next to your torso. Lift your chin off the ground to look forward and inhale and exhale a few times, holding boat pose. Imagine yourself gliding across the water, easily, smoothly, and gently. Envisioning your body gliding along the water energizes the Sacral Chakra, whose element is water. Pressing your pelvis into the earth also brings energy to the Sacral Chakra, which is located below the navel. Release this pose by bringing your legs and arms down, turning your head to the side, and taking a few breaths. Allow your body to take a moment to receive the benefits of the posture.

For a more advanced version of boat pose, instead of keeping the arms by your torso, reach the arms out in front of you while you hold the legs slightly off the ground. Keep your pelvis pressing into the earth, allow the top of the torso to raise while your eyes gaze toward the earth in front of you. Breathe.

After you have released boat pose, take your time and gently come up to standing. If you want to, for this upcoming part, put on music that you enjoy—do these movements at the pace the music moves you. Stand with your legs wider than hip-distance apart. Place your hands on your hips and sway your hips side to side. Breathe as you sway your hips side to side. After several breaths, pause. Now, sway your pelvis back and forth. Breathe as you sway your pelvis back and forth several times. Now, make circles with your hips by putting those movements together, swaying to the right, to the front, to the left, and to the back. Do this smoothly and gently. Luxuriate in this fluid movement, for several breaths, then do it in the other direction. Now, breathe naturally for a few moments and allow your body to move in any way that it feels it wants to. Make the movements fluid, like water, stimulating your Sacral Chakra. If your body doesn't feel the need for more movement, be still, and take note of any sensations in your body.

Come back to a neutral standing position, and leave the music on. Enter goddess pose. Place your hands on your hips. Stand with your feet more than hip-width distance apart. Pivot your feet so your toes are turned out, 45 degrees. Feel your feet rooted into the earth. Gently pull your abdomen in, inhale, and on the exhale sink your sitz bones downward with your spine tall as your knees bend and point away from each other. Keep your abdomen in, and lift your arms up to shoulder height. Bend your elbows 90 degrees and turn your palms to face you. Take seven deep breaths, feeling your belly expand and contract at the level of the Sacral Chakra. Ground yourself into the earth through your powerful legs. If your hips want to move a little bit, allow them some fluid, easy movement. Keep your legs strong, grounded. A balanced Sacral Chakra allows you to feel you are allowed to enjoy life, with stability in the face of emotional challenges. As you stand in goddess pose, you are glowing. Your chest expands as you shine your light, and your strong arms, abdomen, and legs ground you emotionally. Release this posture, straighten the legs and stand up, and you relax the arms down by your side. Pause, and notice how you feel.

Yoga for the Solar Plexus Chakra

Come into the archer pose. The Solar Plexus Chakra is about transformation, using your own fire to make things happen in your life with self-confidence, a positive outlook, appropriate action, and groundedness. The archer pose exemplifies this energy. Come up with an intention for the next step in your life. Face forward, with your legs and feet together. Step your right foot approximately two feet in front of you. Feel stable. If you need to, place your foot a little further in front of you and a little to the right, for balance. Make it stable for your body; everyone is different. Inhale your right arm straight out in front of you at eye level. Make a fist with the fingers of your right hand and point your right thumb up to the ceiling. Bend your left arm and place your left hand on the back of your head. Inhale, pull your abdomen in, gently elongate the spine, and with a soft gaze on your right thumb, begin to twist your torso to the right. Keep your gaze on your thumb as you twist your torso, and your right arm naturally moves with the torso, toward the right side of the room. Keep your gaze on that right thumb, and continue to twist. You are looking over the edge of the arrow. When you come to your stopping point, hold this position and call to mind your intention. Gaze at the thumb, keep your abdomen in, breathe in and out a few times, focusing on the thumb and your intention. See if you can slowly twist further. Pause. Then, gently release this posture by unwinding your torso and releasing your arms down.

"Just as intention seeks its objective, the objective likewise seeks man's intention, for that is what gives our life a meaning: it is no longer just an idea, but the center of the archer's world."

—Paulo Coelho

After pausing for a moment, do the archer pose on the other side. After you have completed archer pose on both sides, step your feet together, bring your hands to your solar plexus, and envision your Solar Plexus Chakra glowing like the yellow sun. As you twisted your torso in the archer pose, you brought energy to the center of your core. This helps wring out energy blockages there, and fills your intention with motivational energy.

Yoga for the Heart Chakra

Lower yourself down onto your back for fish pose. Lie down with your legs straight out along the floor and your arms by your sides. Slide your hands toward each other, placing one hand underneath each buttock. Engage your abdomen muscles, and when you inhale press your forearms down and slowly lift your waist off the floor, creating an arch in your **thoracic spine**, the section of the spine behind your heart. Exhale, press your sitz bones and forearms into the earth. Inhale, expand your chest and bring the back of your head to the floor, chin toward the ceiling. Keep most of your weight on the forearms and on the sitz bones and legs as they press into the floor. Inhale and exhale a few times, feeling the energy come to the Heart Chakra. To release from the posture, exhale as you press through the forearms and sitz bones, and gently take the weight off of your head. Bring your torso back down to the ground, and gently place the back of your head on the floor. Pause and notice the effects. Make any slight movements that your body calls for, in response to the fish pose.

Yoga for the Throat Chakra

Come into table pose, on all fours, on your hands and knees. In this position, do three rounds of lion's breath. To do this, face forward. Inhale, and give a forceful, long exhale as you open your mouth, stick your tongue out and down, and roll your eyes upward. When you've run out of air, release your facial expression to normal. Then, inhale, and do lion's breath again.

Gently sit back into a simple cross-legged position with your hands in your lap. Use the cushion under your sitz bones, and if your knees are

higher than your hips, place cushions or blocks under your thighs to support them. Gently drop your chin down to your chest, and breathe seven deep breaths in this position. Inhale, and on the exhale gently roll your head to the right so that your right ear is near your right shoulder. Inhale and exhale a few times in this position. On an exhale gently roll your chin back toward the center of your chest, and then over to the left. Inhale and exhale a few times in this position. Bring your head back up into a neutral position. Pause.

While looking in front of you do the shell mudra.

Hold your left hand so that the fingers are pointing toward the sky and facing to the right. With the fingers of your right hand, hold your left thumb. As you do this, touch the left middle finger with your right thumb. Hold this shell mudra in front of your chest. Inhale and exhale seven times. Chant the seed mantra for this chakra, ham, on the exhale each time. This will help strengthen the Throat Chakra.

Yoga for the Third-Eye Chakra

Gently lie down onto your back. Get in a comfortable position for relaxation pose, or corpse pose. You may want to have a cushion underneath your knees to help your low back relax. You may want a blanket over your body to keep you warm. Once you are in the position for relaxation pose, rub your hands together vigorously to create warmth, prana. Cover your eyes with the cupped palms of your hands. Feel the prana balancing out the energy of the eyes, behind the eyes, and in the mind. Repeat this palming of your eyes three times. Take deep, nourishing breaths as you do it. Then, release your hands. Relax. Visualize a deep indigo color swirling in the area of the third eye. Hold this visualization for a few breaths. Then, see if your imagination sees anything else: colors, animals, landscapes. Allow your imagination to travel for a few moments. Notice if any symbols or messages come to you.

Yoga for the Crown Chakra

In relaxation pose, use your fingertips to gently massage your head. Make sure you massage the top of your head, gently, bringing energy to the crown. Gently massage your entire scalp. Then, bring your arms down by your sides, and sink into relaxation pose. Let go. Open up to the energy of the universe. There's nothing for you to do in this pose but let go. If you fall asleep, that's okay, too.

After you have stayed in relaxation pose for seven to ten minutes, or longer if you have time, gently roll over to your right side in fetal position. Then, gently sit up. Take a moment to envision each chakra glowing with its associated color. Bring your hands into prayer position at your Heart Chakra, and offer appreciation for the energy that has moved through you.

CHAPTER 13

Meditation and Visualization Practice for Chakra Balancing

Using chakra meditation and visualization, you will access and heal your energy centers. The techniques are versatile: you can add them to your Hatha yoga practice; you can use them in stillness, seated, or lying down; you can choose to focus on one particular chakra, or you can focus on each in a sequence. The benefit of such versatility is if you notice at a certain time of day you want to shift how you are feeling, you can do a meditation on the chakras to bring your energy into balance.

How to Prepare for Chakra Meditation

You can meditate on the chakras for any amount of time, taking the time you need to check in and give yourself the attention your body requires. There is no minimum amount of time, but keep in mind that it will take some time for you to slow down and get centered from whatever your mind has been up to so far in your daily activities.

> If you can only do a short five- or ten-minute chakra meditation, it is better than doing nothing. Taking several minutes to pause and observe your energy is measurably better than not pausing at all. Like taking vitamins, giving yourself some support every day is best.

If you set aside a good amount of time for chakra healing, then you can really let go and not feel rushed. Try to set aside forty-five minutes. You can use that amount of time to include getting yourself settled as well as integration time, so it's forty-five total.

Creating Sacred Space

Sacred space is a way of designating your meditation time as separate from the rest of your day. It doesn't have to be a literal place that you never use for anything else. Sacred space can be an energetic feeling that now is sacred time. While you don't have to, you may find you want to have a special room or corner just for your meditation practice. It's fun to create one, and it's very personal. It also makes it easy to begin meditation because all your items can stay in one place: your meditation cushion or chair, your blanket, and any crystals, props, candles, photos, etc. Sacred space is important when you meditate. It will help you to become energetically open. Be aware that you may become tender during meditation. Harsh noise or words might affect you more easily right after you finish. You will let your guard down. You will just be.

So, that's why it's good to have some time before you meditate to center and time after to integrate the experience, to allow the benefits of meditation to affect you at the cellular level.

Listening to Your Body's Wisdom

When you create the space or time as sacred you are preparing to be with what comes up when you are silent. You are preparing to spend time with the parts of you that you might not often engage with when you are outwardly focused on others, or on what you'll do next. When you create sacred space, you are going to be here *right now*. For chakra healing, when you come to this quiet place, it's time to check in and see how you are feeling. When you notice how you are feeling, those are the clues to which chakras are out of balance.

Become Attuned to How You Feel

When someone asks how you are, perhaps you have an instant and accurate response, "I'm fine," "I'm tired," or "I'm great!' Knowing how you are instantly is helpful; it shows that you are connected to the prevalent sense of how you feel. This instant knowing is good, and then take time to go deeper. Take time to observe.

> You are a living, changing, sensitive being who is connected to all the world. Weather, allergens, other people's energy, and more enter your energy field and affect you. If you judge yourself when you notice what's out of balance, try shifting from judging into neutrality. Remind yourself it's natural. By checking in, you can notice what you're carrying and clear.

Taking time to sense how you are feeling physically, emotionally, mentally, and energetically gives a fuller picture of how you really are right now. When you notice how you feel, it can help you know what to balance in your energy centers so you feel even better. An instant, "I'm tired" response indicates there are chakras out of balance that you might want to look into so you can feel alert and well rested.

Creating an Altar

Objects of encouragement that make you feel supported can make up your altar. An altar is a flat surface decorated with objects and images that support you in meditation and manifestation (what you want to attract into your life). Choose items that will remind you of the energy you want to create, the prayers you want to say, the colors you want to see, the scents you want to smell, and the malas you want to touch in relationship to balancing your energy system.

How to Create an Altar

There's not one way to make an altar. Keep in mind that the point of the altar is to help you with your meditation and manifestation. With that intention, choose and find objects that are meaningful and inspirational to you. Here are some ideas for your altar.

- Choose a small table or shelf just for your altar.

- Drape a colored scarf across the surface, the color of the chakra(s) you want to support.

- Place something from outside on the altar such as seashells from the beach where you felt peaceful and open, or a small vase of dandelions from your backyard.

- Write out mantras that hold special meaning for you, and place them on the altar.

- If there are spiritual leaders or symbols that inspire you, have those images on the altar.

- Place a candle on the altar to remind you of that miraculous natural element that lives outside and inside of you.

- Make an arrangement of crystals whose properties will balance your chakras.

- Place notes from loved ones on the altar.

You can place anything on the altar that brings you the kind of balance you are seeking. If you are fiery and full of energy, use predominantly blue, green, purple, and white as your color scheme to counteract fire. If, on the other hand, you feel tired and unmotivated, then orange, yellow, and red would be great as the main colors for your altar. You could also choose not to have a color scheme, and instead just choose objects that mean something to you. There is no right or wrong way, just make it supportive to you.

Is making an altar necessary?

You do not need an altar. You can meditate on the chakras without any objects. In fact, you could choose to do a short chakra meditation during your day, even at work, where you wouldn't have an altar. For example, if you feel insecure before a meeting, use chakra meditation for your Manipura, Anahata, and Visuddha Chakras.

When you make an altar, keep it simple. Select objects as encouragement and support, and don't overdo it. There's no formula for what is too much: you will sense the limit for yourself, if you cross it. As your energy changes with time, you can change your altar, keeping it inspirational and clutter-free.

Going Inward

Having an altar when it's time to meditate gives you a designated location that is different from everywhere else. When you're in front of the altar, it helps your senses focus on the images and objects that facilitate inward focus and healing. These objects will help you transition to a different place of awareness from where you are when you're catching up with your daily activities. It will remind you of what you want to focus on for your healing journey, which sometimes you will lose sight of with your list of to-dos. Looking at your sacred objects helps you return your attention to all of you, and the bigger picture.

Without an Altar

An altar is not necessary for meditation or for your chakra-healing journey. An altar is way to help create a space for you, to help your senses calm down from outside stimuli, and to honor sacred objects. It's where you can place your crystals or mala beads. You don't need an altar, though. You can meditate anywhere, just make sure you have what you need to be comfortable.

> When you meditate, your body temperature drops. Keeping yourself warm will help you stay comfortable. Staying warm also keeps you healthy. If you get chilly, wear a scarf, even indoors, to keep your neck and throat warm. The neck is one of few body parts often exposed, and keeping it covered will help you feel more comfortable and protect your throat.

Whether in front of your altar or not, you will want a pillow to put under your sitting bones, so you keep the natural curve in your lumbar spine. Or, you will want to sit on a chair, if sitting on the floor is uncomfortable for your body. If you are going to meditate for longer than fifteen minutes, have a blanket or scarf nearby to make sure you stay warm enough.

Chakra Support on an Altar

You can be as creative as you want with your altar. Chakra healing has become popular enough that now you can find items to put on your altar that will have chakra symbols and colors on them. You may also want an image of a rainbow on your altar, in any kind of object: a scarf, a row of healing stones or crystals, a postcard, or a photograph. You can also buy a poster of the chakras, or you could make one of your own: it could be as simple as a drawing of a figure with each chakra as a colored disc.

If you want to focus on one specific chakra, go ahead and make your altar predominantly that color, at least for a little while.

I Am That I Am

One of the simplest and most profound mantras is "So Hum"—"I am that I am." Meditating on this simple phrase, you penetrate your layers of protection and self-criticism. As you repeat "So Hum" over and over, you bring your awareness to who you are at the core. The quiet, still place. You discover simply that you exist, that you are.

So Hum Meditation

Sit in a comfortable meditation posture. Feel your sitting bones rooted solidly. Sit up with a steady spine, without trying to straighten out the natural curves. Make sure that the top of your head is parallel to the ceiling, with the back of your neck long. Take a deep inhale in, and let out a long exhale. Take two more deep breaths, making the exhale longer than the inhale.

Close your eyes and bring your hands into prayer position at the Anahata Chakra. As you breathe in, imagine the syllable "So," and as you breathe out, imagine the syllable "Hum." Do this several times. As you do this, make sure your jaw is relaxed. Begin to feel your entire body relaxing into this mantra.

> When you chant or hear chants in Sanskrit, even if you don't know the meaning of the phrases you will receive healing benefits. The vibrations of the syllables produce healing. So chant slowly, listen attentively, and become aware of how the vibration feels. Let it affect you.

Place your hands, one on top of the other, at your Sacral Chakra. Inhale deeply, and on the exhale, chant "So Hum." It doesn't matter what musical note you chant. Chant a few times with your hands and attention at your Sacral Chakra, which is the chakra that helps you flow through life and connects you to pleasure. Take pleasure in the simplicity and vastness of this mantra: I am that I am. So Hum.

So Hum Japa Meditation

If you really do not have a lot of time for meditation, try Japa meditation with a short mantra. "So Hum" is brief and powerful. To connect this mantra to strengthen a specific chakra, use malas made of the gemstone that will bring healing energy to the chakra you are working on. After you've done at least one round of Japa with So Hum, wear the malas around your neck so the vibrations of the gemstone and the prayers are with you all day.

How to Visualize Healing Colored Light

Because colors, thoughts, and your body are energy, they all work together. When you visualize colors travelling to a chakra, the energy of your thoughts literally affects your energy centers. The energy of your thoughts can also affect your body and your mind.

Color Visualization for the Chakras

You can do visualizations anywhere at any time, when you can be still and focus your energy on the visualization. Don't do visualizations while you're driving because your focus should be on driving. Be focused. The power of the visualization is diluted if you are multitasking, watching TV, cooking dinner, etc.

Can I use visualizations in my Hatha yoga practice?

Yes, you can use visualizations while you are practicing Hatha yoga. Anytime you do something meditative, visualizations can be very effective. Continue to be safe and mindful of your body and breath as you move from posture to posture.

For visualization, close your eyes and take a few deep, nourishing breaths. You can lay down, stand, or sit upright. Then, put your awareness on each chakra one at a time. While your awareness is at each level, breathe in and out a few times until you can envision the color of that chakra in that part of your body. Use the rainbow as your guide for color.

- At the **ROOT** Chakra, envision **RED**.

- At the **SACRAL** Chakra, envision **ORANGE**.

- At the **SOLAR** Plexus Chakra, envision **YELLOW**.

- At the **HEART** Chakra, envision **GREEN**.

- At the **THROAT** Chakra, envision **BLUE**.

- At the **THIRD-EYE** Chakra, envision **INDIGO**.

- At the **CROWN** Chakra, envision **WHITE**, **VIOLET**, or **GOLD**.

Start at the Root Chakra. Take slow, deep breaths in and out, and with your imagination connect to the perineum where the energy center is located. After a few natural breaths, as you breathe this time, imagine inhaling red light into the Root Chakra. Hold your breath in for a few seconds, imagining the colored light sustained there. Exhale, let go. Do this three times, then move up to the Sacral Chakra, and repeat the exercise visualizing the color orange.

Continue up the chakras to the third eye, following the same pattern. When you finish with the third-eye visualization, let your breath flow naturally in and out. Imagine your Crown Chakra glowing white light that envelops your entire body and expands upward, connecting you to the wide expanse. After doing this for a few moments, release the visualization. Cross your arms in front of you, hugging yourself across your chest or waist. Feel the parts of you that are connected to the earth, grounding into the earth. Bring your awareness back into your body. And, when you feel complete, open your eyes.

Deficient or Excessive Chakras and Visualization

In both cases, with a deficient and excessive chakra, the chakra needs healing light. If the chakra is deficient, it doesn't have enough energy. It's moving sluggishly. If the chakra is excessive, it is giving off so much energy that it cannot restore itself or accept what it needs. So, bringing healing light to that chakra can also help balance it. If you use your visualizations on all the chakras, and you can tell which are deficient and which are excessive, you can imagine the excessive ones giving energy to the deficient chakras. Visualizations can be very potent. Precision—visualizing the location as accurately as possible—and sustained focus are your tools.

Healing Mantra

Mantras use the vibration of sound to heal. Each chakra has particular sounds associated with it. You can use these specific sounds, or you can use the mantra "om" for each chakra. Om is the universal sound, said to be the very sound of creation—the vibration from which all vibrations originate.

Bija Mantra

There's a particular bija or seed mantra associated with each chakra. It is said that by chanting the bija mantra that corresponds to each chakra, you connect with the essence of that energy center. Visualize each chakra and repeat the associated bija mantra, shown in the following table.

BIJA MANTRAS AND CORRESPONDING CHAKRAS

BIJA MANTRA	CHAKRA
LAM	Root
VAM	Sacral
RAM	Solar Plexus
YAM	Heart
HAM	Throat
OM or KSHAM	Third-Eye
OM or SILENCE	Crown

Like several things with chakra healing, not all healers agree on the same bija mantras. Chakra healing is both rooted in history and also experiential because each person is unique. Test them out, and see which resonates with you best.

> The *Yoga Sutras* say, "The word expressive of Isvara, God, is the mystic sound om. To repeat it with reflection upon its meaning is an aid."
>
> —Patanjali, translated by Sri Swami Satchidananda

The vibration *om* is often equated to *Amen* as a way to connect to God. It's not just a sound: when you create that sound vibration, you feel your connection to Omniscience, Omnipresence, Omnipotence. By repeating this sound, by connecting to what is Eternal, you connect to the vibration and energy of creation, of healing, of love.

Sound Vibration

Another option for you, if you enjoy chanting one sound, is to chant the vowel associated with each chakra. Again, there are slight variations, so play with it a little bit until you feel the resonance in the right place:

- **O** as in OM for the Root

- **OO** as in POOL for the Sacral

- **AH** as in DHARMA for the Solar Plexus

- **A** as in SPACE for the Heart

- **E** as in FREE for the Throat

- **MM** as in MEDIUM for the Third-Eye

- **NNG** as in WING for the Crown

The key words—om, pool, dharma, space, free, wisdom, and wing—are there to explain how the sounds are pronounced. These words also can be used as mnemonics, to help you remember which sound goes with each chakra. Om is for the Root, and to remember it you can recall that om is the universal sound, the first vibration of physical creation. The Root Chakra connects you to the earth. For the second chakra, a pool is filled with water, the element of this chakra. The third chakra, dharma, is connected to your will and how you create your life with that power and will.

The word *space* is the heart's element. The word *free* relates to the Throat Chakra; when this chakra is in balance you feel free to speak your truth. The word *medium* is what you can cultivate through the third eye. And metaphorically, experiencing bliss at the crown is as if you had wings. Pronounce the vowels when visualizing each chakra to bring the appropriate vibration to that energy center.

Hand Mudras for Chakra Balancing

Eastern traditional medicine maps out how specific points on the hands and feet connect to separate body parts: organs, muscles, and glands. When you intentionally apply pressure to particular places on your hands and feet, you send prana to the corresponding body part and/or chakra.

To practice hand mudras, you will hold your hands and bend your fingers in ways that use this knowledge to develop and heal specific body parts.

Chakras and Your Fingers

In her book *Mudras: Yoga in Your Hands*, Gertrud Hirschi includes a section on mudras and the chakras. She explains that not everyone agrees on how the fingers of the hand correspond to the chakras. Some say that from pinky to thumb, the fingers correspond in sequence from the root to the Throat Chakra. Others illustrate it this way:

- **Pinky** corresponds to Sacral Chakra

- **Ring** finger corresponds to Root Chakra

- **Middle** finger corresponds to the Throat Chakra

- **Pointer** finger corresponds to the Heart Chakra

- **Thumb** corresponds to the Solar Plexus Chakra

Only these five of the seven major chakras correspond to fingers. Because yogis differ in their experience of which finger corresponds to which chakra, see for yourself how the energy works within you. You can use their models as guides.

> Putting light pressure on the fingers that correspond to the chakras can be effective with just a few moments of practice at a time, a few times per day. It's something you can do as a break from your everyday work tasks. Practice first at home, making it easier for your muscle-memory to recall the hand posture later.

A simple way to use your fingers for chakra healing is choose the chakra you would like to work on. Place the corresponding finger of your right hand into the palm of your left hand, and wrap your left hand and fingers around that finger. Breathe in and out naturally, as you visualize healing. Your visualization can be of healing white light travelling through that finger to the corresponding chakra, of the color that corresponds to that chakra, of the chakra itself glowing in health, or you can just witness what happens. If you get the impulse to visualize something in particular that your body needs, follow that impulse. Hold your hands in this mudra for approximately three minutes.

Chakras and Hand Mudras

Hand mudras help strengthen your chakras, and thus your various physical, mental, and spiritual aspects. Practice the mudras that you choose three times per day for fifteen minutes each time. Bring your focus and breath to your intention while you practice the mudra. In this section you will find instructions for four mudras, out of numerous to choose from. The mudras may seem difficult at first; over time they will become easier. As they become more comfortable, it is a sign of the prana and energy working well on your body.

Earth Mudra

Connecting to mother earth is essential. Going on at least a ten-minute walk outside every day will restore and refresh you, or even if you step outside for five minutes and take nice, deep breaths you will create space in your body and mind. If the weather is warm enough, and you can stand outside in your bare feet, you will connect directly to the earth's grounding energy. You also can connect to the earth element with visualizations in your yoga practice, during meditation, and with hand mudras:

1. Hold your right hand so that the palm faces up.

2. Touch the fingertip of your ring finger to the tip of your thumb.

3. Straighten out the other fingers on the right hand.

4. Feel the energy rising up your arms, grounding you. (If you can't feel it, it's okay. Visualize it. Eventually, you will feel something, if not today, another day.)

5. After fifteen minutes, do the same mudra with your left hand.

If you can do this with both hands at the same time, go ahead. Otherwise, if you have trouble straightening out any fingers for the full expression of the mudra, use the other hand to hold the fingers out. Or, use a prop of some kind to keep the appropriate fingers straightened.

And, notice what you feel physically and psychologically as you hold the mudra. You may feel the energy as tingling or heat. Even if you don't feel anything, it's okay. Energy is moving. As long as you are breathing, you have life-force energy coursing through you.

It is good for you to pause several times throughout your day. Stop what you're doing and pause. Try this sometimes when you have the impulse to send a text message or a social e-mail. Before reaching out and contacting a friend, first give yourself some time. Pause. Check in with yourself. Breathe. Do a mudra, if you'd like.

The earth mudra brings energy particularly to your Root Chakra. If you are having any symptoms of a deficient Root Chakra, such as insecurity about your worth, your home life, and your safety, practice this mudra to help strengthen your Root Chakra. Also, to bring your ideas into physical reality, you must be connected to the earth. Do this mudra to help you ground and bring your dreams to life.

Prana Mudra

The prana mudra is designed to help bring life force into the body, and like the earth mudra it is connected to the Root Chakra. These options for bringing energy to the Root Chakra are essential because none of the other chakras can function in sustained health if the root is not balanced.

1. Hold both hands so that the palms face up.

2. Curl the ring finger and pinky finger of each hand to touch the tip of the thumb of the same hand.

3. Keep the pointer and middle fingers straight.

4. Hold this for fifteen minutes three times a day.

As you practice hand mudras, remember to breathe. Sometimes when trying a new posture you will concentrate on getting it right, and you may hold your breath. Return your attention to the breath.

> **Do I hold my fingers firmly in their positions?**
>
> As with all yoga postures, hold the mudras with steadiness and ease. Don't strain, but be firm with the mudra. Keep the integrity of the posture, without feeling pain and without forcing. Release tension from anywhere in the body that doesn't need to be engaged in order for you to hold this position. Do this with lightness. Gently smile.

After releasing the mudra, pause to notice any effects before moving on to your next appointment or activity. Over time, notice if the mudra has become effortless, if your hands are more flexible. As the flexibility of your hands increases, it mirrors a growing openness in your body and in your nature, allowing energy to flow more freely.

Apana Mudra

As you heal your chakras, you will be eliminating what you don't want to carry around with you anymore: physically, psychologically, and energetically. How much are you ready to release? When you exhale, when you sweat, and when you go to the bathroom, you are releasing. These are examples of how your body eliminates waste including emotions, food, and energy that you no longer want or need. There is a hand mudra that can help this process, the apana mudra:

1. Hold your hands out so that the palms face up.

2. Curl the ring finger and middle finger of each hand to touch the fingertip of the thumb of the same hand.

3. Hold this posture for fifteen minutes, three times per day.

Use this mudra to help you eliminate toxicity and make space for new beginnings, new ideas, and new projects. With each inhale, imagine the purifying effects of prana enter your system. With each exhale, know you are expelling what you no longer need.

This mudra is helpful for all the chakras, together. When any chakra is imbalanced it corresponds to illness or disease. By helping with physical, psychological, and energetic elimination of toxicity, the apana mudra supports the proper functioning of all your energy centers.

Hakini Mudra

The Hakini mudra, named after the god Hakini, will help you concentrate, and also remember something you've forgotten. It is connected to the Third-Eye Chakra, where your intuition and imagination reside.

1. Hold your hands with palms facing each other, but not touching.

2. Bring the fingertips of the right hand to touch the fingertips of the left, pinky to pinky, ring finger to ring finger, etc.

3. Direct your gaze upward.

4. On the inhale place your tongue against the roof of your mouth.

5. On the exhale, allow the tongue to relax back down.

6. Do this several times. Pause. Notice if you've remembered what you temporarily forgot.

This mudra can be used in the moment when you forget something. Also use it to strengthen your memory, in general. This mudra is said to balance the hemispheres of the brain, which creates a sense of calm and opens you up to clear thinking, intuition, and wisdom.

CHAPTER 14

Ayurveda and the Chakras

Ayurveda helps you maintain and restore health and vitality in accordance with how the principles of the natural elements—space (ether), air, fire, and water—exist inside and outside of you. With natural, holistic-healing practices that have been used for thousands of years, Ayurveda promotes overall well-being and longevity. Considered the sister science to yoga, Ayurveda's mind-body-spirit approach enhances the effectiveness your chakra healing practices and your understanding of how your mind, body, consciousness, and energy system are affected by your inner and outer environment.

Seeing a Professional

As you learn about **Ayurveda**, *the science of life and longevity*, you will find it feels like common sense. At the same time, it is a vast and intricate science. When you decide you'd like to use Ayurveda as part of your plan for wellness, make an appointment with an Ayurvedic specialist: a **Vaidya**.

> "Ayurveda is the art of daily living in harmony with the laws of nature."
>
> —Vasant Lad, BAMS, MASc

A Vaidya, well-trained in this ancient science, will give you a complete evaluation and sound advice to help bring you into balance. The system of Ayurveda will bring a new sense of youthfulness and vibrancy to your life. It also will mean you have to set aside time for self-care. The success of this relies on your commitment to your own healing, and enthusiasm for doing some things differently than how you've been doing them. Supporting yourself with Ayurveda will enhance and prolong chakra healing effects. It will make it easier for you to stay in balance, energetically, physically, and psychologically. When you are balanced it feels *good* and is good for you—you will be more joyful, more compassionate, and more successful in what you attempt. It also helps bring ease to the aging process.

What follows is a basic introduction to Ayurveda. If you find you are interested in Ayurveda, please see the recommendations for further reading and meet with a Vaidya to help you expand your knowledge and experience. Once you become familiar with Ayurveda, it can become second nature. You can see yourself and your relationship to health in a whole new light.

The Constitution You Were Born With

Each person is born with a particular constitution, or **prakruti**, which describes how prominently each of the three doshas were arranged in you when you were conceived. The doshas—**vata**, **pitta**, and **kapha**— each are described in terms of the principles of elements in nature. The principles are qualities of each element. As these qualities exist in you, they characterize how you function: how you handle stress, how you relate to others, how you structure your life, how you digest your food, and more. Everything you think, say, feel, and do is related to your constitution and whether or not it's in balance. When your parents conceived you, the environment, their health, how the doshas were balanced in them, and the health of their relationship all contributed to making up your constitution. See the table later in this chapter for the elemental principles of each dosha and which functions it instigates in the body.

Determining Your Constitution

To determine your constitution, a Vaidya will use pulse diagnosis. Then she will take into consideration your age, lifestyle, job, family life, and all aspects that help paint the picture of how you are feeling and relating to your life. Considering all of this information with your pulse and the time of year, she will know your **vikruti**, how the doshas are showing up now in you.

Will my constitution change?

Your constitution doesn't change. It's constant, and once you know it, then you know what "balance" means for you. Your constitution will be primarily vata, pitta, or kapha, or a combination of them. When in balance, you'll feel well, and when out of balance you will show various symptoms. Illness is the result of not correcting the imbalance.

Once you know your constitution and the symptoms of imbalance, you can collaborate with your doctor to be an active participant in your healthy lifestyle. You will notice by your thoughts, emotions, physical health, and actions how you are in or out of balance. Then, you can alter certain aspects of your diet and daily activities, to bring yourself into balance naturally and comfortably.

Life and Balance

After your Ayurvedic doctor determines your constitution and notices if there are imbalances, her recommendations will include supplements, oils for your body, and suggestions for eating, sleeping, and exercise. She also will explain why she recommends what she does. As you follow the instructions, you will notice how being in balance affects your life. It will affect everything from how clearly you think to how well you sleep to how well you digest your meals.

Benefits of Ayurveda

Ayurveda as a holistic health system is a natural and time-tested way to nourish your body and help it perform its functions. You can use the advice on a daily basis. The benefits of Ayurveda are overall health, the ability to function well in your life, aging well, and a sense of empowerment over your well-being. Ayurveda works with all of your koshas, from tissues, bones, and organs to your breath, mind, wisdom, and consciousness. And, it gives you the understanding and tools to positively affect your health with the choices you make moment-to-moment and day-by-day.

Body Treatments for Health and Balance

There are a number of Ayurvedic body treatments. They can feel luxurious. Your healing can feel wonderful even though you will also be releasing difficult emotions. Treatments are used to help balance the doshas, improve immunity and circulation, and loosen toxins. The following are explanations of some Ayurvedic treatments.

- **Abyangha** is the application of oil to your entire body. The Ayurvedic bodyworker warms oil infused with herbs, specifically selected for you. Then, she applies the oil to your body in a way that supports physical and energetic circulation, loosens toxins, and relaxes the mind. It's also called Abyangha when you give yourself an Ayurvedic oil massage.

- **Abyangha-Garshana** includes a silk-glove massage before the Abyangha treatment. The silk-glove massage cleans the skin and stimulates circulation, before the oil sinks in to nourish your body.

- **Vishesh** is a treatment of oil infused with herbs applied to the body in rapid, rhythmic movements. This helps facilitate energetic, arterial, and lymphatic flow throughout the body.

- **Shirodhara** is a steady stream of warm, herbalized oil poured onto the forehead, balancing and calming the mind.

Often Ayurvedic bodyworkers will combine treatments. For example, you could request Abyangha-Shirodhara.

> The best way to receive the deep benefits of bodywork is to allow yourself time to rest afterward. Allow the oil to penetrate the surface of the skin, going deeper into the body. At the very least, see if you can schedule the treatment so you can rest for an hour afterward. Or, leave the oil on overnight.

Ayurvedic bodywork will also help balance the chakras because the bodywork affects all the koshas. When the koshas are nurtured, the energy centers receive healing energy as well. For example, for the Annamaya kosha (physical sheath), bodywork helps you feel grounded and safe, which reinforces the Root Chakra. The balancing and relaxing effects of bodywork on the mind support the Third-Eye Chakra.

Panchakarma

Panchakarma literally means *five actions*, and it's the best way to purify the body of toxins, especially if disease has set in. Also, the goal of panchakarma is to balance you, guiding you back into your balanced state, prakruti. It is a special and thorough practice that requires supervision by a properly trained Vaidya. And, you must make sure you are feeling up to it. Do not begin panchakarma if you have a cold, anemia, or anything that means your body is particularly low-energy. After getting the "okay" from your doctor, panchakarma will literally clean your body out, giving it time and support to release what's blocking you physically, emotionally, mentally, and energetically.

> In his book, *The Complete Book of Ayurvedic Home Remedies*, Dr. Vasant Lad outlines how to do panchakarma at home if you cannot go to a place that offers the treatment. Even so, as he recommends, do it under the supervision of an Ayurvedic doctor who can recommend the herbs and treatments for you.

Panchakarma has profound healing effects. Toxins that have become stored in the body from emotional, physical, and mental stress will be released. The process lasts several days, and includes internal oleation (you will drink specific amounts of ghee), external oleation (oils and massage), a specific and light diet of kitchari, plenty of rest, and methods for eliminating the toxins. Kitchari is the food of choice for panchakarma because it gives you enough protein to sustain you, and it's easy to digest. This way you won't be spending a lot of energy on digestion.

Making Kitchari

The basic recipe for kitchari is simple. This recipe will nourish you, and it won't make your digestive system work too hard. You can have kitchari anytime, not just during a panchakarma. Heat 1 tablespoon of ghee (clarified butter), and add 1 teaspoon each of cumin, coriander, fennel, and turmeric. Add 1 cup of yellow split mung dahl, and sauté for a few minutes. Then, add 3 cups boiling water. Cover and simmer until the dahl is nearly cooked (approximately thirty minutes). Then, add 1 cup of basmati rice (and more water, if necessary) and simmer until the rice is cooked (approximately one half hour). Add more water if you need to, to cook the rice. Try to add only enough water so that it will be fully absorbed by the mixture. Once the rice is fully cooked, stir in a pinch or two of sea salt.

To add more vitamins and nutrients to kitchari, add vegetables. Either cook them separately and add them at the end, or add them when you add the basmati rice. This will ensure they are well-cooked, keeping in line with the benefit of kitchari as easy to digest.

> Before cooking kitchari, rinse the mung dahl and rice two or three times to make sure they are clean. Pick out and discard any debris. To make the mung dahl even easier to digest, soak it for a few hours before making the kitchari.

If you can, go to a supervised panchakarma rather than doing it at home. If you are able to go to a center that offers panchakarma, they will prepare the kitchari and everything for you. In a fully supervised program, you can step out of your life for a little while and give your body the chance to release. Those who supervise the panchakarma will make sure you rest, and you'll receive Ayurvedic bodywork there, as well.

The Doshas: Elemental Forces Within You

Each of the three doshas contributes to your overall health and daily performance, and there are specific symptoms you will notice when the doshas are out of balance. The way to help bring the doshas back into balance is to remember: like increases like, and opposites balance. The following table shows each dosha, its associated element, and the energetic processes in the body that it primarily supports. If you notice something isn't functioning well, then it might be that the associated dosha is out of balance.

DOSHAS AND THE ELEMENTAL PRINCIPLES

DOSHA	ELEMENT	SUPPORTS
VATA	Space and Air	All movement in the body (e.g., blinking, exercising, muscular movements of organs)
PITTA	Fire and Water	Biochemical processes (e.g., digestion, assimilating information for intelligence)
KAPHA	Water and Earth	Form and lubrication (e.g., holds body together, brings water to all cells, lubricates joints)

When you know how each dosha correlates to processes in the body, you can assess the state of your doshas by how your body is functioning. While your own constitution is unique in the ratio of vata-pitta-kapha, the qualities of each dosha remain constant from person to person. By answering questions about your physical body and your temperament you can determine a lot about how the doshas are at work inside of you.

Vata

Vata is associated with air and space. The qualities are exactly what you'd associate with air: cold, dry, moving; and space: ethereal and expansive. If you have a lot of vata in your constitution, you may have a thin physical body frame, as well as dry hands, hair, and nails. You may have poor circulation, demonstrated by cold hands and feet. Your eating habits will be variable (tending toward hardly eating). Because you are mostly of the airy qualities, you will want to move often: meaning in daily life you will not enjoy sitting still for long, and you will enjoy travelling. You may be easily constipated and have trouble focusing your attention.

When you think of vata and want to determine how much it makes up your vikruti, there are questionnaires that a Vaidya or ayurvedic specialist can give to you. Ayurvedic questionnaires list several kinds of temperaments and attributes associated with each dosha. By noticing how many qualities apply to you, you can find out how active each dosha is.

Over time, you can also use your own common sense and experience. For example, in addition to vata attributes listed above, vata types are said to be cold and variable when it comes to sex, and that is considering "air" side of vata. But there's another side to vata: imagine the expansive aspect of it. When vata is in balance, then vata-types can be expansive in relation to sex. Notice that for each dosha there are certain effects when there's too much of that dosha plus there are benefits when there is balance.

> Every dosha has qualities that help you succeed in life, and every person has some of each dosha in his make up. Getting to know the attributes of each dosha and your constitution will remind you where your natural tendencies are and how to use them to your benefit in all aspects of your life.

Because vata is of the air, you will be comfortable in the energy of the upper chakras. So, if you're experiencing a lot of vata energy you will be clear-minded, alert, imaginative, bright, and even clairvoyant. At the same time, you could feel disassociated with the grounding and stabilizing qualities of the Root Chakra.

Pitta

Pitta gives you your fiery qualities. With the pitta energy your temperature runs hot, you have a good appetite, and your metabolism is strong. Your weight will not easily fluctuate. You may have freckles, and tend to sweat even in mild weather. Pitta energy makes you active, productive, and magnetic. You'll be thinking, solving, and doing. Because of pitta's nature to be active mentally and physically, you may be perfectionistic, critical, aggressive, and domineering when out of balance.

Pitta can be related to the Solar Plexus Chakra and third eye (fire, intellect, and connection to wisdom). With pitta as predominant, you may feel disconnected from the subtle, profound energies associated with the Heart and Throat Chakras. When it comes to these chakras, you will be a good public speaker and advocate, but perhaps you will have trouble with true connection and good, comfortable communication in personal and intimate relationships.

Kapha

Kapha is associated with the principles of water and earth. A kapha person likes structure and stability. If you're predominantly kapha, you may have a rounder, bigger body type, and gain weight easily. Your skin will be smooth and you have large eyes. You give great hugs, and are quite happy lounging around. There is a tendency for kapha types to be prone to depression, procrastination, and weight gain.

Kapha energy can be linked to the Root and Sacral Chakras. If you're predominantly kapha, you may not have a strong Manipura Chakra, which will affect your digestive fire as well as your self-esteem.

Helping Your Doshas Balance

A simple way for you to work with dosha imbalance is first to notice your appearance, mental activity, and emotional reactions. Notice:

- Your skin (dry, soft, shiny?)

- Your elimination (constipated, diarrhea, well-formed, daily?)

- Your energy level (sluggish, hyper, balanced during the day?)

- How you're thinking (spacey, clear, productive, imaginative, overwhelmed?)

- Your emotions (erratic, appropriate, distant?)

- Your reactions to situations/people (calm, with perspective, fearful, irritated?)

- Your temperature (hot, cold, comfortable?)

After you've assessed these aspects of yourself, compare them to the table below to find out what doshas are strongest in you, now. For a more complete list of attributes for the doshas and a questionnaire, see *The Complete Book of Ayurvedic Home Remedies*.

EVALUATING YOUR DOSHAS

DOSHA	BODY	MIND	EMOTION	ELIMINATION
VATA	Thin frame; dry skin, hair, nails	Flexible, intelligent, creative	Fearful, anxious, loving	Hard, dry
PITTA	Medium-build; shiny skin, red hair	Sharp, active	Irritable, jealous, passionate	Loose
KAPHA	Large, round; pale skin, thick or wavy hair	Slow, steady, exact	Steady, greedy	Thick, oily

There are several additional attributes to notice about yourself, before determining your prakruti and your vikruti. The table is meant to give you a basic sense of how the principles of the elements appear in your physical, mental, and emotional bodies. From the basic table, you can get a general understanding of how the doshas are working inside of you.

Creating Internal Harmony

When your doshas are out of balance you can feel off-kilter in one way or another. When your doshas are balanced according to your prakruti, you will feel balanced, with a sense of internal harmony that will radiate outward. A Vaidya will be able to give you a comprehensive plan that will work precisely with your prakruti and vikruti to create balance and harmony. In the meantime and in between visits, you can help by doing your best not to aggravate your doshas. To this end, notice which attributes in the table apply to you and which doshas those refer to. In addition take into account what season it is, and what its attributes are where you live. Once you determine which qualities are the most prominent, you can then act and eat in ways to create balance.

The Seasons and Your Constitution

The seasons play an important role in the state of your body, mind, emotions, and energy. Because you are intimately connected with nature, the qualities of what's happening in the natural world affect the doshas. The depths of winter have kapha qualities (heavy, wet, thick), and this carries on into early spring. Later in spring, the season is hot (pitta) and that carries into summer. The end of summer has vata qualities (dry, cold), which carry on into the beginning of autumn. The end of autumn, as it gets darker still and colder, takes on the qualities associated with kapha. Monitor how these relate to your tendencies and which seasons may naturally balance you and which may naturally aggravate your constitution.

Creating Health in Winter

In winter, the cold will affect you beyond the surface level of your skin. Your skin and other areas that need moisture (such as your nose and eyes) can become dry. The cold penetrates beneath the skin—bringing cold and dryness to your bones and organs. These qualities are also associated with vata: the start of winter can aggravate vata. So, if you are already prone to vata tendencies, and you are experiencing very cold weather, your vata qualities can become exaggerated. When vata continues to be aggravated, this affects how you age and your health. Dryness can lead to cracking of hair, nails, and bones. It also can increase your anxiety, fear, ungroundedness, and difficulty focusing. In the long run, it can lead to disease. Winter also can increase your kapha energy. It can make you sluggish and lethargic.

To create balance, bring elements into your life that counteract the overly active conditions, whether vata or kapha. For example, if you notice you have mostly vata tendencies such as dry skin, anxiety, and constipation, you can help balance those qualities by making sure you use oil for your skin each day, eat foods that are warm and moist, drink plenty of warm water, and meditate to calm your anxiety. If winters are cold in your area and you are feeling sluggish and slipping into depressive tendencies, find ways to bring activity into your life. Enjoy winter sports, dance around your room, and take classes at an indoor gym. Wear bright colors, get outside with friends, and make dates to be out and about. Activity will help balance out the sluggishness.

You can give into the seasons a little bit, however, without harming yourself. Allow your body to adapt to the seasons. You may sleep more hours in winter and naturally be more inward. Just notice that if you begin to feel depressive and/or dry, you need to do things for balance.

Springtime Health

In spring, the weather becomes moist and rainy. There are puddles to splash in, and the refreshing rain mixes with the soil to form mud. The beginning of spring has kapha qualities. As spring progresses it gains qualities of pitta, heading into summer. For health in the springtime, notice how your constitution is affected by kapha and then pitta. Nourish yourself in ways you do in winter for kapha, and look at how you adapt to summer to pacify pitta.

Cool Down in Summer

Summer increases pitta. In order to stay balanced in summer, you want to balance the heat that is outside. If you already are predominantly pitta, you will want to minimize your exposure to direct sunlight, wear light clothing, and drink cool beverages. Go swimming, and try Shitali Pranayama.

> Shitali Pranayama is a cooling breath, great for pacifying pitta. Stick out your tongue and curl the sides up and together to form a tube. Inhale through the tube and notice how cool that air is. Exhale through your nose. Do several rounds. If you can't curl your tongue, purse your lips as you'd do to whistle.

Also to pacify pitta in the summer, avoid strenuous and vigorous activity. For exercise, take leisurely walks in the shade and go swimming. If you want to play sports, try to avoid playing during the hottest hours of the day. When pitta is aggravated you'll become easily angered, jealous, and judgmental—not only toward others, also to yourself. So, keeping your pitta pacified has benefits for everyone.

Get Cozy in Autumn

As autumn begins, nature has vata qualities. Compared to the hot, bright, and long days of summer, autumn is dry and cold. During this season as the days get shorter and shorter, the body begins to feel internal effects of the external reality. Naturally as the seasons change from summer to fall, pitta will calm down, especially if you were able to balance it somewhat during the summer months. To balance vata during autumn, keep your body warm. Wear your vests and sweaters. Drink hot apple cider. Also, be mindful for children, teens, and teachers that school starts in autumn: vata calms down with routine and schedule, and can also be aggravated by all the mental stimulation and potential for stress.

Choose Foods that Support Your Body, Mind, and Spirit

There's a lot of talk nowadays about the connection between food and emotions. The latest teachings point out that people use food as a replacement for love. It's become common knowledge that when people feel emotionally empty or ungrounded they will try to fill up and ground with food. This is not enjoying food. This is using food as a substitute for something else. This will actually cause you to gain weight and feel worse. There is, however, a way to use food to feel good, and that is to eat in a way that helps you stay balanced in each season.

What if I live in place that doesn't have four seasons?

Use the summer, fall, winter, and spring analogies in a way that reflects your climate. Also, the analogies can apply to times of day. For example, perhaps the morning has qualities of winter, the middle of the day feels like spring, summer comes in the afternoon, and then it feels like fall at night.

Even if you don't have the four seasons where you live, you can notice the qualities also at different times of day and life. Your youngest years are known as the kapha years, your middle years are pitta, and your senior years have vata qualities. When you eat in a way that balances you for the season of the year and of your life, you are working with your body's needs. When you go against what's natural your body's metabolism and health will be adversely affected. And, you may notice this as weight gain, weight retention, illness, fatigue, insomnia, constipation, poor memory, or irritability.

Eating for Vata

Whether it's that your type is predominantly vata, if it's vata season, or if you're in your vata years of life, create balance by eating foods that are moist and warm. Cook your vegetables and fruits. Add extra-virgin olive oil or ghee to your food, and drink sips of warm water throughout your meals and throughout the day. This will help lubricate the body, add warmth, and soothe the dryness of the season or time of day. Don't fill up on raw vegetables, salads, and cold juices.

Eating for Pitta

Pitta types have great digestion and metabolism. They also are hot, so calming the body with cooler food and drinks helps pacify pitta. Choose foods that are not spicy or sour. Drink cool (not cold) beverages, and avoid alcohol. In general think about avoiding what is very acidic, hot, or heating to the body.

Eating for Kapha

For predominantly kapha individuals, you want to avoid what will add more kapha qualities. So, dairy products, cold foods, and heavy food should be avoided especially at times of year when nature exhibits kapha qualities.

Kaphas gain weight easily, so learning good eating habits is of particular importance to kaphas. As you will do for all doshas, eat what is in season, and eat a variety of colors. Be aware of overeating, which means eating too much at one sitting or snacking. For each meal, don't eat more than what you could fit with your two hands cupped together.

If you get hungry between meals, try drinking a large cup of warm water with a few squeezes of lemon or lime juice and honey to curb your appetite. Oftentimes, many people don't drink enough water anyway and think they are hungry when they are really thirsty. Drink lemon or lime water, and also notice if you want to eat for emotional reasons. If something's bothering you, take out a journal for a few moments. Take a few breaths. Write out your feeling on the page. Start with, "Right now, I feel . . . " Allow the words to flow as they will, without thinking or planning what to write.

> If you are used to eating too much, when you eat the right amount you may think you are still hungry because your stomach won't feel full. To eat enough you don't have to feel stuffed. Your stomach just needs to be one-third full. Once you get accustomed to eating the right amount, the "full" feeling will feel uncomfortable.

If you do need to snack between meals, don't reach for sugar or starch. Those can be addictive and also not satisfying.

Healthy Snacks

You know those types of snacks where you can't eat just one? That's not a good thing. Instead, eat a handful of almonds, or spread almond butter on celery or slices of apple. You'll be getting protein, which is good for you and satisfying.

Kale crisps are a great snack. They are crispy, light, and very healthy. They can satisfy you, and you can add salt, seasonings, and/or olive oil to them.

KALE CRISPS

1. Preheat the oven to 350°F.

2. Lightly grease a baking sheet with extra-virgin olive oil.

3. Rinse a bunch of kale and pat it dry.

4. Rip up the kale into pieces the size of your palm.

5. With your hands lightly coated with extra-virgin olive oil, pick up the kale in clumps and smoosh the kale in your hands so that you lightly coat the pieces with oil.

6. Spread the kale onto the baking sheet.

7. Sprinkle sea salt onto the pieces of kale. Or make up your own recipe of seasonings.

8. Bake the kale in the oven until it is crispy, approximately eight minutes. Be careful not to burn the kale.

9. Serve and enjoy!

Having this type of light and dry snack is a great way to counteract the heavy and wet kapha qualities.

Transition Smoothly from Sleep to Activity

Ayurveda gives instructions for a daily morning routine: a short list of how to help you transition comfortably from sleep to the movement of your day. The immediate benefits of the routine help you to wake up, and the long-term benefits multiply over time supporting equilibrium and health. Instead of jumping right out of bed and checking e-mail, set aside time for the transition into your day. Take time to notice how you are today, as each day is different. Spending time with a morning routine will help you be mindful during the day, which is necessary for your health.

Waking Up the Body

When you first wake up, stay in bed for a moment. Take a few nice, deep inhales. Notice the breath flow in and out. Take a moment and notice how you feel. Roll onto your back and very slowly and gently inhale and stretch the legs out and the arms up. Exhale and release. Wiggle your fingers and toes, and rotate your ankles and wrists. Slowly roll your head side to side. Do these gentle exercises in the order that feels comfortable for you. Then, gently begin to get out of bed. Place your feet on the floor. Feel the solid earth beneath your feet and stand up. Do any movements that your body asks you to. And take another nice deep breath.

Taking Care of the Senses

After getting out of bed, begin what Ayurveda calls *Dinacharya*, which means to become close to the day. This is a nourishing practice, use this as a time to give love to yourself. For well-being it's important to love and accept yourself. When you really do, it won't be arrogance or conceit, it will be radiance. To remember how to do Dinacharya, just think of all of the senses and koshas of your being. Once you are used to it, this whole routine will take less than fifteen minutes:

- **EYES:** Rub your hands together vigorously to create heat and energy. Close your eyes and gently place your cupped palms over your eyes. Feel the heat. This is called palming the eyes. Now open the eyes and look down, to the left, up, to the right, and down again. Do this a few times. Reverse the direction. Spray rose water (a brand specifically designed for this purpose) into your eyes. This is cooling and refreshing.

- **NOSE:** Use the neti pot and then drop a few drops of nasya oil into each nostril. To use the neti pot, place about 1 teaspoon of non-iodized sea salt into the pot. Fill the pot with warm water. Tilt your head to the left, and place the tip of the pot in your right nostril. Adjust the angle of your head so that the salt water goes into the right nostril and flows out of the left. Do the same on the other side. Then, use nasya oil in each nostril. If you don't have nasya oil, you can also use warm sesame oil (not the sesame oil used for cooking; see the additional resources for suggestions of where to buy pure sesame oil).

- **MOUTH:** Use a metal tongue scraper to scrape your tongue several times until it's clean. Brush and floss your teeth. For healthy teeth and gums, swish warm sesame oil around your mouth and gargle with it. Then, spit it out and massage your gums with your finger.

- **EARS:** Place one drop of pure sesame oil into each ear.

- **BODY:** Oil your entire body, head to toe. Take your time, massaging in long strokes along the limbs and gentle circular motions around the joints. Even oil your hair. Massage the oil into your scalp.

Each of these steps helps purify and nourish your body in numerous ways. Most importantly, if your body gets dried out, it can crack in ways you wouldn't even see. Bacteria and allergens can enter your body through those openings. By rinsing your eyes and nose you are washing out pollutants each morning rather than letting them absorb into your body. By oiling the ears, nose, and body you are keeping yourself from drying out, from cracking. You can choose oils that will be particular for your dosha and the time of year. For example, in the summer coconut oil will be cooling, and in the winter sesame oil is warming.

Will the oils stain my clothes?

If you really rub the oil in, and allow it to sink into your skin (for about five minutes), it will typically not stain your clothes. For your morning routine, oiling before you take a bath or shower is recommended. The heat opens your pores so oil can sink in more deeply.

When you scrape your tongue, you are scraping off *ama*, undigested metabolic waste. In other words, you are scraping off the waste that overnight your body was working to eliminate. It ends up on the surface of your tongue, by morning. If you don't scrape your tongue, then you will ingest the waste.

Purifying the senses with a daily routine is so important: they are how you take in, enjoy, and make meaning in the world. They are also how you get your nourishment; everything you see, hear, taste, touch, and feel is ingested into your bodies. Everything has an impact on you.

Morning Evacuation

After you've cleansed the sense organs, drink a glass of warm water. This will help you with your morning evacuation. Go to the bathroom every morning: your body has been digesting overnight so waste is ready to be eliminated. Drinking a glass of warm water will help. Then, even if you don't have to go to the bathroom, sit on the toilet for a little while. Relax. Intend to go to the bathroom. Eventually, even if not the first morning, this will work. If you are having trouble, there are gentle yoga postures that can help.

To help get your system going in the morning, some kind of exercise is wonderful. You can do even just a ten-minute gentle yoga routine or take a nice walk outside. Going outside is a wonderful way to bring yourself into the physical world after having been in dreamland. It's always a good thing to take a few deep breaths of fresh air in the morning.

> Constipation creates disease. What you aren't eliminating is what your body already converted to waste. It rots if it remains inside. Triphala is an Ayurvedic mild laxative you can take. Also, lie on your back, and bend the right knee in to your chest, then do the same with the left. Hold this position for five deep breaths on each side.

Meditation and Prayer

Even just five minutes of meditation and prayer in the morning helps you start your day from a more centered place than if you just rush into work or e-mail inbox. Meditation and prayer in the morning connects you to the bigger picture, even if just for a few moments. You'll be starting your day off from a positive place, with good intentions for how you will feel during the day.

CHAPTER 15

Chakra Healing and Your Constitution

Ayurveda can support and help you sustain the results of chakra healing. Ayurvedic oils, supplements, and nutrition start at the level of your physical body and then have deeper, broader effects. As Ayurveda helps you flush toxins and correct imbalances, all aspects of your being benefit. You'll notice the effects on your mind and your connection to equanimity. Disease at any level—physical, psychological, or spiritual—needs to be healed physically, psychologically, and energetically. Ayurveda supports all aspects of you, complementing your chakra-healing practice.

Chakra Healing for Vata

If you have excess vata tendencies, you will be feeling spacey. You will have trouble focusing, organizing, and staying on task. Your skin and nails might feel dry and brittle, and you could have poor circulation. You may be variable in your desire for sex, and you may feel ungrounded. To help with this, your Ayurvedic doctor will recommend specific oils, herbs, and foods. As you work with Ayurveda to help combat the vata symptoms, you can also use chakra healing as more support to bring you out of the clouds and back down to earth.

Vata and the Root Chakra

The qualities of too much vata are similar to the symptoms of a deficient Root Chakra. The symptoms of too much vata—feeling ungrounded, spacey, variable appetite, and difficulty completing tasks—are the same qualities of a deficient Root Chakra.

According to Ayurveda to help balance too much vata, you will eat warm, wet, heavy foods such as kitchari, cooked vegetables with extra olive oil or ghee, cooked apples with honey and cinnamon, squash soup with pumpkin seeds, and vegetable stew. You will massage your entire body with warm sesame oil daily. Be sure not to use sesame oil that is used for cooking. You want pure sesame oil that you can get from stores that sell Ayurvedic products. Ask at health-food stores, and see the additional resources at the end of this book for suggestions of where to order Ayurvedic products. Both of these lifestyle habits—giving yourself an oil massage and eating moist, warm foods—cause you to bring awareness to your physical body. This will help you feel "in your body." When your Root Chakra is imbalanced, just like when you have too much vata, you need to feel grounded in your body. Calm vata and strengthen the Root Chakra with the above suggestions as well as meditation, yoga postures, and visualization.

Vata and the Sacral and Solar Plexus Chakras

One quality of excess vata is dryness. The Sacral Chakra is the water chakra, fluid and flowing to ameliorate the effects of dry vata, which can be constipation, fear, and uncertainty. A balanced Sacral Chakra will help you flow through life with less fear in the face of the unknown, and balance in this area will help evacuation. Sex is also an issue of vata and the Sacral Chakra. Bringing more energy to this chakra will help balance your sexual desire, which means you will have a healthy psychological relationship toward the sexual energy in you.

> Ayurveda recommends that to stay hydrated, sip warm water throughout the day, instead of drinking big glasses of water a few times per day. Avoid cool water since it will cool off your digestive fire. Warm water is best. Warmth helps correct vata and kapha imbalances.

The Solar Plexus Chakra is associated with fire. Healing your Solar Plexus Chakra will add heat to your body, which balances out the cold, dryness of vata. It will also stoke your digestive fire, supporting a good appetite and metabolism steadying the variability of vata's appetite.

Vata and Downward Movement

If you have a lot of vata energy, it can manifest in an inability to focus, complete tasks, and stay calm. Bringing energy down in the body helps because you literally move energy down from your thinking mind into your grounded body. This will help you stay on task, reduce anxiety, and produce results.

Grounding Vata for Manifestation

Bringing energy down through the chakras is the path of manifestation. You are bringing energy from universal consciousness and your thinking mind down through the throat (your truth), the heart (your connection to others), the solar plexus (your strength), the Sacral Chakra (your creativity), and your root (connecting you to the earth). This is the way to bring ideas into physical form. Bringing your energy down through the chakras brings it from the imagination to physical reality.

Pitta and the Chakras

If your pitta feels too strong, you will experience the effects of too much fire. Fire is associated with the Manipura Chakra. It's the chakra you would send more energy to if you wanted more heat. To temper your pitta, you want to cool down and spread the energy more evenly throughout the chakras. So when you feel excess pitta, you will want to dissipate energy from the Manipura.

Pitta and Svadhistana

Firey qualities are primarily associated with Manipura Chakra. And, yet, each chakra affects the ones above and below. When pitta is aggravated, you may also notice symptoms that correspond to the chakra directly below Manipura, the Svadhistana Chakra. Symptoms of excess pitta such as needing to be in control and emotional imbalance can mean there's excess energy at the Svadhistana Chakra.

If you notice your symptoms indicate excess energy at Svadhistana, do healing exercises that focus on the Root Chakra and the chakras above the Anahata. This will coerce energy from the second chakra to other energy centers, encouraging it to spread out.

Pitta and Anahata

When pitta is aggravated it can also mean that Anahata, the chakra above Manipura, is overactive. This manifests in possessive feelings toward someone else, and trying to use love for control, i.e., not loving unconditionally.

> Pearls balance all the doshas. According to Dr. Lad in *The Complete Book of Ayurvedic Home Remedies*, "Pearl ash is used internally to treat many ailments." He suggests putting four to five pearls in water overnight and in the morning removing the pearls either with a clean hand or spoon and drinking the infused water.

If pitta is spreading to the Anahata, giving it too much energy, you risk high blood pressure and heart disease. The heart is located where Anahata flowers into the front body. So, taking care of your Heart Chakra and pitta will calm your reactions in love, support the health of your heart, and cool down your judgments of yourself and others.

Chakra Visualization for Calming Pitta

One of the qualities of pitta is to spread. Pittas are interested in knowledge and will want to spread what they've learned. A pitta type may be a teacher, a lawyer, or a public figure. So it's not surprising that pitta energy will spread to the nearby chakras causing them to be excessive. Try this visualization to help calm pitta and cool down:

1. Sit in a comfortable posture for Pranayama.

2. Close your eyes.

3. Begin Dirgha Pranayama.

4. Do a few moments of Shitali breathing, and envision cooling waves as you hear your breath flow in and out.

5. Release Shitali, return to Dirgha breath, and continue visualization of blue, calm waves for several breaths. Blue is a cool color.

6. As you take slow, deep inhalations and exhalations, begin to gently massage the top of your head. Gently and lovingly give yourself a soft head massage. Imagine the Crown Chakra glowing a soft white like the shine of a pearl.

7. Slowly and carefully, wipe down your energy field, carrying this pearl-colored light down your entire body. To do this, hold your hands

an inch or two in front of your face and sweep gently in a downward motion. Dusting off any turbulent energy as a soft white glow emanates from your hands.

8. Continue this over your whole body, slowly as though you are wiping away cobwebs from your torso and limbs. As you brush each area, visualize pearly white healing energy emanating from your hands. Gently clear your energy field, and send cooling energy.

9. After you've wiped head to toe, release control of your breath. Allow your breath to flow naturally.

10. Sit quietly for a few moments. Notice any difference in how you feel.

As you clear your energy field with this gentle sweeping downward motion you initiate a grounded, stable, and calm state. Ground your energy as though you were a lightning rod, giving your fiery energy to the earth.

Kapha and the Chakras

Excess kapha can manifest as slow digestion, lethargy, and cold extremities. Predominantly kapha types, when kapha is aggravated, can become greedy, lustful, and materialistic. Slow digestion, lethargy, and cold extremities point to low digestive fire and low heat in the body: low Manipura energy. And, greed and lust can be symptoms of an unbalanced Root Chakra.

Lower Chakras and Kapha

When in balance kapha is comfortably grounding—rooting you to the earth and physical reality. When kapha is overactive you are prone to greed, lust, and materialism. When you have so much kapha, that it's showing up as attachment and hoarding, you can do Ayurvedic treatments to balance kapha in combination with chakra work.

One way to get the benefits of color therapy is to fill a clear, glass jar with spring water. Wrap the jar in plastic that's the color you want the water to absorb. Place the jar in the sunshine for a few hours. The color's vibration will enter the water. A few times a day, take sips of the water.

Ayurveda recommends bright colors to help balance kapha, such as red, orange, and yellow. These colors also will bring healing energy to the lower chakras. The red helps balance the root, orange helps to balance the sacral, and yellow helps to balance the solar plexus. As you bring energy into your system like this, you are creating more healthy and heating fire: this helps balance kapha's lethargy, coolness, and unctuous qualities.

Kapha and the Upper Chakras

Kapha can make the mind foggy. You could be slow to comprehend, though you have strong retention. If the kapha energy increases, your mind could become frustratingly foggy. To help with this, continue to move energy up the chakras.

Moving energy up to the Throat Chakra and the third eye can help with your clarity. Energy at the throat relates to your ability to see clearly and express what is going on within you. It helps with self-knowledge and self-expression. As you bring energy up to the third eye, it helps with your wisdom, your intuition. Bringing energy to these upper chakras balances the grounding and earthy energy of kapha.

Morning Chakra Check-In and Intention Setting

Adding a chakra check-in and intention-setting period to your morning is a great way to be mindful of how you want to feel during your day. After you have done your Dinacharya, take a moment to see how you are feeling, and set an intention.

Intention Setting and Chakras

The intention you set can come from what you notice in the moment about your chakras. For example, if you feel that your heart is heavy this morning, set an intention such as, "Today my heart is well, open, and strong," and visualize sending green energy to your heart space. Use that as your mantra for the day.

> Write your intention on a piece of paper and bring it with you. You can put it in your pocket, tape it to the back of your mobile phone, or tape it to the dashboard of your car. If you put it somewhere where you'll see it, then you'll have an easier time remembering it throughout your day.

If you are feeling ungrounded and separate from your body, sit on the floor and notice that you are held up by the earth. Or, stand tall and feel your feet firmly connected to the earth. Then, say to yourself "All day I am safe, stable, and connected." Feel the support of the earth underneath you. Repeat the intention three times, with your eyes closed, envisioning it to be true. As you envision it as true, you are creating that reality. If you think you'll be anxious all day, then it would be hard for you to feel otherwise.

When you notice an imbalance in your psychology or physical body in the morning, ask yourself which chakra that connects to, then set your intention in a way that supports that chakra's function.

Pranayama for Doshas and Chakras

Pranayama can balance your doshas and your chakras. For example, for cooling pitta you can perform Shitali Pranayama. Shitali Pranayama brings cooling effects into your entire body, affecting the energy system. Cooling in the body will cool Manipura, and this further supports cooling off pitta.

If you notice you are predominantly kapha or vata, you will not need to do a cooling breath for those doshas. For kapha it would be helpful to do an invigorating breath like Kapalabhati. As you perform Kapalabhati for kapha you are also stoking your inner fire—Manipura. And, as the Manipura gets balanced, that heat with help you continue to balance your kapha.

> When I practice Pranayama, how long should I do it?
>
> Start in small increments. Over time you can increase repetitions. For Kapalabhati breath, start with ten to fifteen repetitions and increase to thirty at a time. For Dirgha, Ujjayi, Nadi Shodhana, and Shitali start with five minutes, and increase to as long as you'd like with practice.

For excess vata, Nadi Shodhana is a great practice. As you practice Nadi Shodhana to balance vata, you are also balancing the hemispheres of the brain. Calming vata is wonderful for your Third-Eye Chakra. When your third eye is out of balance, you could have nightmares, experience memory trouble, and feel spaced-out—qualities that can be caused by too much vata. Calming vata with a slow and deep Nadi Shodhana will also help with the Third-Eye Chakra.

Ayurveda and Chakra Healing for Specific Conditions

You can use Ayurveda and chakra healing together to treat disease in the body. Using Pranayama, yoga postures, visualization, and Ayurvedic remedies, you can heal various ailments. Following are some common conditions and ways to use Ayurveda and chakra healing to bring relief.

Clear Up Acne

According to Ayurveda, acne is the result of too much pitta underneath the skin. To pacify pitta, you can drink coriander-cumin-fennel tea a few times a day. According to Dr. Lad, to make coriander-cumin-fennel tea, use $\frac{1}{3}$ teaspoon of each, steep in boiling water for ten minutes, strain, and drink. You can also infuse spring water with the energy of blue light, which is cooling, and sip the water a few times during the day.

In addition to what you put into your body, visualizations help. Here's an example of a visualization to help with acne:

1. Sit upright in a comfortable position, with your hands resting in your lap.

2. Notice several breaths flow in and out.

3. Begin Dirgha breath and imagine blue light filling your torso as it expands with the breath: first in the belly, then the ribs, then the chest, and up into the third eye. As the blue light travels up your torso imagine it passing through each chakra, from the root to the third eye, bringing cooling energy to all the chakras. Exhale it out. Repeat this visualization several times.

4. Continue deep breathing. Change your visualization to the image of your skin clearing. Imagine how it looks clearing up and then all clear. As you breathe in and out several times focus on the image of your clearing and clear skin.

As often as possible when you think of your skin, imagine it cooling down and clearing up. Do not focus negative attention and frustration on how you look. This will continue to aggravate your emotions and pitta, which counteracts the healing work you're doing. The negative visuals and emotions cancel out the positive ones.

Staying emotionally balanced and calm helps cure acne. Throughout the day, notice if you are carrying tension in your face. Bring your internal awareness to your face, notice if your jaw is relaxed. Create space between the top and bottom rows of the back teeth to help relax the jaw. Use your fingers to gently massage in circular motions the spot where the top jaw bone connects to the lower. Next, bring the fingertips of the first two fingers of each hand together at the third eye. Inhale, and as you exhale draw the fingertips away from each other across your forehead—from the third eye to the temple on each side. Do this a few times. Close your eyes, inhale and exhale a few times imagining your face relaxed, clear, and healthy.

When choosing what to eat, favor a bland diet. Spicy, fried, and acidic foods increase pitta. Remember that you want to bring cooling, calm, and positive energy to your mind, body, and spirit.

Anxiety

Anxiety can be relieved by calming down vata. To counteract excess vata, which makes you dry and cold, find ways to bring heat and moisture to your body. If you have a hot tub, go in the hot tub before or after work. Make a habit of taking hot baths when you can. You don't have to do this type of heating therapy at the time of the anxiety. In other words, if you notice you've been feeling anxious at work, taking a hot bath before and/or after work can help. You can also sip hot water throughout the day. Eat warm, moist food, and oil your entire body with self-massage daily. Finally, before going to bed, massage warm oil on your feet and on the top of your head.

Bringing your focus to all the chakras will help calm vata. Start your visualization at the Root Chakra, and imagine the Root Chakra glowing bright red. Feel your sitting bones stable, supported by the earth. Inhale and exhale with your attention at the root. Place your hands one on top of the other on your torso at the location of the Sacral Chakra. Notice how your own hands on your body are grounding, comforting. Hold your hands at the area where the Sacral Chakra blossoms, and imagine a bright orange color as you inhale and exhale. Move your hands up to the solar plexus. Imagine the bright yellow glow of your third chakra. Continue this up your body at the Heart, Throat, and Third-Eye Chakra. Finally, place your hands on top of your head at the crown. Through your hands, visualize calming, healing white light flooding your brain through this chakra. Visualize yourself relaxed. Release your hands. Take a moment, notice if there have been any changes in how you feel. Notice your breath, your level of physical tension, and your mind.

Low-Back Pain

Low-back pain can be caused by many factors. It is commonly associated as a vata disorder. Along with treatments that your doctor recommends, follow a diet that will balance vata, and reduce vata aggravating activities. Stay warm, meditate, and relax.

> **Is there any specific Ayurvedic oil that could bring warmth to my low back?**
>
> Mahanarayan oil is recommended for low-back pain. Warm the oil, and massage it into the area of your back that hurts, or better yet have someone else do it for you. Massage in slow, long strokes. Remember, to calm vata, move slowly and make sure you're breathing with nice, long exhales.

Low-back pain is in the area of the Sacral Chakra. This is the seat of your emotions. When you have low-back pain, slow down and look at what is happening in your emotional realm. Are you angry? Are you concerned about your sex life? Are you emotionally or obsessively attached to someone else? Do you deny or indulge too much in pleasure? Whatever you notice, accept it. Allow it to be there, and then carefully and gingerly find ways to deal with that emotional fire. Grounding practices can help: visualizing the fire moving from the Sacral Chakra through the

Muladhara Chakra and into the earth. Low-back pain can be related to an emotional issue that is deeply rooted, so do more than one practice. You may decide to do chakra healing plus journaling, Ayurvedic support, and dancing in addition to seeking advice and help from healers and medical doctors.

If you have strong emotions, it can help to journal, talk to a good friend, and seek a good therapist. Other people, especially trained professionals, can help you deal with emotions and physical manifestations of pain that might seem too overwhelming for you.

When emotions get stirred up, energy accumulates and takes up space. It can push organs and other body parts out of their usual place, or at least put pressure on them. Acknowledge the emotions you are having, and give them your attention. Repressing or ignoring them will not help them go away. They will stay buried, causing other illnesses and likely weight gain and retention. Your cells store your memories and emotions. You may notice that sometimes in a yoga class or after exercise you will cry, perhaps without knowing why. In those cases it could be that you dislodged a past feeling or memory, and finally released it. That means you've created more space in your body for prana to flow, which brings overall health.

Bad Breath

To freshen your breath, practice good oral hygiene. Scrape your tongue each morning. Floss your teeth two to three times per day. Brush your teeth for two minutes twice per day—taking two minutes ensures you've brushed well. Swish warm sesame oil in your mouth, then spit it out. Massage any excess oil into the gums. Sesame oil is nourishing for your teeth and gums, and it helps to prevent and soothe receding gums.

Be mindful when you are cleaning your teeth and gums. Care for yourself as you would care for a loved one. If you notice your mind thinking about your workday, draw your attention back to caring for your mouth. Enjoy it. This stimulates and encourages the healing effects, and gives you time to relax before starting your busy day.

Also, after meals chew a pinch of a combination of roasted fennel and cumin seeds. You can carry the mixture in your purse, backpack, or briefcase. This combination helps aid digestion. Poor digestion and toxicity in the body can produce bad breath.

The Common Cold

According to Ayurveda, a cold is a kapha-vata disorder. Kapha creates the mucous, and the increase in vata leads to low appetite and chills. You will be more prone to colds and flu at kapha and vata times of year. When you start to become more aware of seasons in relationship to vata, pitta, and kapha, you can prepare to support your health in relation to the seasons.

Both kapha and vata can make you feel chilled. Steaming with tea tree essential oil can help. The steam will carry the properties of the oil into your nasal passages, sinus cavities, and even down your throat. The heat will help combat the cold your body feels, and the moisture will help combat dryness. You can also use fresh ginger instead of tea tree oil—ginger, in general, is highly recommended if you're suffering from a cold or flu, but if you are taking aspirin do not use ginger at the same time. Both thin the blood, so if you want to use both, take them a few hours apart.

Eucalyptus oil will also help fight the common cold. If you steam with it, the steam will bring physical relief while the antimicrobial, germ-fighting properties of the oil enter your system.

When you have a cold, your immune system is compromised. Rest and drink warm liquids. Ginger tea and even plain hot water work well. The chakra healing that will complement your healing process will be to visualize heat coming into the body, combating mucus and chills. Work on the Manipura Chakra, stoking your internal fire.

1. Lie down; cover yourself with blankets to stay warm.

2. Close your eyes, and imagine the glowing sun.

3. Imagine the brightness of the center, and the power of its rays. Visualize this for several moments.

4. Inhale deeply, and imagine that you are inhaling the warmth of the sun on a very warm day. Feel the heat enter your nostrils, rise up to your third eye, and then travel down through your energy centers. Exhale toxins. Relax.

5. Again, inhale rays of sun, and when you exhale, release toxins. As you repeat this a few times, imagine your Solar Plexus Chakra beginning to glow brighter and brighter. This is your fiery chakra; ignite it with light and warmth.

6. After you've repeated this breath and visualization, allow your whole body to let go. Relax. And, when you are ready, open your eyes and sit up. Notice how you feel.

Every time you do anything as a healing practice, take time to notice if there's a difference. This brings awareness to the effects, shifting your focus to any improvements and what your body needs next. Are you warmer? Ready for a restorative nap? There is no right or wrong answer, simply notice. If you're thirsty, do not reach for cold water. Instead, sip warm water.

Constipation

By now you may be able to guess which imbalances will cause certain conditions. Constipation is caused by excess vata—the qualities are dry, cold, and hard. Ayurveda follows common sense: to remedy the situation you want to add heat, moisture, and digestive fire. Vata increases with movement, so give yourself some time to stop moving. Relax and allow your digestive system to work. Drink warm water. The Ayurvedic herb triphala will help your bowels move. Other natural remedies are to eat prunes, take a relaxing walk, and try wind-relieving pose.

1. Lie on your back with your legs straight out on the floor.

2. Take a few deep breaths, relax into the support of the earth.

3. Bend your right knee and draw it up to your chest as far as is comfortable. Keep the left leg straight on the ground. Use both hands to hold the right knee into your chest. Breathe deeply several times, feeling your belly rise up against your right thigh.

4. On an exhale, straighten the right leg back onto the floor.

5. Repeat steps two through four, using the left leg.

6. Gently roll over onto your left side. Then, slowly get up. You start this exercise on the right side and then move to the left because that follows the direction of digestion in your colon. Your colon ascends up the right side, then descends on the left. You're physically helping it along with this exercise, and you're relaxing.

If you have diarrhea, pacify pitta. Dr. Lad recommends eating cooked apples or uncooked bananas with 1 teaspoon of ghee, a pinch of cardamom and of nutmeg. Choose foods that are binding. Lad recommends this recipe, "1 cup of cooked basmati rice, add 1 tablespoon of ghee, and 3 or 4 tablespoons of plain fresh yogurt, stir together, and eat."

To help keep your digestion strong and good, be mindful when you eat. Choose foods carefully according to what your body needs. And, when you eat, sit down. First look at your food and take a moment before diving in. Spend a moment being thankful for what you have. Even take a moment to smell the food. This helps your digestive process begin. Have you ever noticed when you smell something baking or cooking in the kitchen you start to get hungry? As you eat, take your time. Enjoy your food. Pause between bites. And when you're finished, sit for a moment before rushing off to the next task.

CHAPTER 16

Aromatherapy
for the Chakras

One of the fastest ways to create and notice a change in your energy field is to use aromatherapy. The aromas from essential oils can promote relaxation, clear-thinking, positive outlook, and greater health. There are a variety of ways to experience aromatherapy. You can use quick-and-easy methods to feel more relaxed, or you can create longer and more luxurious experiences. Whichever you choose, as you inhale the aromas your body will begin to respond, and if you surrender you will notice a change in your mental, physical, and energetic bodies.

What Is Aromatherapy?

Aromatherapy is a healing modality that uses **essential oils** to heal the body, mind, and spirit. Essential oils are natural products. They are highly potent, concentrated oils from trees, plants, and grasses. The scents, energy, and properties of the oils heal and protect you from illness, disease, and imbalance. There are many different essential oils and ways they can be used, so it's best to have training, buy a comprehensive guide on aromatherapy, and/or talk to someone who is well-trained for sound advice about which oils to use for the results you desire.

> The National Cancer Institute has found through studies on rats in Europe and Japan, "that exposure to various odors can result in stimulation or sedation, as well as changes in behavioral responses to stress and pain." And they noted "improvement in immunological and behavioral markers in rats exposed to fragrances while under stressful conditions."

Not everyone agrees on which essential oils support each chakra. That doesn't meant it's not a valid support for the chakra system. It means that each person is slightly different, and responses will vary. Seek advice from someone who is experienced and well-informed and combine that information with your own experience of how the essential oils affect you. Their knowledge combined with your personal experience is the best indicator for which essential oils you will favor for balance.

Aromatherapy Massage

A trained professional gives aromatherapy massage by selecting the appropriate oils to mix in a base carrier oil. The essential oils are highly potent, and so are not meant to be applied directly to the skin. A base carrier oil is a pure oil, such as extra-virgin cold-pressed olive oil or sesame oil, that can be used to dilute essential oils.

If you do get expert advice and would like to do self-massage with essential oils, get the best carrier oil that you can, from a specialist store.

What you put on your body gets absorbed into your body, so you want only the purest and best oil when you apply it to your skin.

Then, add drops of the essential oil to the base carrier. A typical recipe is to measure the amount of base oil in milliliters, and then divide that number in half to give you the maximum number of drops of essential oil that you will need.

> Test the mixture of essential oils and base carrier on the skin of the receiver, first, by applying a small amount to the inside of the wrist, behind the knee, and/or in the crease of the elbow. Check the spot twenty-four hours later to see if the skin had a reaction or not.

After testing the oil on the skin to make sure there is no allergic reaction, you can do a healing self-massage. First put a couple of drops of the mixture of base oil and essential oil onto your hands and rub your hands together to stimulate the scent of the oil. Bring the palms of your hands up to your face, and inhale the scent for several breaths. Then, gently begin to massage the top of your head, at the crown. Then, slowly progress down the body, giving your body the attention it deserves. Continue to inhale the aroma that gently wafts through the air.

When you've finished with the massage, relax. Allow the effects of the massage to sink in. Envision the healing occurring, enjoy the process.

Energetic Massage

You can do an aromatherapy energetic self-massage without touching your body. For the energetic massage, mix the essential oils with a high-quality base carrier oil, as directed above. Place a few drops of the elixir into your hands. Rub your hands together to release the scent of the oils. Bring the palms of your hands to your face to inhale the scent for several breaths and call to mind the healing properties of the oils. Inhale and exhale several times. Then, hold your hands about six to ten inches from your body and do an energetic sweep of your entire body. Slowly sweep downward, brushing away unwanted disturbance in the energy field. After you've completed this, relax for several moments. Notice the effects. Then, wash your hands with cold water.

Historically, lavender has been used as an antiseptic and for mental health support. Today, it's used for its sedative and calming qualities. It's used to treat anxiety, insomnia, and depression. It can also be used to alleviate headaches and upset stomach.

Diffusing Essential Oils

Instead of applying a mixture of base carrier oil and essential oils to the skin, you can receive the healing benefits of essential oils by diffusing them. There are specific diffusers made to use with essential oils. Read the directions, each diffuser works differently. The point of the diffuser is to release the aroma and the healing properties of the essential oil into the air. This has both a humidifying benefit to combat the dryness in the air, and it helps sanitize and infuse the air with healing properties. For example, you can diffuse lavender in the air to promote relaxation and serenity, or tea tree oil for its antiviral and antibacterial properties.

Steaming with Essential Oils

Especially at times of year or in climates where the air is dry, steaming with an essential oil is a wonderful way to receive therapeutic benefits.

1. Have a towel and your essential oil nearby.

2. Get a bowl that is approximately ten to twelve inches in diameter.

3. Boil enough water to fill the bowl one-half to two-thirds full.

4. Pour the steaming water into the bowl, and then add one drop of the essential oil to the bowl.

5. Lean your head into the flow of the steam, and put the towel over your head to cover your head and the bowl.

6. Inhale deeply through both nostrils, exhale gently through the mouth. Repeat this several times.

7. If you would like to, also close one nostril with your finger, and inhale and exhale through one nostril at a time to make sure that each side is receiving the benefits.

8. If one drop of the essential oil wasn't strong enough, or if the scent diminishes, add another drop. It's doubtful you will need more than two drops of the essential oil.

9. When you are finished steaming, sit down. Take a moment to notice the effects. Practice this two to three times per day if you're working with a particular imbalance or onset of a cold.

Steaming with an essential oil is a fast way to get the benefits of the essential oils. The vapor infused with healing properties rises into the nasal passages, entering your system immediately. Steaming is an effective, easy, and soothing way to feel the benefits of essential oils.

> Essential oils contain the healing properties of the plant from which they came, so when these properties enter your system they help boost your immunity. In addition, essential oils carry the energetic vibrations of the plant, the life-force energy sustained within it. That vibration interacts with your energy system. Particular oils are said to balance specific chakras.

Another way to enjoy steaming with an essential oil is to use the elixir in a warm bath. First, dilute the essential oil in a base carrier oil, then pour about a fourth of a cup of the mixture into your bathtub. The oil will absorb into your body through your skin, and as you inhale you will bring the oil's healing qualities into your body through your nostrils. This is a soothing, relaxing, and natural way to feeling healthy.

Aromatherapy for the Root Chakra

As your connection to the earth, when the Root Chakra is balanced you will feel grounded. To balance this chakra you may choose essential oils from a plant that has earthy and red-toned colors. Suggested oils are patchouli, myrrh, and cedarwood.

Root Chakra Aromatherapy and Ayurveda

If you notice that you need to balance your Root Chakra to feel more grounded, check to see what Ayurvedic imbalances you have, as well. Ayurveda also works with essential oils. See if there is a correlation between what you notice about your dosha and your chakras. For example, if you are feeling ungrounded, it could also be a symptom of a vata imbalance.

Aromatherapy and Vata Imbalance

For calming vata, essential oils cinnamon, sandalwood, myrrh, rose, and jasmine are recommended. Dilute these in sesame, almond, or olive oil. You can use this mixture as part of your daily self-care routine, when you massage oils into your body.

Even if you don't have a vata imbalance, some of these oils are also good for pitta and kapha imbalances. As a rule, the flowery ones are usually recommended for pitta (such as jasmine), and the warming stimulating oils that are good for vata are also useful for kapha (such as cinnamon and myrrh).

If you don't want to massage the diluted oils into your entire body, it's particularly helpful for grounding to massage the oil into your feet, scalp, and third eye. Or, another way to receive the benefits of the essential oil is to put one or two drops on a cotton ball, and inhale the aroma from the cotton ball.

Aromatherapy for the Sacral Chakra

The Sacral Chakra is associated with fluidity, creation, sexuality, and emotions. You want essential oils that will calm the emotions and ease fear of change. Recommended essential oils are sandalwood, jasmine, and rose.

Sacral Chakra, Aromatherapy, and Ayurveda

When the Sacral Chakra is blocked you could experience fiery emotions, which is different from the balanced state that is full of sweetness, fluidity, and trust. With a fire in the Sacral Chakra, you could look to Ayurveda for balancing pitta if you also have other qualities that show pitta is acting up in you.

Aromatherapy for Sacral and Pitta Imbalance

The same essential oils are recommended for balancing pitta as for balancing the Sacral Chakra: sandalwood, jasmine, and rose. You can dilute these in coconut oil, which is cooling, and rub it particularly on the lower half of your torso—front and back, in the area that surrounds your Sacral and Solar Plexus Chakras.

> Ayurveda supports essential oils as healing aids, with cooling and heating properties that affect the doshas. According to Dr. David Frawley in *Ayurvedic Healing*, "essential oils can be placed directly on various sites on the skin, like the points of the seven chakras (especially the third eye)."

To calm pitta, rose is among the recommended essential oils. In addition to any aforementioned techniques for receiving the benefits of aromatherapy, you can also buy rose water that is designed to be sprayed into your eyes for cooling and cleansing effects. It's very healthy for the eyes, and can be part of your routine even if you don't need to balance pitta or your Sacral Chakra.

Aromatherapy for the Solar Plexus Chakra

The solar plexus is also a fiery energy center. While the Sacral Chakra can be fiery with unbalanced emotions and sexuality, too much fire in the solar plexus is associated with becoming judgmental, controlling, and angry. So, again, you will want scents that calm down fire: cooling, flowery, calming scents.

Solar Plexus, Aromatherapy, and Ayurveda

An imbalance of the solar plexus can have the same qualities as a pitta imbalance: being judgmental, controlling, and angry are also signs that pitta is overactive in you. Some recommended essential oils to try for the Solar Plexus Chakra are sage, geranium, and ylang-ylang.

Aromatherapy for Pitta and Solar Plexus Imbalance

Because of the placement of the solar plexus, its imbalance can affect your digestion. If you're feeling overly fiery in that region, you may want to try mint to help calm the fire of pitta and the fiery solar plexus. Mint can be cooling and can be very effective at calming a nervous or upset stomach.

> Ayurveda chooses essential oils based on their scent as well as color. While some scents will pacify certain doshas, they may aggravate others. Based on your prakruti and vikruti, it might take some experimentation and work with an expert to find what works best for you. Be patient, for when you do find the right combination, you will find relief.

When you inhale the scents of the aromas, you can also practice visualizations. Visualize the healing energy travelling to the parts of your body that need it most. With every inhale, envision the healing mist entering your body, and with every exhale release the toxins. Always, visualizations help the healing process.

Aromatherapy for the Heart Chakra

The Heart Chakra is such a powerful transmitter for love, compassion, and maintaining authentic relationship. When it's out of balance, not only will you feel unsatisfied in your relationships, you also will have diminished perceptive abilities. Your heart really perceives what's going on in and around you, and if that chakra is imbalanced your perception won't be as keen as it could be. This could lead to more misunderstandings and miscommunications, and fuel the pain of an imbalanced Heart Chakra because of cloudy perception.

The Heart Chakra, Aromatherapy, and Ayurveda

Essential oils recommended for the Heart Chakra are rose, melissa, and neroli. It isn't obvious which dosha imbalance you may have if you are noticing that your Heart Chakra is out of balance. It can be connected with an imbalance in any of the doshas. Rose oil is best for pitta and vata imbalances. Neroli, rose, and melissa have sedative qualities, which could be soothing to vata or pitta imbalance.

Aromatherapy for Heart Chakra and Kapha Imbalance

When there is a kapha imbalance, while you may be drawn to sweet scents, it will be more healing for you to find stimulating scents. Cedar and pine are among the scents recommended for kapha imbalance. If your Heart Chakra is imbalanced and you have a kapha imbalance, both will benefit from these tree scents because the Heart Chakra responds to green, and the cedar and pine tree are green in their natural form.

Aromatherapy for the Throat Chakra

Chamomile and thyme are two herbs recommended for an imbalance in the Throat Chakra. If you notice you are constantly talking, monopolizing the conversation time you share with others, and feeling needy for conversation, you may have an overactive Throat Chakra. If you are withholding your opinion and voice, you may have an underactive Throat Chakra. In either of these cases, using chamomile or thyme could help. Lavender is also an option. It's an all-around useful oil, and notice that it's a color that can be associated with this and the Third-Eye Chakra.

The Throat Chakra, Aromatherapy, and Ayurveda

If the Throat Chakra is imbalanced, it doesn't give much of a clue as to which dosha could also be imbalanced. If you're too talkative, switching from one subject to the next, it could be an indicator of a vata imbalance. If you are domineering in conversation, it could be a symptom of pitta. And, if you are withholding and aren't coming up with anything to contribute to the conversations, it could be a kapha imbalance. When you use additional, more definitive methods to find out which doshas need support, then you can bring that to your chakra healing practice.

The Throat Chakra and Steaming

Particularly when the Throat Chakra is out of balance, you may want to take the oils as a steam. At these times, instead of inhaling through your nostrils, inhale through your mouth and envision the steam travelling down to your Throat Chakra. You can also envision the steam travelling down to your Throat Chakra if you inhale through your nostrils. Try it both ways, alternating a few inhalations through the nostrils, and a few inhalations through the mouth.

Moisture is soothing, and steaming with essential oils is a great way to bring moisture to your nasal passages, sinuses, mouth, and throat. Keeping these areas from getting too dry will help you in the winter months. Steaming is also useful in the summer months if it's a dry heat and if you are exposed to a lot of air-conditioning, fans, or wind.

Humidifiers are also a good option, as long as you are vigilant about keeping them clean and not creating too much humidity in the room.

Aromatherapy and the Third-Eye Chakra

The Third-Eye Chakra is enhanced by frankincense, basil, and rose geranium. Frankincense promotes deep relaxation, and breath-awareness. It helps you access dreams states, past lives, and deep meditative states. Basil helps with clear thinking, and helps to decrease stress and nervousness. Both frankincense and basil help with congestion and respiratory infections.

The Third-Eye Chakra, Aromatherapy, and Ayurveda

Frankincense is recommended for vata types, rose geranium is great for pitta, and basil is supportive for kapha types. If you have any of these dosha imbalances, you can use the appropriate essential oil to both heal the Third-Eye Chakra and support your dosha.

The Third-Eye Chakra and All Essential Oils

Because of its placement near the olfactory senses and the brain, the Third-Eye Chakra is a prime place for you to rub any healing oils. Even if you want to heal a chakra that is located in another part of your body, you can always include the Third-Eye Chakra as place for putting the oil.

Aromatherapy for the Crown Chakra

The Crown Chakra, like the third eye, is a prime location for putting any of the essential oils because of the proximity to the brain. The essential oils that are recommended for this chakra are ylang-ylang and rosewood. Both these scents are said to connect you to the universal energy, helping you to experience out-of-this-world states of relaxation and bliss.

The Crown Chakra, Aromatherapy, and Ayurveda

Because the Crown Chakra is your energetic gateway to bliss and one-ness with the universe, it doesn't correlate simply to any of the doshas. The Crown Chakra isn't reliant on the workings of the physical body or how the elements of nature are at work within you. If your Crown Chakra is excessive, it can make you feel ungrounded. And you can use the aromatherapy recommendations for vata imbalance to help. If your Crown Chakra is sluggish, you could experience depression and inability to focus. For this, try aromatherapy for kapha.

The Crown Chakra and Vata or Kapha Imbalance

Because both vata and kapha benefit from warming and stimulating oils, when your Crown Chakra is out of balance and you feel as though you are experiencing vata or kapha imbalances, try any of these essential oils: camphor, musk, or cinnamon. If your experience feels more like a vata imbalance, use sesame oil as the base carrier. For kapha, it'd be better to use mustard or flaxseed oil as a base carrier. Once you mix the base carrier with the essential oil, massage it into the top of your head, for the benefit of the Crown Chakra and your overall sense of balance.

CHAPTER 17

The Law of Attraction

The Law of Attraction explains the way that you actively create your life. Your thoughts and desires are vibrations that emanate from you. In response, the universe begins to answer your request. Like attracts like: as you have thoughts, more related thoughts come to you and bolster your thoughts/desires. The universe conspires to make it so, as you continue to give strength to the original thought. You may not notice this to be true yet in your life, if you haven't heard of the Law of Attraction. Once you understand the Law of Attraction you will be able to look back at the events of your life, and notice how this has been true so far even without your full awareness of it.

Creating a State of Receptivity

The Law of Attraction is not activated based on whether or not you believe in it. The Law of Attraction is working right now, everywhere, all the time. As you begin to learn about it you will begin to understand how to lead the life you want to lead, how to attract circumstances you desire, and how to create fewer obstacles for yourself in the process.

Believing in Well-Being

If you've picked up this book, you are interested in overall well-being. You are interested to learn more about overall health and happiness, and you believe—even if deep down—it's possible. You believe that there is a way that you can positively influence the course of your life and your connection to joy, and you're right!

Just as the yoga sutras explain how to benefit from yoga practice, the Law of Attraction explains how your desires and thoughts attract what you want into your life. A foundational premise of the Law of Attraction is that the universe is interested in well-being, not disease. The universe is basic goodness: things work together in harmony. Even in the Judeo-Christian model the Bible says repeatedly, after God created something, he saw that it was good.

> "And God said, Let there be light: and there was light. And God saw the light, that it was good . . . And God saw everything that he had made, and, behold, it was very good. And the evening and the morning were the sixth day."
>
> —Book of Genesis

This belief isn't only found in religious texts. Just by looking out the window or into the eyes of a beloved, you notice how the universe is good. The universe creates and sustains life, and what's more, it creates and sustains beauty. From the bright stars in the dark sky to the tiny clovers in the green grass, the earth is more than life-sustaining—it is full of beauty. How about that for goodness: the earth is pleasing to human senses.

Just as the earth is interested in well-being and harmony, so are you. Your body, when in a state of balance, can perform all its functions to keep you healthy. If you can now believe that the universe and you are both interested in well-being, you can begin to live from a place of belief that harmony is the natural state of things. The world is not out to get you, trick you, or make your life difficult. In fact, the universe provides you with all you need for health, joy, and fulfillment.

You Communicate with the Universe

You are not separate from the earth. With every inhale and exhale you are plugging in to the same energy that sustains the entire universe. The healthy food you eat and the water you drink come from nature. You receive your energy and physical sustenance from the earth, which means your vibrations and needs are compatible with the vibrations and gifts of the earth. The fuel of the earth is fuel for your physical body. You thrive when you exist in harmony with nature.

Just as your physical body is compatible with earth's produce, on an energetic level your vibrations are compatible with the other vibrations in the universe. This includes the vibrations of plants, animals, and water. Your vibrations resonate outward into the universe and the universe answers your request. According to the Law of Attraction, the universe works to match the vibrations you send out, bringing your desires into being as soon as seven seconds after you feel the desire. Your task, after putting your desires out there, is to be receptive.

Sending Mixed Messages

The universe responds to what you are feeling and desiring to be so. It doesn't need words. So, for example, what if you would like to have more friends? The way that you attract more friends is by feeling the feeling you would have with more friends. To do this, imagine it to be already so. Stand in whatever your feelings are in relation to more friends. Now, you are sending out the vibration of "plenty of friends." Your desire for friends, felt in the affirmative, puts an affirmative vibration out there that can be matched accordingly. You desire "plenty of friends," and the universe begins to send "plenty of friends." There will be a bit of a time difference between the asking and the receiving, but it will be in the works as long as you continue to hold that desire in that positive way.

A mixed message to the universe occurs when you are also feeling the feelings you associate with not enough friends. If you are dwelling on the negative feelings you feel and the image of not enough friends, you are sending out the vibration, "not enough friends." And that is the vibration that will be matched. The more you are living in that feeling and belief of "lack," the more you are putting out the message for more of that.

> "Even though a clear desire has emanated from you as a result of the contrast you have considered, you often, rather than giving your attention purely to the desire itself, focus back on the contrasting situation that gave birth to the desire. And, in doing so, your vibration is more about the reason you have launched the desire than it is about the desire itself."
>
> —Esther and Jerry Hicks, *Ask and It Is Given*

Contrast is important in life because it helps you identify your desires. By knowing what you do not want, you give rise to the desire for what you do want. Once you have determined what you want, after considering its contrast, stay focused on the feelings of "having" to bring the results.

If you notice that you still are not getting what you want, examine what contrast you are focusing on and why. For example, if you feel you do not have enough friends and you are still focusing on the lack, maybe you also have the feeling that you don't want more friends. Look into your own real feelings to see if there's a reason you are putting out the lack. Why are you telling the universe you do and don't want friends? Are you feeling too insecure to meet new people? Do you feel safer not being social? Think about if you really are comfortable, truly, having what think you want. It's okay if you are unsure about what you want, but realize that you are the one who is unsure. It's not that no one is listening. In fact, the universe is responding to all the vibrations. You are thoroughly heard.

Getting Clear About What You Want

Once you understand that the universe supports you, and your thoughts and desires can become manifest, you can see the value in finding out who you are, how you can contribute to the world, and what you want. The truth is, perhaps you don't know the answers to these questions, and that is all right. You can take the time through meditation, yoga, chakra healing, and other methods to discover or remember your talents and how you can do what you love and attract what you love.

Notice How You Spend Your Energy

If you don't already know what you most desire, spend time getting to know what your heart's desire is. If you don't spend time on self-inquiry and self-care, notice if you spend too much of your energy focused on others. Focusing on others can come in the form of replaying over and over what someone has said to you, putting lots of interest in what others are doing (or not doing), dwelling on what's not right with you or the world, and wishing other people would change. Caring about others and their well-being is compassionate and beneficial. It can be a slippery slope, though. If you are focusing so much on others that you do not attend to what you need and can create in your life, then focusing on others could be an escape. Cultivate the balance between giving to others and nourishing your health and dreams.

> When looking at other people's lives, it's possible at times to experience envy. One good way to deal with envy is not to spend time focusing on what that other person has. Instead, shift your attention to what you really want. Move your attention from envy toward what you are grateful you have and what you'd like next.

If you are used to focusing so much on others, and then you see them get what they want, this can cause you to have negative feelings toward them. You could have resentment or jealousy when someone else succeeds and you are dissatisfied with something in your life. If this happens, re-examine how you are spending your time. Are you productively seeking out what you want and need? It is your responsibility to create time for self-care and self-development. Someone else's success and happiness is not a threat to your own. Spend your energy wisely. Make time for others, and make time for you.

Effort Without Struggle

The beauty of manifesting your desires is that you don't have to struggle to attract what you want. You have to know what you want and then enjoy the process. Enjoyment is an important part of the manifestation process.

The effort is the part where you strip away the chatter and the noise to find out what you really want in your life. You examine where you are, what you are grateful for, and what you would like to attract. In this process, it's important to be very specific. There's no need to feel guilty or embarrassed about what you want. Make the list detailed. Whether it's a list of the qualities you want in a partner or a detailed description of a house you would like to buy, go for it! The more specific you are, the more you will get exactly what you want.

As you make this effort, you don't need to struggle. Make this easeful. You are creating what you want in your life, doesn't that sound good? Enjoy the process.

You Are the Archer

For an exquisite metaphor on you as an archer in life, read Paulo Coelho's *The Bow, the Arrow, and the Target*. It's a short work, describing you on the path of life as an archer with a bow, arrow, and target at your disposal. His work is poetic and poignant. He describes the bow as your body and your energy. He advises you to take care of it. Know that you can use it to harm others or to create goodwill; be mindful with this bow.

He calls the arrow your intention, the force that connects you to your desired object (the target). Then, he describes the target. You have chosen the target, and "If you look on the target as an enemy, you might even make a good shot but you will not manage to improve anything in yourself. You will spend your life just trying to put an arrow in the center of something made of paper or wood, which is absolutely useless. And when you are with other people you will complain all the time that you do not do anything interesting." The metaphor illuminates and describes self-empowerment, your work in creating your life.

Making Space

Once you have specific ideas about what you want, you need to make space in your life for your desire to enter. To return to the example of wanting more friends, if someone with similar interests reaches out to you and you don't have time to call him back, then you won't be able to cultivate a friendship. Or, if you are so hung up on your last relationship that your thoughts still are constantly focused there, then there isn't space for something new. Do not be afraid to let go of the old, and have some empty space before the new enters.

What Are Your Priorities?

Before you decide how to make space in your life, make a list of what your priorities are. What are the things in your life you want to make the most important? Even if you don't already have one of the things in your life, list it. For example, say you want marriage to be a top priority, but you aren't married. It's okay, list it. List your top three to five priorities in life. Does the way you spend your energy right now match up to how you want your life to look? If not, why are you spending energy on other things? What are the other things that are taking up your energy? Is it possible to make a shift?

Once you have noticed what you would like to be your priorities, with patience and intention start making your energy and focus aim toward those things. Notice where else your energy might wander, and see if it goes in useful directions. Once you know what your priorities are it's much easier to determine what you can cut out of your life to make space.

Fresh Start

To make space in your life for new things, change your physical environment. For example, go through the rooms in your house and make small changes or big changes. You can start in the bedroom. Get rid of clothes you don't wear anymore. Trust that when you need something, you will be able to find it or buy in it the future. Trust that you have everything you need, without having to hold on to all the clothes in your closet. Give away what you don't need that someone else could use; throw away what is too worn-out for anyone. Remember when you create space, something new and better can enter to fill it. Give away your unwanted earrings, belts, and ties.

Go through old letters, papers, and files. Get rid of what you don't need. It's clutter that is holding you to the past. Look through old things one last time, keep what you feel is worth keeping, and throw away what you will not miss.

> Many people sleep on their pillows for too many years. Dust mites live and breed in pillows. Buy new pillows for your bed every three to five years; this will help you sleep well and give your body less allergens to contend with. You can also encase pillows in protective covers. Covers create another layer between dust mites and you.

Freshen up your life by releasing what you no longer need, creating space for something new. And, as you do this, you are recognizing that you don't have to hold on to all things from the past for your sense of happiness. You are learning to trust that good things are not just in the past.

It's Already Happening

As soon as you feel your desire, it's out in the universe. And within seconds, the universe is responding. While you may not immediately see the results, it's in the works. Sometimes it takes time for what you want to come to you based on several factors that you may not know. Things will not always happen according to your desired timing; cultivate patience and belief that it's already happening.

Waiting Patiently

The experience of waiting isn't easy if you're ignoring the present moment and only focusing on what you want. After you've put your desire into the world, know that it might take some time and you must still be present to what is. Be patient for what you want, change doesn't always happen overnight.

While still holding the vibration of your desire, stay present to what is now. Don't ignore what's happening in your life by daydreaming only of what will be. Stay present to what is, deal with your to-dos, and also enjoy knowing that you are creating the life you desire. Step by step. It's happening.

You Don't Have to Know It All

The universe can bring things to you that you desire without you planning everything, knowing how every step must unfold, or understanding how everything works. Good things can happen in your life when and how you least expect it, and without your total control.

> "The Stream of Well-Being flows even if you do not understand that it does, but when you *consciously* become aligned with it, your creative endeavors become so much more satisfying for then you discover that there is absolutely nothing that you desire that you cannot achieve."
>
> —Esther and Jerry Hicks, *Ask and It Is Given*

When you let go of needing to know "how" everything will come to pass, you will find that things can come into your life without your understanding of how they come to be. If you put your desire into the universe, relax, and have fun with it, then you allow the universe to answer your request in the time it takes to do it.

Receiving What You Asked For

After you've asked for what you desire and you've become patient to allow the universe do its part, the last step is receiving it. This step can sometimes be thwarted because if you have given up too soon, and/or if you have focused your attention elsewhere or on the "lack" of it, then you won't be in the place to receive what you asked for.

Joyful Expectation

While your life is unfolding, and you know what you've asked for, the Law of Attraction is supported by your joyful expectation. It's the same as when you go to pick your friend up at the airport. You go to the passenger pick-up area, and you wait. His plane landed at 8:00 P.M., and now it's 8:20 P.M. He could still be at baggage claim, or he may have stopped in the bathroom. Who knows? It doesn't matter right now what he's doing on the way. What you do know is that he is coming, so you wait for him. You don't think that maybe he isn't coming so you'll leave the airport before he gets to you. If you did leave the airport, then you would definitely not see him. So, you wait, knowing he is on his way. This is a metaphor for waiting for what you are creating with the universe.

Delightful Change

With each new creation that you manifest, you will experience change in your life. If you've asked for a new partner, a new house, a new career, more money, etc., inevitably the new circumstances will create change. Sometimes people resist change. Even if something "good" comes their way, they may not be ready to take it and make the change they thought they wanted.

When what you asked for comes into your life, trust that you can handle the newness, the unknown. In the time it's taken the desire to manifest, you've grown and changed with the thoughts you've had about this new idea. Know that with each new step comes the invitation for yet another one. You are constantly changing, life is constantly changing, and you play a part in how it unfolds. Change can bring about delightful experiences.

The Feeling of Appreciation

Appreciation is one of the most wonderful feelings to experience. Once you receive what you've asked for, take time to appreciate it. Appreciating is pausing to notice the beauty and support that you have in the universe. When what you've asked for comes to you, appreciating the creative process and the new circumstance is a part of the joy of receiving. By noticing the qualities of what you've asked for and received, it reminds you why you desired it in the first place.

Charting Your Course

When you cultivate appreciation for things large and small that enter your life, you will enjoy your life more. As you enjoy your life more, you will come up with ideas for what comes next. You will begin to see there are so many options in life, and you will begin to notice which ones appeal to your sensibilities and talents.

> Your preferences will change over time. Maybe for years you have enjoyed travel. It may surprise you that one year you start to wish you could stay put. You may worry that it's not possible, that you've set your life up in this one way. That's not true. You can change your preferences, ask the universe, and receive.

You may have short-term goals and long-term goals. You may find that once you achieve your short-term goals you have different feelings about your previous long-term goals. This might come as a surprise to you. You may have thought the entire reason for the short-term goals was to achieve the long-term goal. That's not always the case. Sometimes what you find through short-term goals is a new path that diverges from anything you could have imagined before. As you go through life, you gather new experiences and information. When something comes to your life in a surprisingly good way, take time to appreciate that circumstances, ideas, and opportunities appear in time, in ways you cannot foresee or predict.

Your Appreciation Creates Health

Being in a state of appreciation, it is an antidote to stress. Worry, anger, and fear are not states of appreciation. When you are appreciative you are thankful, you feel supported, you feel good. Good feelings create good health.

Here's how you can feel appreciation now:

- Take a moment to recall something you appreciated or can appreciate. It can be something that happened recently or a while ago. If nothing comes to mind, think of someone you love and appreciate having in your life. If no one comes to mind, then think of anyone who has been of service to you lately, the person at the grocery store, at the bank, or your postman.

- Hold your attention on that person or circumstance. Now cultivate a feeling of appreciation for what transpired with that person or circumstance. If you can't feel appreciation, first imagine how difficult it would have been if that person or circumstance had not happened. This can help you understand the positive impact on you.

- Notice that the object of your appreciation has supported you, uplifted you, or taken care of you in some way. Notice how it feels to be the recipient of goodwill.

- After you've experienced this for a few moments, let it go.

Feeling appreciation not only is healthy for you, it is healthy for those around you. When you appreciate someone you are letting them know that you accept and benefit from the time and energy that they've spent thinking of you and supporting you. Oftentimes people do not do what they do for you in order to receive your appreciation, they do it for the pleasure of giving. However, your appreciation validates that what they've done has been of use to you. Your appreciation lets them know that they got it right when trying to give you what you need or want. It's affirming to them to know that they were supportive of you.

CHAPTER 18

Combining Chakra Healing and the Law of Attraction

You always can connect to the healing and creative energy of the universe. Both chakra healing and the Law of Attraction explain that when universal energy flows through you in a balanced way, you experience overall health and the life your heart desires. When you are unhealthy or unsatisfied, it doesn't mean you are separate from all that is good. It means the flow of energy is blocked in you. With mindfulness and intention behind your thoughts, words, and actions you can create space for energy to flow.

Picking Your Practice

This book outlines various ways to balance and support the chakras including yoga, visualization, meditation, color therapy, diet, movement, Ayurveda, and more. At first, if all of this is new to you, it might seem overwhelming. It might be difficult for you to choose how to begin or how to incorporate this into your life.

If so, one way to begin is to take a deep breath and relax. Remember that this is a self-nurturing, healing process. This is not a race, a test, or a competition. Chakra healing and understanding the Law of Attraction is an exploration of you, what your needs and preferences are, and how to gently incorporate new practices into your life. You don't have to do all of the exercises suggested in this book, even though you may want to. Try all or as many as you like. Allow the process to unfold, and don't be afraid to go out of your comfort zone and try something new.

> "Insanity: doing the same thing over and over and expecting different results."
>
> —Albert Einstein

Especially if you've tried other ways to cultivate health and you've not had the results you want, try something new. You already know and have experienced what happens in your life if you continue to do things the way you're doing them. Try something new, and see what happens.

Guilt-Free Pleasure

Think of the things you do for pleasure now that you might feel guilty about: eating too much cake, drinking too many alcoholic drinks, or sitting in front of the TV or computer so much that you don't exercise. Are these things you do for pleasure that you feel guilty about? If so, first, allow yourself to experience then release the guilt. You do not need the guilt to help you make change. You can decide to make a change or not, and there's no positive effect from feeling guilty.

If you want a change, try chakra healing. A variety of options are presented in this book so that you can mix-and-match to find the practices that work for you. If you have a habit of eating too many sweets, the next time you go to reach for something unhealthy see what happens if instead you go outside for a walk or follow the chakra meditation practice below. Change the habit. Or, if after a long day of work you always sit in front of the television for several hours, once in a while try something new. If your impulse is to watch TV, try going in to your meditation space or your room, instead. Sit in a comfortable position and follow this chakra meditation practice.

SELF-CARE CHAKRA MEDITATION

1. Sit in a comfortable position for meditation, with your sitting bones firmly planted on the chair, or on a cushion if you are on the floor. Sit upright, allow the natural curves of the spine to be as they are. Make sure the top of your head is parallel to the ceiling. Gently rest your hands in your lap.

2. After you've read all the following steps, then close your eyes to do them.

3. Relax your jaw, and all the muscles of your face. From top to bottom notice each body part and relax it. Relax the forehead, the jaw, the neck, the shoulders, the arms, the hands, the torso, the belly, the hips, the thighs, the calves, the ankles, and the toes.

4. Breathe naturally for several breaths, and notice the breath as it flows in and as it flows out. Watch and observe how your torso expands on the inhale, and lets go on the exhale.

5. Now with your eyes closed, do a chakra scan: at each chakra envision its corresponding color glowing. Start at the Crown Chakra. Envision it glowing white, and notice how it and you respond. Relax for several breaths, and notice.

6. Draw your attention down to each chakra, envisioning the color of the chakra for several breaths. Noticing how you feel.

7. After you've done this at the Root Chakra, continue to observe the breath for a few moments.

8. Place both of your hands on your body over your heart. Position your hands either in prayer position or with one hand on top of the other facing your heart. Imagine your hands giving your heart energy, loving, restoring energy.

9. When you feel complete, release your hands, and open your eyes.

What you might need at the end of the day is some "me" time, in this way, especially if in your job you have to be "on" or managing others. If you are a stay-at-home mom, you also focus a lot of your energy on others. So, instead of always relaxing in a way that takes you out of yourself (like television or going out for drinks), try coming in to yourself for a change. See how it feels to check in with your chakras. This isn't to suggest you give up television or going out altogether. It's about trying something new and seeing if it feels better. You don't have to sacrifice TV altogether to do chakra healing. You can take time for a chakra meditation in the evening as well as watch television or go out. One doesn't exclude the other. The chakra visualization helps you connect your body, mind, and spirit. It's good for your mood, too, especially after a long day. What's more, there's nothing to feel guilty about: it's free, it's nonfat, and it produces well-being.

If You Like to Try It All

If you are the sort of person who wants to dive right in and try everything, as you enter into the chakra-healing journey, do not rush. Take your time. Chakra healing is about having an experience; take it on in small, luxurious doses. Really enjoy it as you go. It's not necessary to do everything outlined in this book to receive the benefits. You can pick and choose. In other words, you don't need to drink color-enhanced water, take an aromatherapy bath, practice yoga, wear clothes of the color of the chakra you want to balance most, and journal every single day. As you get more used to chakra healing, you could incorporate all of that into a day, or you could try one or two of the practices every few days. Since everyone is different, there's no one way to do it. You can decide if you want to do something every day or not. Know that every step you take makes a difference, and don't pressure yourself to do it all at once.

Just as you don't need to spend your whole day on chakra healing, you don't need to spend hours of your day every day focusing on what you want to attract into your life. The Law of Attraction works with positive thoughts and intentions, though they don't have to occur all day long. What's most helpful is to notice if you have negative feelings or positive feelings toward the thought of want you want to call into your life. If you have positive feelings, then you are in the space of allowing what you want to come to you. If you have doubts or resistant thoughts to it, you are not allowing. So, you don't have to focus all the time on what you want, instead cultivate positive feelings around the desires when they come up.

What if I don't feel anything different during or after I meditate on the chakras?

Give yourself and the process time. If various things about you and your lifestyle are out of balance, it may take time to notice results. Stay with the practices, and give them time to work on you. Illness and negative thinking patterns don't develop overnight, and so they won't heal overnight. This is a process. Subtle changes can occur without you noticing.

If You Need Motivation

If you are the kind of person who reads a lot about healthy lifestyle choices and then doesn't have the motivation to follow through, here's an idea: pick two practices to start with and commit to doing them tomorrow or the next day. Write them in your daily planner or put a sticky note on your mirror as a reminder.

One easy first thing to do is to buy a piece of jewelry in the gemstone or color of the chakra you wish to balance. To decide which chakra, either do a chakra meditation or decide based on the physical or psychological qualities that correspond to each chakra when it's in and out of balance. If you don't wear jewelry, buy any item of clothing in that color. If you don't normally wear colors, buy socks or underwear in the color you are choosing, so no one outside will know.

> "With all the messy stuff, no matter how messy it is, just start where you are—not tomorrow, not later, not yesterday when you were feeling better—but now. Start now, just as you are."
>
> —Pema Chödrön

A second easy thing to start with is one of the hand mudras with the corresponding visualization. You can practice the mudra just for three to five minutes in the morning. And, there you go: two practices that you can begin with. Then, after a couple of weeks, see if there are other things you would like to do. Make sticky notes or write it in your planner to revisit this book and explore. As you commit more time to the practices you will begin to see more results.

Make a Day of It

While chakra healing and using the Law of Attraction can simply be incorporated into your life, you may also really enjoy making a day of it, or an afternoon of it, now and then. For example, go online to find a labyrinth near you, and take an afternoon getting to the labyrinth, walking it, and journaling afterward. You can bring a picnic, or a thermos of tea, and spend the afternoon creating health and intentions for your life. Doing something like this weekly, biweekly, or monthly will be nourishing. If you don't have a labyrinth nearby, find a comfortable spot in a place where there are books to enjoy. Read poetry that inspires you or look through a book of photography or art while drinking a refreshing or calming drink. Or, if you like to go for a run, make time for that. Admire the beauty and appreciate the feeling you get from appreciating what's beautiful.

Envisioning the New Reality

When you practice chakra healing and the Law of Attraction, visualize the healed state, the new place you want to be. If you're visualizing any part of your body, even if not a chakra, envision it healing and envision it healthy. Spend time envisioning the healing and the healed image, and imagine sending healing breath and light to that area. Where you envision the breath going, healing energy will go. Do this for your chakras, your body parts, your mind, and anything about your reality that you want to create.

Retrain Your Brain

Your mind goes from thought to thought throughout the day. You may not even realize how many negative, suspicious, or insecure thoughts you have each day, if you've never taken time to notice. Make it a practice to become more mindful of where your mind goes. Notice if the thoughts are putting you in a negative state of mind. And, notice how those negative thoughts make you feel, probably not so good.

When you notice yourself having positive thoughts that affirm you, others, and how life unfolds, notice how those thoughts make you feel. These are the kinds of thoughts that will help you sustain health and create what you want.

Sometimes something someone else says or does could "trigger" you, sending your thoughts quickly along a typical path that might not be healthy for you. It happens so quickly and is so ingrained in your mind that you may not realize it until you become more mindful of your thought patterns. Here's an example:

Every time someone compliments Eleanor, she becomes silent and looks down. Eleanor realizes that she doesn't like to be complimented, so she decides to try to figure out why so she can retrain her brain. She decides to be mindful of where her mind goes the next time she receives a compliment.

Her kind friend Fredrick says, "You have stunning eyes." Eleanor notices that she feels scared, looks down, and says nothing. She doesn't understand why she would be afraid. So, she later replays the situation in her mind to try to unlock what she's afraid of. She notices she's afraid of several possibilities: she's afraid Fredrick is hitting on her and wants more from the friendship than she does; she's afraid that if she does have stunning eyes she will stand out in the crowd, making her vulnerable to the criticism and jealousy of others; and she's reminded of the times in the past when as a child her mother would compliment her and then a few moments later criticize her until she went to her room and cried. After Eleanor writes this in her journal, she looks over what she's afraid of and notices that now, in her life, she's not really afraid of those things anymore. She can deal with any of those scenarios, should they arise. She notices that while each of those scenarios isn't always comfortable, she doesn't fear any of them. Those fears come from experiences she remembers she had several times in her childhood and young adult life: unwanted sexual advances; hurtful comments from classmates when she was very young, that the principal of the school said were because the other students were jealous; and the nature of her mother's compliments and criticism. All of these used to cause Eleanor fear, but as an adult they do not. Now, Eleanor sees she can try to retrain her brain as she rethinks about the new scenario and the next time she gets a compliment. Instead of allowing her mind to go where it will unconsciously, she can take into consideration who is saying it and that she isn't a child anymore. The brain will respond and can be retrained. And, then Eleanor can work on taking in the positive energy in the affirmations from her friends.

> It's healthy for your brain when you learn new activities or games. Pick up a new hobby! For example if you've never grown herbs, try it! Buy a package of seeds, read the instructions, talk to the person at the store if you need more advice, and read up on recipes for how to incorporate your fresh herbs into your diet.

The more healthy information and sensory input you are open to, the more your brain can learn new habits. Be friends with people who have your best interest at heart. Even they will be willing to tell you where you might be slipping into an old pattern: good friends are those who can do it in a way that feels safe and supportive and who wait until you ask for their advice on sensitive issues such as how you are wired. Or, if they really want to offer advice to you without you asking for it, they will gingerly ask if you would like their advice, support, or thoughts on the issue. Accepting other people's points of view can really be helpful, so don't be afraid to ask dear friends for how they would handle a situation or what they think. That doesn't mean you have to listen to what everyone says or do things the way they would. Be mindful about what you watch on TV, what you read, and whom you listen to. You pick up on their energy, and in a good way, other perspectives remind your brain that there isn't just one way to think about things.

Make Choices from a Place of Love, not Fear

According to the Law of Attraction if you have resistant thoughts to what you desire, you are blocking what you want from coming to you. For example, if you want a new house, and also you are afraid that you can't perform all of the upkeep, worried about moving all of your things into a new home, and concerned that you won't like the new house as much as your present home, then you are sending out the signals that you don't really want a new house. See if your fears are really telling you something important, and if not, see if you can shift your attitude to contentment around the new house. This will allow the positive outcome to flow to you.

In the *Yoga Sutras* of Patanjali, he explains that there is a natural evolution and flow, and the purpose of practice is to remove obstacles that are in the way. Sutra 4.3: "incidental events do not directly cause natural evolution, they just remove the obstacles as a farmer removes the obstacles in a water course running to his field."

Taking time in your life to practice chakra healing and getting used to keeping in mind the Law of Attraction is a perfect combination to create the conditions to allow the natural flow of energy. To use chakra healing and the Law of Attraction to help cultivate fearlessness, buy a clear quartz or amethyst crystal that you can hold in the palms of your hands. It will support your Crown Chakra for this exercise.

1. Have the crystal nearby, but not yet in your hands.

2. Take a moment to bring to mind one big thing that your heart desires. Allow your mind to go to what fears you may have around receiving this next thing. If you want, write the fears down, now. Then, place the paper to the side.

3. Pick up the crystal, and hold it inside your cupped hands: one hand on top of the other, with the crystal inside.

4. Feel the energy of the crystal in your hands. Feel the energy travel through your arms, into your entire body, cleansing your body of doubt, fear, or anxiety. If you don't feel it, it's okay. Visualize it.

5. Breathe in and out naturally for several breaths while envisioning the pure, vibrant energy replacing insecurities held in your body and mind.

6. Put the crystal down, and on a new piece of paper write down how you are feeling now. Notice if there have been any positive shifts in your energy.

7. Throw away or burn the piece of paper with your fears on it.

Notice if you feel more relaxed after these several moments of breathing and visualizing new energy pulsing through your body. Feel a connection to love, and from this place, think about your choices. Envision how you want things to be, and fill that vision with your pure, positive intentions.

Letting Go

Once you have cultivated a clear vision of what you are attracting into your life, relax around it. Let it go. Give it time to manifest. When what you want comes to mind, feed it with positive thoughts, take the appropriate actions to bring it into being, but don't cling to it. Don't overdo. Don't worry that you have to push, push, push to get what you want. Give it space.

What to Do While Letting Go

While you wait for your desires to become manifest, continue your chakra healing practices. Continue to create health in your life. Continue to make healthy choices for you and those you care about. Every moment is a moment to practice being skillful amidst the uncertainty of life.

> "Moving into our experience—whether it's the opening experience of love and compassion or the closing-down experience of resentment and separation—brings us an enormous sense of freedom: the freedom of nothing solid . . . This moving away from comfort and security, this stepping out into what is unknown, unchartered, and shaky—that's called liberation."
>
> —Pema Chödrön

When you start to let go, and stop focusing on what's next and how to keep yourself busy, you will feel groundlessness. You will experience the feelings you try to escape when you are constantly on the go or occupying your time with distractions. The truth is, even when you are trying to escape from feelings, they are there. They will come up in your interactions with friends, coworkers, and family. They will come up even if you think you are protecting yourself from them. The solution is to sit with them; to watch and allow them to be. As you watch and allow them to be, they will pass. Like a wave, the emotions will pass if you allow them to flow.

Not Giving Up

When you let go, it doesn't mean you give up. You just allow things to unfold as they will. You do your best in the practical and real ways to set up for your success, and then you relax. If something doesn't happen in the time frame you've set out for, do not give up. If it feels appropriate, take another action, and do it from a place of security and openness.

A practical example is when applying for a job. Do all the required things to apply for the job. Do them to the best of your ability. You can even call to make sure they received the application, and send a note of appreciation after the interview. And, after you've done what's required and perhaps just a little extra to show you are interested and on-the-ball, let go. Find that balance between showing what you have to offer and not acting out of desperation or fear. Work hard on the parts that are laid out for you, then relax.

Chakra Exercises for Letting Go

When you want to let go and allow things to take their course, strengthening any and all of the chakras always helps. Specifically, if you are feeling insecure, it can be mainly in the Solar Plexus Chakra. If you are not feeling anxiety, you are feeling insecure; try this exercise.

1. Sit in a position for meditation.

2. Place your hands one on top of the other on your solar plexus.

3. Practice Kapalabhati breath. If you are new to it, just practice ten exhales. If you are used to it, do thirty. Relax, then repeat two more times.

4. Notice how you feel.

5. Keeping your hands where they are, and while breathing normally, envision glowing yellow light emanating from your hands into your third chakra. Do this for several moments.

6. When you are done with this visualization, take a moment to come back to the present moment.

This visualization and Kapalabhati exercise is meant to strengthen Manipura. Do not perform Kapalabhati if you have uncontrolled high blood pressure, if you are pregnant, if you have recently had surgery, if you are menstruating, if you have stomach or digestive trouble, or if you have high anxiety. If you have these conditions, try Nadi Shodhana for fifteen minutes each morning and/or evening. And, do the visualization of steps five and six, above, for Manipura.

Enjoy Your Work

Whether you want big change or small change, while things are always in flux, see what you can enjoy now. If you already love the work you do, that's great. If you love the work you do, in theory, but don't really enjoy it most of the moments of the day, is that something you can change? Take a look at the following questions:

- Does your work help others?

- Does your work support you financially?

- Do you feel your job is secure?

- Do you feel competent at your job?

- Do you give input or feedback to your boss or coworkers?

- Do you feel heard?

- Are you able to take vacations, and breaks during the week?

- Do you feel appreciated and supported by those you work for and with?

- Do you feel mentally engaged, yet not overworked?

After answering the questions, you can get a picture of how you feel at your job. The questions also relate to the issues of the different chakras. As you look at those questions, if you feel that you answer "no" to several of them, check in with yourself. Do you think it's because you are in an unhealthy work environment, and/or do you think you could do some work with your chakras in order to help the "no" answers turn into "yes" answers? How would it feel if you could say "yes" to all those questions? Do you think it's possible at this job? If not, is it possible somewhere else? Your work environment and attitude about your work is an essential part of your overall well-being.

Forty Hours per Week

Most people work an average of forty hours per week. Those are a lot of hours of your life, and many people work even more hours than that. Imagine how different it would feel to enjoy your work versus dreading it. If your job is a good job, and yet you are noticing that you really don't like being there, is there a way you can approach the work with a different attitude. Were there appealing reasons why you chose this job? Do those reasons still appeal to you today? Are there other things you can see about this job that make it worth your while to be there? If you can remember those reasons and they still are valid, allow yourself to find ways to enjoy those forty hours per week, so you're not always waiting for your time off.

> Vacations are essential to maintaining good health. No matter how much you enjoy your job and how much you have to do, talk with your employer about your vacation days. Do they really respect you taking the time off? They should. And, if so, take those days. You will be more productive and healthy in the long run.

When you do take your weekends off and your time off, cultivate those other components in your life that are separate from work. Enjoy your family, friends, and alone time. Practice healthy habits that support you, so you can be fresh and happier when you are working.

Be Creative

If you generally enjoy your job but have been feeling bored, think of what would spice it up for you. Often, you end up knowing your job better than those around you and those whom you work for because you are the one actually doing the work. If you find you are getting bored at work, think of suggestions for how to make things better. And, in a positive and helpful way, suggest these ideas to your boss and those you work with. If you are proactive and your ideas are helpful, this is a good thing. It will help you and your place of business.

To help spark your creative juices, focus on all the chakras, specifically the Sacral, Solar Plexus, Heart, and Throat Chakras. These chakras combined are your centers for adapting to change, feeling empowered, feeling connected to others, and speaking your truth. Chakra healing can help with these practical situations, allowing the energy to flow so you can be your most productive, creative, and empowered self.

Keep an Open Heart

As you are practicing enjoy the moment now and also manifesting things for the future, keep an open heart. This is not as easy as it sounds. The heart is very perceptive, and as such it will close down to protect itself. If you are expending too much attention outward or if you are being overloaded with too much needy attention, the heart will become blocked. Allow for that to happen, when you notice it's necessary. Sometimes you do need to protect yourself from others' energy. Learn, too, how to open your heart at times when it will serve you.

Loving Your Friends

Friendship can be the most valuable treasure in the world. They are your mirrors. Your friends mirror your good qualities back to you and also mirror the qualities about you that are difficult. The good thing about true friends is that they have your best interest at heart, and you have theirs. In real friendship, you don't mean to hurt each other, though sometimes it will happen. One of the best things you can do is, if your friend does hurt you in the same way several times, try to find the most gentle way to discuss it. This could be enlightening for your friend, and healing for you. This is a tricky thing, though. You must come to the conversation with an open and gentle heart, even though you are feeling hurt and possibly closed off. If you know your friend doesn't mean to hurt you, before talking to your friend about what's hurting you check these points:

- Tell your friend you want to set aside some time to talk about something important to you, time when you both can relax and have a talk.

- Journal ahead of time about how you are feeling, get it all out on paper.

- Practice Nadi Shodhana for ten to fifteen minutes.

- Now write down the conversation you would like to have: precisely what he did, simply; precisely, how it made you feel; and precisely what you think he could do differently.

- Be open to the fact that he might have an adverse reaction to your comments.

- Send loving thoughts from your Heart Chakra to your friend, before having the conversation.

This might sound like more preparation than you are used to for having a talk, but friendships can be sensitive because both people are usually doing the best they can in the relationship. Especially if they care about you, your friends won't feel good hearing they have hurt you or let you down. With time, hopefully you and your friends will understand that these talks are meant to bring you closer, not tear you apart. Of course, this won't work with all friends. Some friendships cannot withstand this kind of authenticity, and you'll have to decide if those are friendships that work for you.

Wishing Happiness for All Beings

Truly wishing happiness for all beings can take practice. There's a special kind of meditation that is used for cultivating this ability. It's called *metta meditation*. There are variations, but in general this is how you practice metta:

1. Sit in a comfortable, seated position for meditation.

2. Close your eyes, follow your breath as it goes in and out several times.

3. Say this to yourself: "May I be happy. May I be healthy. May I know peace."

4. Bring to mind someone you love dearly. Hold this person in your mind's eye. Repeat the same wish: "May you be happy. May you be healthy. May you know peace."

5. Bring to mind someone who is an acquaintance whom you have good feelings toward, and don't know very well. Perhaps it's someone who works in the same building as you or the person at the post office who always helps you mail your packages. Hold this person in your mind's eye, and say: "May you be happy. May you be healthy. May you know peace."

6. Now repeat this for all beings: "May all beings be happy. May all beings be healthy. May all beings know peace." When you are finished, open your eyes.

Once you have become accustomed to doing metta mediation with sincerity there is a step to add. Before you repeat the wish for all beings, call to mind someone with whom you have a conflict. Hold that person in your mind's eye, and send him or her the same wish: "May you be happy. May you be healthy. May you know peace." Then, for the last wish, do it for all beings.

When you are truly able to wish everyone peace and happiness, even those with whom you feel conflict, you sincerely know that they, too, have struggles. Even if you have trouble getting along with someone else, you can feel compassion for the light within him. There is a way to believe that he is doing the best he can, and because of how he is acting, he is struggling.

When you practice metta you are balancing your Heart Chakra, and as the effects of metta transform you, you are connected to the feeling of oneness of all that is. That's the space to be in as you create your path.

CHAPTER 19

Creative Projects for Attracting What You Want

Your thoughts become your reality. Being intentional about your thoughts, words, and actions is how you create your path, moment by moment. Being intentional also leads to good health. You are healthiest and happiest when what you think, say, and do all line up. Creative projects are an ideal way to meditate and manifest your beautiful and bountiful desires. These projects put you in the playful, imaginative space for balancing the chakras and attracting exactly what you want. The universe responds to joyful, open, and trusting enthusiasm.

Ideas for Collage

Collage is an activity you can do alone, with your children, and with your friends. It's a versatile, simple, and vivid way to manifest your desires and balance your chakras. It's fun, colorful, and light-hearted, just the way manifestation works best.

Kitchen Table Collage Day

Prepare your kitchen table for collage time. Invite family members or friends to join you. Make a play date out of it. Before you do, make sure to pick up supplies such as:

- Magazines with lots of photos and words of the kinds of things that appeal to you: look for words and photos about health, vacation spots, jobs that appeal to you, cars, homes, computers, smiling faces, etc.

- Crayons, markers, and colored pencils

- Glue sticks

- Construction paper

- Scissors

Once you have the supplies, place them on the table along with a few crystals or candles as reminders of your connection to the energy of the universe that is answering your request.

Sit at the table and do at least a brief meditation or centering to bring yourself into the inner place where you can listen to your heart's desires. What is it you've been longing to bring into your life? Take some time to let the answer bubble up.

When you are ready, choose a piece of construction paper as your canvas. Then, look through the magazines for photos that resemble what you want. Cut inspiring words, images, and colors from the magazines. You can cut and paste directly onto your paper as you go, or collect bunches of images and words before gluing anything. Then once you have enough for your collage, decide how to arrange them on the page. There's no right or wrong way to arrange your images on the page, so have fun! If you don't find a representation of everything that you want to bring into your life, draw what you want with crayons or pencils. *Whatever* you want, put it on the collage. Usually collages have images that overlap each other and are placed on the page in all sorts of angles. Be playful with the arrangement: whatever is pleasing to your eye will work well.

> Collage material isn't limited to flat magazine cut-outs or drawings with crayons. You can use other objects on your collage like tissue paper, clay, pipe cleaners, popsicle sticks, and cotton balls. Use whatever you like that conveys what you want to bring to life.

Choose images that are uplifting reminders of what you truly want. Then, when you are finished, keep the collage as a visual reminder and support for attracting what you desire. You can make more than one collage at a time, or start over with a new one whenever you like. The point is to enjoy using your hands to create your vision.

You can also focus on colors that will energize the chakras that you notice are out of balance. If you're feeling fiery and judgmental lately, make your collage with cool tones to help move the energy from the Manipura and to pacify pitta. If you're feeling sluggish and heavy, use brighter colors to help ignite your inner fire.

Computer Collage

For those of you who love to be on the computer, you can do a similar type of collage onscreen. Pull up a blank page on the screen, and then cut and paste images from the Internet. A good way to look for images online is to go to a search engine and type in the name of the image you want to find plus the word "image." Then, often, you can copy and paste that image onto your blank screen. You can crop and move images on the page. As long as you are only doing this for personal use, you won't be infringing on intellectual or creative property rights.

Decoupage Furniture or Other Items

Collage doesn't have to be limited to paper. You could collage the top of a table, the cover of your notebook, gift boxes, picture frames, or the cover of your journal. When you cover the tops of surfaces, like boxes or notebooks, you can then cover them with a special decoupage coating from an art supply store. When wet, the coating will help the cutouts stick to the surface, and when the coating dries it will be clear and smooth. This process of making collage on a surface and then covering it with a clear varnish is called *decoupage*. The visual results of your collage and decoupage help you envision in your mind's eye what you want to attract and how you want to feel. As you create it, believe it is already happening.

Painting, Drawing, and Coloring for Everyone

You don't have to think of yourself as an artist, artistically talented, or creatively gifted to receive the benefits of painting, drawing, or coloring. Everyone can enjoy their creative expressions: expressive arts are not just for children. Nor are they frivolous, a waste of time, or incidental. Everyone's expression matters, and you may be surprised by what you can create.

Being in Your Right Brain

When you paint, draw, and color you strengthen the right side of your brain, the creative side. The creative side of you enjoys forging into unknown territory to see what happens next. Starting out with a blank piece of paper or canvas is a fresh beginning. Whether or not you have an idea about how the finished product will look, you are forging into new territory. You are the creator of the piece of art, you are creating something out of nothing. There are no rules, there is no one to impress. In the same way, you are the writer, director, and audience to your life.

What will you produce? Practice creating on paper to strengthen your comfort with making creative choices in your life.

Spending time using the right side of your brain will feel different from using the left side. When you are in the left side you construct viable plans, make your grocery list, and succeed in the details of your job. That feels useful and productive, not to mention essential. And, it is. The left side of your brain is a wonderful part of being you. Being in the right side doesn't have that same feeling of "essential" to people who are more interested in logic. Your left brain may judge the right brain activity as not essential. The right side of the brain is essential. It is connected to your intuition, interest in holistic thinking and living, and seeing the big picture. While living in this side, you may feel more open to new ideas and full of wonder.

Your left brain may get threatened, and say to you, "this is a waste of time. Come back to me. Let's plan something important." The reality is, only by practicing being in the creative space can you be open to the unexpected miracles and create even grander things. And "grand" can mean whatever you want it to mean: different career, stronger love, more peace. Only by being in the right side can you dream up bigger plans that your left brain won't come up with. Don't worry, though, both sides will be a big part of your life. They work together: your right side can have big dreams, and your left side can help you execute the details. The experiences feel different, and learning to switch back and forth can be a challenge. Most people are naturally more comfortable in one side, or have trouble switching back and forth. With practice, though, it becomes much easier and fun to be the creator of your life.

Many of the yoga, meditation, and chakra healings in this book all can help you balance the hemispheres of your brain. Practicing Nadi Shodhana and walking a labyrinth are two particularly good practices for creating balance. You can add the following exercise to your repertoire, specifically to initiate stepping into the right side of your brain from left-brain-centered activities.

Find a spot where you are out of the range of anything work-related. Be out of sight and energetic range of your telephones, computer, fax machine, and cluttered shelves. Find a place where there is free space in front of a wall, or where you can bring a chair for one of the physical postures you will be doing. This sequence will help you see things from a new perspective.

1. Find a spot where there is wall space, or have a chair handy. Sit comfortably, close your eyes, and relax. Let out a sigh of relief: inhale, and exhale with a sound. Sigh a few times, relaxing the lines in the forehead, relaxing the jaw, relaxing the shoulders.

2. Now position yourself in "legs up the wall" pose. You will use the wall or a chair to lean your legs up against. Sit sideways on the floor so that your right side is facing the wall or chair. Sit so that your right hip is approximately one foot away from the wall or the chair. If you are new to this pose or not too flexible, start further away, and explore the next two steps at different distances to see what feels comfortable. This is not a contest: what feels good for your body is healthiest. Also, it may be more comfortable to put a bolster or folded blanket close to the wall or chair to support your low back. See the following figure.

3. Lean over to your left onto your left forearm while you begin to gently raise your legs up and to the right. As you do this, pivot your body, so that you end up on your back with both legs leaning up against the wall. If you are using a chair, remain on the floor, and raise your legs up onto the seat of the chair. Using the chair, have thighs at a 90-degree angle in relationship to your lying-down torso, and your knees bent so your thighs and calves create a 90-degree angle. Your calves rest on the seat of the chair.

4. With your legs up the wall, your legs can be at an angle. The point is for your legs to be up, and for you to feel no strain. Now, let your entire body relax, with your legs up the wall or on the chair. Feel your back body sink into the floor: head, shoulder blades, back, and buttocks release into the support of the earth.

5. As you lay here, with your legs up the wall, open your eyes for a moment and look at your feet. This is a different perspective from how you are most of the day. Normally, your feet are beneath your head, now they are higher than your head. Acknowledge that your feet now have time to rest from the physical weight they carry. Notice that gravity is now working on your legs in a different way. Down is now up, up is now down: different perspective.

6. Take several deep breaths, with a longer exhale than inhale. Relax.

7. Palm your eyes by rubbing your hands together vigorously to create warmth, prana. Once you've generated heat, close your eyes and carefully place the cupped palms of your hands over your eyes. Breathe in the prana and warmth. As you do this, prana comes into the upper part of your body, including the upper chakras.

8. Keep your palms here. Breathe and relax. Envision your Throat Chakra a glowing, azure blue. Breathe a few breaths with this visualization.

9. Envision your Third-Eye Chakra as a lotus, glowing a deep midnight-sky indigo. Breathe a few times with this visualization of the indigo lotus at your third eye.

10. Now, envision your Crown Chakra projecting a brass-colored golden sphere above your head in the shape of a globe-like sun. It shines with a mirroring quality.

11. Reach your hands above your crown, and grasp that solid ball of gold, that energy that you've just imagined into being with your thoughts. Carry that ball of energy from above your head to above your solar plexus, and allow the energy to charge your Manipura Chakra. Hold your hands over that spot, nourishing the Manipura Chakra. Breathe a few times.

12. To release this posture, spread your hands and arms wide, let the ball of energy go. Slowly bend your knees into your chest. Roll over onto your right side. When you are ready, sit up. Slowly move on to whatever activity you have planned next.

This exercise helps you begin to see things from a new perspective while lying with your legs up the wall. While you do this, the visualization strengthens your Throat, Third-Eye, and Crown Chakras, before you bring that universal energy into your Manipura Chakra. With a stronger Manipura Chakra, you have self-confidence and will to create something new. This pose and visualization is great to do whether you have left-brained or right-brained activity next. Getting into your right brain won't hinder your left brain.

Resisting the Right Side of the Brain?

If you experience resistance to going into activities that correspond to the right side of the brain, do you know why that is? Are you afraid you don't have time? Are you afraid you can't do it? Are you attached to logic and needing to know the outcome ahead of time? Look at your answers to the question, why won't you venture into a more spacious, creative space? When you find the answer, strengthen the chakra that is associated with that feeling. That will help. Then, slowly add some creative time into your life. Find a friend to join you, or spend time doing something creative with a child—she will enjoy the attention, and you will get your creative time.

> It's fun to do something creative with others. To get out of your routine, sign up for a class. Learn to do something new or strengthen your skills by signing up for a drawing, painting, photography, or pottery class. You'll meet new people and get to know a new side of yourself.

If you aren't excited about unexpected miracles, yet, it's okay. That said, life feels infinitely more magical when you step into unknown territory and have a "let's see" attitude. The good news is, if you step into unknown territory, and you don't like what happens, you aren't stuck there. Life keeps changing. If you try an adventure, a type of food, or a vacation that you don't like, you can choose not to do that again. It's not a waste because the more you step into the unknown, the more you will have some experiences you don't like that will lift you to heights you never imagined you could experience. More often than not you'll try things that lift you up. Those infinite gems, those pleasing surprises, exercise your Heart Chakra and remind you that the world is more vast, more beautiful, and more surprising than you know. The more open you become, the more often life will be there to carry you on. Yes, there will be some struggle, but you can't avoid struggle even with a closed heart. The degree to which you follow your heart into the creative unknown is directly proportional to how much heart-expanding joy you will attract.

Creative Art Box or Art Closet

If you don't often explore your creative side, you may not have a creative art box or an art closet at home. It's really useful to have a stash of materials so that you can create something when you get the impulse. To be prepared, mark a day in your calendar to get supplies. This can be just as fun as the creative process itself. It's important to mark it in your calendar because if you don't have the supplies available, you will have to get in the car and go shopping for supplies on a day when you get a creative impulse. And, that could kill the creative energy. Having supplies handy means you can get right down to it, and take a creative arts break when the spirit moves you. You could even stay in your pajamas if you already have the supplies at home.

Suggestions for your creative arts box or art closet include:

- A simple set of watercolors, with brushes included
- Paper that takes watercolors; construction paper; and plain white paper
- Colored pencils, pencil sharpener, and good erasers
- Fun, smooth markers or colored pens
- Crayons
- Scissors
- Some fun things that appeal to you when you walk around the art supply or craft store
- Magazines
- Glue sticks and rubber cement glue
- Coloring books, stencils, or activity books
- Plain cardboard boxes

Once you have supplies, make sure you also buy a box to put them in. Keeping them neat, tidy, and protected is good for your supplies and it also means you won't add a mess to your house. You may want to make sure the box is big enough so you can put some newspaper in there or a tablecloth that you can get dirty, so that when it's time to create you can cover a table with the paper or a tablecloth. For fun, you could get yourself an apron, too, to protect your clothes.

Coloring as Meditation

Take time to find arts-and-crafts things at bookstores, toy stores, and other places that have themes that appeal to you. There are coloring books and kits of mandalas, gods and goddesses, and other images of what you want to manifest in your life. When you color something, focus on what you are doing. As you focus on this object, you are practicing the ability to shut out the distractions of the world and focus on the project and what you want to bring into your life. The vibration of the image that you choose can be healing and supportive. It's a very worthwhile endeavor, and if your supplies are handy, then anytime you want color it doesn't have to be an unnecessarily long break from other to-dos.

Photography as Appreciation

Photography is capturing an infinitesimally small moment out of the eternity of time and space. You crop a section out of space by deciding how to capture an image when you position the camera for the photograph, and you crop a section of time by capturing that moment on film. Taking a photograph is a beautiful metaphor for seeing life. You can only see one small section at a time with the eyes. Your desire to capture an image, hold onto it, and share it shows your appreciation of it. When you are in the place of appreciation, you're in the right mindset for manifesting your desires. Also, the sweetness of life resides in appreciation, and sweetness is a quality of the Sacral Chakra in balance.

Creating and Immortalizing a Moment

By taking the photo of a flower, a friend, or a house on the lake you participate in the creation of the captured image by your choice of angle and proximity. You may at first think you are just photographing reality, but reality is constantly changing and too vast for one photo frame. What you are doing is creating a work of art that, to you, speaks volumes. You choose to photograph something in a certain way, and your choice is new to the world.

When you take a photograph you immortalize that moment. Just like a poet uses poetry and a sculptor uses clay, when you create a photograph you immortalize your object.

Photography as Manifestation

Taking photographs can be a meditative and manifestation practice. You focus on the object and on getting a particular representation of it. In this focused inquiry, you're able to become present to what is and your relationship to what you're photographing, disregarding what else might be going on in life or what your next "have-to" might be.

You can use photography as part of your manifestation. You can be intentional about what you photograph or what photograph you choose to own. Then, put the photographs on your collage, on your altar, or in your wallet as inspiration. It can be a literal representation of what you desire, or a representation of an action you hope to experience one day. It can also be a photograph of anything that brings you bliss, inspiration, hope, comfort, joy, or any feeling associated with the chakras that you want to strengthen. Photography is a powerful tool. It demonstrates to your eyes that what you want is manifest in physical reality.

Journaling for Self-Discovery

Journaling is a way to have a conversation with your higher self. Just like in conversations with other people, you cannot know ahead of time how conversation may take twists and turns. Journaling is like taking your mind for a walk down a path, and you don't know what you'll encounter today. You may pass familiar landmarks, go down familiar valleys, or pass through familiar tunnels. In the same way, you may be surprised by where you go when you journal.

How to Journal

To journal, you can start with a prompt. Meaning, you can start with a question or a beginning of a sentence. You may start with "In this moment, I feel . . . ", "What I am avoiding is . . . ", "I have a new intention to . . . ", or "What I learned today was . . . ." Start with what is going on right now, and see where it leads. See Appendix C for writing prompts and space to write.

You also could start with free-flow writing. In that case, you don't have to think about where to start, just write. Just let the words flow without discretion about what comes out. Then, later, you can read what you wrote. That is a great way to see if your feelings are positive or negative and how it relates to what you are attracting in your life.

A third option is to have a gratitude journal. At least once a day, open up your journal and write about what you are grateful for. You can write it as a list, write it in paragraph form, or write it in poetry. Whatever you're inspired to do in the moment, focus on the feeling of gratitude.

What You Don't Want to Manifest

As you go through your day, you may not be aware of every vibration you are putting into the universe. You may be putting out contrasting vibrations without being completely conscious of it. If you journal, you will write down your thoughts and see what you are thinking right now. You will see if you have contrasting thoughts. If so, after you see what came out during the beginning of your journaling time, then you can decide how to continue the positive thoughts or turn the negative thoughts around.

Journaling and the Throat Chakra

Journaling is a great way to strengthen your Throat Chakra, which is about expressing yourself in the world. As you express yourself in writing, you are practicing hearing and seeing your own voice. What thoughts do you have toward your own voice? What thoughts do you have about your own writing? Do the thoughts about your writing mirror thoughts you have about yourself in general? Notice which chakras match up to the feelings you are having. Then, balance blocked chakras. Always, in addition to any chakras you strengthen through journaling, the act of journaling itself strengthens your Throat Chakra.

How could I journal to bring energy to a specific chakra?

To bring healing to a particular chakra, write how you experience the physical and psychological issues of that chakraw. If your experience indicates a blocked chakra, then write, "what emotions are associated with this imbalance?" Then, put pen to paper and see what answer you write. Once you find out what emotions are involved, you'll know which chakra to heal.

Often, journaling allows you to discover what answers will come. You can journal for self-discovery and to reveal your own inner wisdom that you don't always access throughout your day. If you allow the thoughts to flow with patience and an open heart, you will find the answers that you seek. The more you find answers to who you are, what you need, and what you desire, the more intentional you can be about placing your energy on what you want to manifest in your life.

Engaging the Senses to Access Basic Goodness

When you feel basic goodness, that life is good and gravitates toward health and wholeness, you are reminded of the natural beauty of the world. The senses are a direct link to the basic goodness of the universe. Bringing yourself into a space of awe about the fundamentals of existence is a ripe place for enjoying your life and attracting what you want.

Awaken Through Smell and Taste

Awaken to the basic goodness of *now* through your senses of smell and taste by gardening and cooking vegetables and herbs. Gardening and cooking are both creative and scientific. These activities put you in touch with the art and science of the natural world. The smells and tastes that nourish you are the result of the miracles of nature. Take time to become present and appreciate that the earth supports you with a myriad of smells and tastes that support your existence.

Touching Basic Goodness

Use your sense of touch to appreciate texture. Spend time petting your animal friends, appreciating the cotton bed linen, and touching the soft petals of flowers. If you're cooking, enjoy running the flour or rice through your hands. Be appreciative when you're kneading dough. Using your sense of touch to become present to being right here, right now, reminds you of the basic goodness in the moment and of all you have to appreciate.

The Vibration of Sound

Learning to play a musical instrument or listening to music gets you in touch with harmonious vibrations, which affect your cells positively. Everything you touch, taste, smell, see, and hear can be digested by the body. What you experience becomes part of your life-experience. Choosing pleasing sound and learning to create music either through singing or playing a musical instrument allows you to contribute your voice to the sounds in the world.

Affirmations

When visualizing the future, it's important to continue to give yourself affirmations. Whatever creative medium you choose—whether paint, clay, photography, music, or journaling—encourage yourself. See your creations as beautiful, as supportive of the life you want to lead, and as true expressions of you and what is possible in the world. If you can imagine it, it can be so. If you can create a representation of it, it can be so. Create and allow.

Trust in the validity of your imagination. It's not always fantasy, it's also your lifeline to the creative impulse of what is yet to be.

> "I am enough of an artist to draw freely upon my imagination. Imagination is more important than knowledge. Knowledge is limited. Imagination encircles the world."
>
> —Albert Einstein

Looking in the Mirror

Pay attention to what you think about yourself when you look in the mirror. If you notice that you start your day saying negative things to yourself, change that. If you look in the mirror and can't possibly like what you see, can you find at least something that you like? Can you look into the mirror and say something good? Do not start your day already telling yourself something negative. If this is a struggle for you, work with this every day, trying to think of something positive. Learn to look in the mirror and tell yourself something affirming. The way to create what you want into your life is to start from a place of positivity.

Greeting Card Inspiration

The next time you're at a place that sells greeting cards, browse for a quotation that feels inspirational to you. look through them, and buy yourself a card. You can turn it into a bookmark, place it on your altar, or write the quotation in your journal and send the card to a friend. Never underestimate the power of laughter from a funny card or the kind words of an "I'm thinking of you" missive. Take it in for yourself, then pass it on.

Affirmation Cards

In bookstores and online you can find cards with affirmations on them. Sonia Choquette, SARK, and Louise Hay have created beautiful and supportive decks. Look also for power animal cards, fairy cards, and other soul-supportive cards. It's fun to pick one daily, and they always hit on something that resonates with your innermost being. Before picking a card, say a short prayer, asking for guidance for your highest good and the good of all.

Chakra Healing Affirmations

All affirmations are good and healing for your chakras. There are affirmations you can attach to each chakra, based on the psychological issues associated with each.

When you do chakra-healing affirmations, you strengthen each chakra with the vibration that supports its proper functioning. You can envision colors while you do this, you can hold appropriate crystals to bolster the healing energy, or you could simply do the affirmations and be with what comes up. All of these ways are valuable and effective methods for bringing energy to the chakras. It's amazing how helpful self-affirmation is. The messages you tell yourself directly affect your overall health and the life you create.

AFFIRMATION	CHAKRA
I am safe, I am supported	ROOT
I feel, I flow	SACRAL
I act, I can	SOLAR PLEXUS
I love, I receive love	HEART
I speak, I listen	THROAT
I see	THIRD-EYE
I am	CROWN

Acknowledgments

The open-heartedness, humor, and encouragement of friends, colleagues, and family make it possible for me to discover who I am and how to do my work in the world. Each person who has crossed my path, whether listed here or not, has been a teacher to me. To all of my past, present, and future teachers and friends, thank you.

Specifically, I want to thank Paula Munier for staying in touch and thinking of me, Lisa M. Laing for her edits and guidance, and Brett Palana-Shanahan and Khrysti Nazzaro for their editorial work. Thank you to all the authors whose work I've quoted, your work inspires me. For supporting me on the journey to and through the writing of this book, thank you: Abby Irwin, Adam Occaso, Alan Inglis, Beth Haydon Bodan, Carol Williams, Cindy Samuel Kalachek, Colleen MacCallum, Cristie Newhart, Dahlia Dawood, Dale Garson, Danny Arguetty, Devarshi Steven Hartman, Erin Gleason Leyba, Erin Mashburn Moulton, Evelyn Gonzales, Grace Welker, Henry I. Schvey, Hallie L. Deen, Heather Bilotta, Irma Gurgon, Janna Delgado, Jeannie Bull, Jill Esterson, John Tunnicliffe, Jonathan Dahari-Lanciano, Joshua Needleman, Jovinna Chan, Jurian Hughes, Karen S. Li, Kelley Johnson Boyd, Laurie Magoon, Liam McDermott, Lily Ruffner, Lois Rosenbaum, Lyn Williams, Marjorie Balter, Megha Nancy Buttenheim, Mia Scarpa, Michael Parsons, Misha Kellner-Rogers, Nina Dawe, Noushin Bayat, Patricia Lemer, Patrick Spottiswoode, Pauline Reid, Rhoda Thompson, Sadie Cunningham, Sally Segerstrom, Stacey Staub, Stanley Rosenbaum, Sudha Carolyn Lundeen, Susan Maier-Moul, Susan Olshuff, Suzanne Kent, Toni Bergins, Vandita Kate Marchesiello, Vicki Baird, Vici Williams, and Vila Maya King.

I thank my mother for teaching me to follow my heart, despite any fear. I thank my father for teaching me to appreciate every breath, every snowflake, and every moment. I thank my brother for being indispensable in my life: a source of unparalleled laughter who touches me with his talents, thoughtfulness, responsible decisions, and adventurous spirit. I thank Swami Kripalu and the Kripalu lineage for the teachings and guidance on "the path of love." Thank you, all.

Adrenals:

Part of the endocrine system. They support your body in stressful situations, activating your fight-or-flight response. The adrenals attach to the kidneys.

Ajna:

The Third-Eye or Brow Chakra. It means *to perceive*. The chakra is located between the eyes and slightly above the brow line. The Ajna Chakra is said to radiate an indigo glow.

Allopathic medicine:

Uses surgery and drugs to combat disease, also considered *conventional medicine*.

Alternative healing practices:

Healing modalities that are not considered conventional practices by Western medical standards. Alternative practices include, but are not limited to, mind-body medicine, natural remedies, energy work, and bodywork. These practices are considered alternative when used instead of allopathic treatments.

Anahata:

The Heart Chakra. The name means *unstruck*, and the chakra is said to have a green glow.

Anandamaya kosha:

Bliss sheath.

Annamaya kosha:

Food sheath.

Aromatherapy:

The use of the scents of essential oils to soothe and heal body, mind, and spirit.

Asana:

Any of the physical postures of Hatha yoga practice.

Atman:

The soul, higher self.

Aura:

The energetic field surrounding the body. It can be seen by the naked eye and in kirlian photography.

Auric field:

See Aura.

Ayurveda:

Called *the science of life*, it is a comprehensive medical system of health considered to be the sister science to yoga. It is a holistic system, caring for the health of the mind, body, and spirit.

Causal body:

Bliss sheath.

Cervical vertebrae:

The upper part of the spine, made up of seven vertebrae.

Chakra:

Sanskrit for *wheel* or *disc*. Spinning vortices of energy.

Complementary healing practices:

Healing modalities that are used in conjunction with allopathic medicine to support the healing process. Complementary modalities include, but are not limited to, mind-body medicine, natural remedies, energy work, and bodywork.

Dharma:

Your life's purpose and calling.

Dinacharya:

Literally means *close to the day*, and details how to care for the senses.

Dowser:

A divining rod, or a person who uses it, to help find water or minerals.

Essential oils:

Potent oils distilled from flowers, plants, trees, and grasses that are used in aromatherapy to promote and sustain wellness.

Ganglia/ganglion:

Masses of nerve tissue originating in the spinal cord and branching out to other parts of the body.

Gonads:

Part of the endocrine system, responsible for the secretion of sex hormones.

Hatha yoga:

The physical practice of yoga postures.

Ida nadi:

One of the three major energy channels in the body. The ida nadi starts at the Third-Eye Chakra and first curves to the left before crossing the sushumna at the Throat Chakra, then curving to the right. It criss-crosses with the pingala nadi back and forth all the way down to the Root Chakra.

Islets of Langerhans:

Part of the endocrine system, located in the pancreas. They are responsible for the secretion of insulin.

Kapha:

One of the three doshas, according to Ayurveda. Kapha has the properties of water and earth.

Kireji:

A "cutting" word or phrase in haiku that marks a transition from one thought or image to another.

Kirlian photograph:

A photograph that captures an aura as visible light.

Kirtan:

Call-and-response chanting, usually of mantras from the Indian spiritual traditions.

Koshas:

The five *sheaths* or *layers* that are the physical, energetic, mental, knowing, and spiritual parts of the body.

Kundalini:

The serpent goddess who is said to be coiled around the Root Chakra, until she is awakened and travels up the seven chakras to unite with divine consciousness at the Crown Chakra.

Lumbar vertebrae:

The lower part of the spine above the sacrum, consisting of five vertebrae.

Mandala:

A geometric design used for meditation, usually consisting of a square inside a circle with sacred images or patterns evoking the order and beauty of the universe.

Manipura:

Referred to as *lustrous gem*, the Solar Plexus Chakra, is said to glow a bright yellow.

Manomaya:

The mind sheath.

Meridians:

Energy channels in the body mapped out in Chinese medicine, especially useful for acupuncture, acupressure, and reflexology.

Muladhara:

The Root Chakra, said to glow a deep red.

Nadi:

Energy channel in the body.

Nirvana:

State of liberation from the physical body.

Niyama:

Special observances for how to take care of your mind, body, and spirit on the eight-limbed path of yoga.

Om:

The universal sound; the primordial sound; the sound of God, energy, spirit.

Parasympathetic nervous system:

Creates the relaxation response.

Pericarp:

The fleshy part of the fruit or flower, the part that protects the seed.

Perineum:

The area of the body between the genitals and the anus.

Petroglyph:

Rock carving.

Physical body:

The mortal part of the body.

Pineal gland:

Part of the endocrine system that secretes serotonin and melanin.

Pingala nadi:

One of the three major energy channels in the body. The pingala nadi starts at the Third-Eye Chakra and first curves to the right before crossing the sushumna at the Throat Chakra, then curving to the left. It criss-crosses with the ida nadi back and forth all the way down to the Root Chakra.

Pitta:

One of the three doshas, according to Ayurveda. Pitta has the properties of fire and water.

Pituitary:

A gland of the endocrine system that influences growth, metabolism, and many chemical processes in the body.

Prakruti:

According to Ayurveda, the constitution you were born with.

Prana:

Life-force energy.

Pranamaya kosha:

The breath/energy sheath.

Pranayama:

Breath and energy control.

Raja yoga:

The yogic path of self-awareness, learning to develop witness consciousness.

Sadhu:

A student on the path of yoga.

Sahasrara:

Literally means *thousandfold*, it's the Crown Chakra, that glows white, gold, or violet.

Samsara:

Scars, trauma, and karma that gets carried from one lifetime to the next.

Shadow sides:

Aspects of one's personality that the individual rejects.

Sitz bones:

The sitting bones.

Subtle body:

The wisdom, mental, and breath/energy sheaths.

Sushumna:

The central energy channel of the body that is located in the spine.

Sutra:

See Yoga sutras.

Svadhistana:

Meaning *sweetness*, this is the Sacral Chakra, said to glow a bright orange.

Sympathetic nervous system:

Activated when you are in fight-or-flight response, increases your heart rate and prepares you for action.

Theosophist:

A student of theosophy.

Theosophy:

A school of mystical thought founded in 1875, inspired by yogic philosophy.

Thoracic vertebrae:

These twelve vertebrae make up the central part of the spine.

Thymus:

A gland in the endocrine system responsible for supporting your immune system.

Thyroid:

A gland in the endocrine system that supports metabolism.

Upanishads:

Vedic philosophy.

Vaidya:

A doctor trained in Ayurveda.

Vata:

One of the three doshas, according to Ayurveda. Vata has the qualities of space and air, particularly the quality of movement.

Vijnanomya:

The wisdom sheath.

Vikruti:

How the doshas are showing up within you, now.

Visuddha:

The Throat Chakra. In Sanskrit it means purification. It is said to have a blue glow.

Whole systems of health:

Medical practices that are comprehensive in theory and practice, and separate from conventional Western medicine. These include Ayurveda, Chinese medicine, and homeopathy.

Witness consciousness:

A state of awareness that can observe the thinking mind, the emotions, and the body without identifying with them.

Yama:

Special observances for conducting yourself in the world, as part of the eight limbs of living a yogic lifestyle.

Yoga nidra:

Yogic sleep.

Yoga sutras:

The philosophy of the practice of yoga as outlined in writing by Patanjali. *Sutra* means "thread."

BOOKS

Arguetty, Danny. *Nourishing the Teacher: Inquiries, Contemplations, & Insights on the Path of Yoga.* (Canada: Danny Arguetty, 2009).

Avalon, Aurthur (Sir John Woodroffe). *The Serpent Power: The Secrets of Tantric and Shaktic Yoga.* (New York: Dover, 1974).

Butler, David S. and G. Lorimer. *Explain Pain.* (Adelaide, Australia: Noigroup, 2003).

Chödrön, Pema. *Comfortable with Uncertainty.* (Boston: Shambhala, 2002).

Chödrön, Pema. *Taking the Leap.* (Boston, MA: Shambhala, 2009).

Chopra, Deepak. *Journey Into Healing: Awakening the Wisdom Within You.* (New York: Three Rivers Press, 1995).

Coelho, Paulo. *The Alchemist.* (New York: HarperCollins, 1993).

Emoto, Masaru. *The Hidden Messages in Water.* (Atria: 2005).

Frawley, David. *Ayurvedic Healing: A Comprehensive Guide.* (Salt Lake City: Passage Press, 1989).

Hicks, Esther and Jerry. *Ask and It Is Given.* (Carlsbad, CA: HayHouse, Inc., 2004).

Hirschi, Gertrud. *Mudras: Yoga in Your Hands.* (San Francisco: Weiser Books, 2000).

Hoffmann, Yoel. *Japanese Death Poems: Written by Zen Monks and Haiku Poets on the Verge of Death.* (Tokyo: Tuttle Publishing, 1998).

Judith, Anodea. *Eastern Body Western Mind: Psychology and the Chakra System as a Path to the Self.* (Berkeley: Celestial Arts, 2004).

Judith, Anodea. *Wheels of Life: A User's Guide to the Chakra System.* (Woodbury, MN: Llewellyn, 2010).

Kern, Hermann. *Through the Labyrinth.* (New York: Prestel, 2000).

Lad, Vasant. *The Complete Book of Ayurvedic Home Remedies.* (New York: Three Rivers Press, 1998).

Mercier, Patricia. *The Chakra Bible.* (New York: Sterling, 2007).

Satchidananda, Swami. *The Yoga Sutras of Patanjali.* (Yogaville, VA: Integral Yoga, 2009).

Simpson, Liz. *The Book of Chakra Healing.* (New York: Sterling, 1999).

DVDs

Grilley, Paul. *Chakra Theory and Meditation* [DVD]. (2007).

Judith, Anodea. *The Illuminated Chakras: A Visionary Voyage Into Your Inner World* [DVD]. (Llewellyn, 2010).

Lundeen, Sudha Carolyn. *Kripalu Gentle Yoga* [DVD]. (Lenox, MA: Kripalu Center, 2005).

Websites

BanyanBotanicals.com

Buy Ayurvedic herbs and oils, take a quiz to discover your Ayurvedic type, and learn ways to balance your doshas.

Chopra.com

Timeless tools and healing principles to nurture health, restore balance, and create greater joy and fulfillment.

eomega.org

Omega is a wellness and retreat center that has been a pioneer in exploring, teaching, and embracing new ideas, focusing on health and wellness, personal spiritual growth, and self-awareness.

Eslaen.org

The Esalen Institute was founded in 1962 as an alternative educational center devoted to the exploration of what Aldous Huxley called the "human potential," the world of unrealized human capacities that lies beyond the imagination.

JourneyDance.com

JourneyDance moves you through deep, personal exploration into a loving, intimate relationship with body, mind, and source energy. Join Toni, the founder of JourneyDance in workshops throughout the country and beyond, or practice in your own living room with her CD.

JurianHughes.com

Join Jurian for YogaDance teacher training and other workshops to free your body and feed your spirit.

Kripalu.org

Kripalu Center for Yoga & Health is an invaluable resource for books, DVDs, CDs, gemstones, Ayurvedic products, and more. As the nation's largest retreat center for yoga and health, you will find daily classes and workshops as well as weekend and weeklong programs with internationally known presenters and teachers. Visit the website for information on Kripalu's workshops, and check out the online store for products to support your path toward overall well-being.

LetYourYogaDance.com

Let Your Yoga Dance is a fusion of chakra-yoga and joyful breath-based power movements. It is a dance of the multidimensional self, bringing levity and healing to the seven energy centers (the chakras) and the body in its entirety.

Index